*The Story of Denmark*

# THE STORY OF
# DENMARK

by
STEWART OAKLEY

FABER AND FABER
3 Queen Square
London

*First published in 1972*
*by Faber and Faber Limited*
*3 Queen Square London WC1*
*Printed in Great Britain by*
*Latimer Trend & Co Ltd Plymouth*
*All rights reserved*

*ISBN 0 571 09951 3*

# Contents

# Contents

# *Illustrations*

9

# *Illustrations*

MAPS

TABLES

# *Preface*

---

THERE has, up to the present time, been comparatively little interest in the history of Denmark (at least since the end of the Viking period) among scholars of either Britain or the United States. One of the reasons has doubtless been the language barrier, though this is little higher than that which divides English-speakers from other countries whose languages are not normally taught in schools and certainly not higher than that around the more distant Sweden, which has attracted a good deal more attention. In addition, it may be argued, Danish emigration to the New World in the late nineteenth and early twentieth century was comparatively slight, so that the number of Danish-Americans wishing to investigate their European heritage is smaller than that of descendants of settlers from many other countries.

The fact cannot be escaped that Denmark is a small nation which has for a long time been unable, nor indeed has wished, to play a leading role on the European diplomatic stage. She has been liable to fall victim to the belief, unfortunately common even among historians, that the history of a country which makes little immediate impact on contemporary international affairs is not worth bothering with. It is also true that, though Denmark was for most of her history the richest and most populous of the Scandinavian powers and even as late as the early nineteenth century could, largely because of her fleet, force larger nations to take her attitude into serious consideration, she has never made her mark on a larger stage to the extent that Sweden did in the seventeenth century. Nor has she produced, at least in modern times, rulers of the stature of Gustavus Adolphus or the psychological fascination of Queen Christina or Charles XII. Yet her story is certainly not lacking either in striking personalities or dramatic incident. And, at a deeper level, it contains peaceful developments which—like the late eighteenth-century reforms—are distinct enough to offer fruitful comparisons with those in other lands and help towards an understanding of historical processes in general.

In its scope and purpose this book is very similar to my short history of Sweden. As there, I have attempted to do justice, as far as has been possible in a rather limited space, to all periods and aspects—economic, social and cultural as well as political —of the country's evolution. I hope that English-speaking visitors to Denmark (where they will find no real language problem, so many Danes having an excellent command of English) will, after reading my account, be able the better to understand and enjoy a most delightful country and people. At the same time I have kept very much in mind students of history who wish for a reliable introduction to a neglected corner of their art, and I trust that they will be encouraged, with the help of the bibliographical appendix, to delve more deeply into it, perhaps even themselves to contribute to its literature.

It is with great pleasure that I record my thanks to Folketingsbibliotekar cand. mag. Kristian Hvidt and amanuensis mag. art. Kai Hørby, who between them painstakingly read all the chapters of the book in draft and made many constructive criticisms on them, and to Mrs. Janet Mawby of the University of East Anglia, who generously took time off from thesis-writing to help improve the presentation and accuracy of the final manuscript. For errors, misinterpretations and infelicities of style which remain I apologize to them and to all future readers. For assistance in providing the illustrations and granting me permission to use them, my thanks are due to: the National Museum, Copenhagen; the Royal Museum of Fine Arts, Copenhagen; the Thorvaldsen Museum, Copenhagen; the National Historical Museum at Frederiksborg; the Royal Library, Copenhagen; and the Danish Tourist Board.

Norwich                                  STEWART P. OAKLEY
August 1971

# NOTE ON THE SPELLING OF PROPER NAMES

In cases where there is a familiar form of a Danish place-name (e.g. Jutland for Jylland, Copenhagen for København and Elsinore for Helsingør) I have chosen to use it, while noting the Danish version on the first occasion. In the case of the two duchies which have played such a prominent part in Denmark's foreign relations through the centuries, I have compromised by using the German 'Holstein' rather than the Danish 'Holsten' for the southernmost, which had for almost as far back as we can trace a purely German character, while referring to the northernmost, with its large Danish-speaking population, as Slesvig. I have, on the other hand, been compelled to keep the form Schleswig-Holstein. With personal names I have been rather less consistent. In general I have preferred the Danish form where the difference is largely one of spelling (e.g. Frederik) or where the name is purely Danish, even though there might be an English transliteration (e.g. Knud (Canute) ). Danes often refer to their writers, politicians etc. by the initials of their first names rather than, as is more usual in English, by a first name itself. The most striking example of this practice is Hans Andersen, known to Danes as H. C. Andersen (and to most Americans, incidentally, as Hans Christian Andersen to make matters more complicated!). Again I have tried here to make the best of both worlds by giving a first name in full, followed in brackets by the initials if these are more commonly employed in Danish sources.

# NOTE ON DANISH PRONUNCIATION

Danish pronunciation is the main stumbling-block which faces the learner of what is not otherwise a difficult language. No attempt can be made here to explain the intricacies of the characteristic glottal stop (even if the author felt himself qualified to do so) nor to list the exceptions to practically any rule which can be given. The following very rough guide may, however, save the reader, when quoting the Danish words used in the text, from causing his or her Danish friends too much pain:

| | |
|---|---|
| å[1] (formerly aa) | when long, like *aw* in f*aw*n (e.g. Neerg*aa*rd) |
| | when short, like *o* in t*o*p (e.g. h*å*ndfæstning) |
| æ[1] | like *e* in f*e*d (e.g. F*æ*drelandet) |
| au and av | often like *ou* in s*ou*nd (e.g. St*au*ning and st*av*nsbånd) |
| d | usually like *th* in *th*ere after a vowel (e.g. O*d*ense); usually silent after 'l' and 'n' (e.g. Roskil*d*e); and always silent before 's' and 't' (e.g. Ma*d*sen-Mygdal) |
| eg and ej | often like *i* in m*i*ne (e.g. r*eg*nskabslen and D*ej*bjerg) |
| g | sometimes silent after a vowel (e.g. Ri*g*sda*g*) |
| j | like *y* in *y*et (e.g. *j*arl) |
| k | always pronounced (e.g. *K*nud) |
| ov | like *oe* in r*oe* (e.g. Kongel*ov*) |
| ø[1] | like French 'eu' and German 'ö', i.e. roughly *u* in h*u*rt with lips more protruded (e.g. M*ø*n) |
| øj | like *oi* in s*oi*l (e.g. H*øj*re) |
| u | when short, nearly like '*o*' in l*o*ng (e.g. M*u*nk) |

[1] æ, ø and å come at the end of the Danish alphabet in that order.

14

|   | when long, like *oo* in m*oo*n (e.g. Glimminge-hus) |
|---|---|
| v | see av and ov |
| y | like French 'u' or German 'ü', i.e. the *ea* in m*ea*n with rounded lips (e.g. F*y*n) |

The accent generally falls on the first syllable.

1. Modern Denmark

# CHAPTER I

## *Earliest Inhabitants*

---

DANISH scholars were prominent among the founders of the modern science of archaeology. To Christian (C. J.) Thomsen (1788–1865), founder and first director of the National Museum in Copenhagen, we owe the now familiar division of prehistory into Stone, Bronze and Iron Ages. And it was Thomsen's successor, Jens (J. J. A.) Worsaae (1821–85), who first divided the Stone Age into Old and New. In the early and middle years of the nineteenth century these two men and their assistants began to unearth and interpret the rich deposits left behind by the early settlers in their homeland and hidden for centuries beneath its soil.

Later researchers have revealed evidence of man's presence in Denmark at least as far back as the time when, about 14,000 years ago, the country was first freed from the great ice-sheet which covered most of it during the last Ice Age. This is late compared with southern and central Europe—as indeed was, until recently, the arrival of nearly every new development in a land so far removed from the Continent's great cultural centres. There do seem, however, to have been human visitors to Denmark before the last advance of the ice, about 50,000 years ago, blotted out nearly all traces of them. In 1912, bones of fallow deer dated to before this happened were dug up in a sandpit at Hollerup near the town of Randers in north-east Jutland, and in 1955 they were shown to have been split open by what can only have been men's hands to extract the marrow. And western Jutland (Danish, *Jylland*) was never covered by ice, although no proof that men inhabited the area during this period has so far been discovered.

The oldest human settlement site uncovered not only in Denmark but in the whole of Scandinavia is at Bromme in the middle of Zealand, the largest of the Danish islands (Danish, *Sjælland*). Crude tools of flint, a material in which Denmark is particularly rich, and bones of reindeer, elk and beaver indicate occupation during a brief warm spell around 10,000 B.C., when lush grassland and trees like willow and juniper covered the region. Then came a return of bitterly cold temperatures and tundra vegetation, conditions which lasted for a further 2,000 years or so. Yet men continued to live in, or at least to visit, Denmark in small numbers during the summer months. They came from the south in pursuit of the reindeer which provided them with not only food but also clothing and tools like axes, arrowheads and harpoons made from their antlers.

About 8000 B.C. the climate began to change yet again. Though the winters were still very cold, average summer temperatures eventually approached 20°, warmer than today. Great forests of birch, hazel and fir sprang up, providing shelter for elk, bear, lynx, wild boar, deer and the primitive giant cattle known as aurochs, as well as for a wide variety of birds. At the same time the retreat of the ice sheet toward the north of the Scandinavian peninsula caused the land to rise. The Baltic became an enormous freshwater lake; a single land mass stretched from Britain to what is now southern Sweden; and the Belts, which now separate the Danish islands from each other and from the mainland, were simply large rivers flowing northward. The human remains left from this period are, as might be expected, richer. But the population was still very small by later standards and migratory; little family groups with the dogs which they had tamed still had to follow the game on which they relied and could settle for only brief periods by the banks of rivers and lakes to fish and collect berries with which to supplement their meat diet. The culture which they evolved in the east of the country takes its name from Maglemose in Zealand, where the first objects characteristic of it were found. While these include small flint tools, bone was still the principal material used in the making of harpoons, needles and knives etc., often decorated with simple figures and patterns which may have served a magical purpose. Consequently the Maglemose period is sometimes referred to as the Bone Age.

Further west, in what is now Jutland, a similar but distinct culture emerged which left remains along the banks of the Gudenå.

Towards the end of the Maglemose period (around 5000 B.C.), the climate changed once more; the winters became milder and the summers more humid. The forests grew denser, and the oak and the elm took over from the fir as the commonest trees in them. As a consequence, the larger game animals were less plentiful, and, while Maglemose and Gudenå hunters continued to eke out an existence in the interior, many men drifted towards the new coastline which was forming and began to rely heavily on the harvest of the sea. This new coastline emerged as the weight of the water released from the melting ice cap caused the land around what is now Denmark to sink again; the sea eventually broke through to the Baltic by way of the Sound and divided Zealand from the Scandinavian peninsula, while Zealand was separated from Fyn to the west by the Great Belt, Fyn from the Jutish peninsula by the Little Belt and Jutland from Britain by the wide expanse of the North Sea. Denmark took on something like its present shape of a peninsula jutting northward from the mainland of Europe with to the east of it a number of large islands (Fyn, Zealand, Lolland and Falster) and over 450 smaller ones.

We owe a great deal of our knowledge of the new way of life which was created by the coastal dwellers of north Zealand and Jutland in this last period of the Old Stone Age to the enormous piles of refuse which grew up on their summer sites, an example of which found at Ertebølle on Limfjorden has given its name to the culture. These 'kitchen middens' as they are called are to be found also in other parts of western Europe, but they were first fully investigated by Worsaae in Denmark. They have revealed a very varied diet, including birds, shellfish (especially mussels and oysters), seal and game from the surrounding forests. Human skeletons also among the remains suggest a very unceremonious treatment of the dead, and there is even evidence of cannibalism. Bone had now finally given way to flint as the commonest material for the making of tools and weapons, many of which were indeed exported to more northerly parts of Scandinavia which lacked the raw material. But the most interesting objects found in the middens are the earliest examples of pottery in Denmark: large conical storage and cooking jars with pointed bases so that they could be placed upright in the sand, and crucibles to hold blubber which provided a feeble light when lit.

The Danish countryside is dotted with a very large number of striking man-made structures consisting of great upright stones arranged in a rough circle, often capped with a further slab of rock and surrounded by a kerb of smaller stones. Each of these 'dolmens' (Danish, *dysser*), whose sides were originally covered with earth, concealed a body and artefacts associated with its owner. They imply not only a considerable degree of technical skill on the part of their builders but also a higher degree of social organization, a more settled existence and more sophisticated religious beliefs than any hitherto described. They belong in fact to the early part of the New Stone Age, which began in Denmark about 2700 B.C. Small bands of immigrants from the south-east at that time brought with them into Jutland a knowledge of crops like wheat and barley, which they could grow on land first cleared from the forest with the aid of fire and a new type of polished stone axe set in a wooden haft, then possibly prepared with a primitive plough and finally harvested with finely chipped flint sickles. These people had also domesticated the cow, the sheep, the goat and the pig, but, in spite of these accomplishments, they appear to have had to continue to rely to a considerable extent on the produce of wood and stream. The climate was still warm and drier than in the Old Stone Age, so that elaborate dwellings were not needed, but traces of small villages from this period have been unearthed, the oldest being at Barkær in eastern Jutland. They apparently consisted of long, narrow houses of wood or wattle and daub, together with smaller round huts.

The first farmers settled in Denmark some time before the dolmens began to be built. Though such megaliths are more highly concentrated in Denmark than anywhere else, they are widely spread all along the coastal regions of western Europe, and it has been suggested that the idea of building them was carried northward by sea by small bands of missionaries from the Mediterranean, where the Mycenean civilization was flourishing. In time dolmens gave way to larger and more elaborate communal graves—oblong chambers of upright slabs

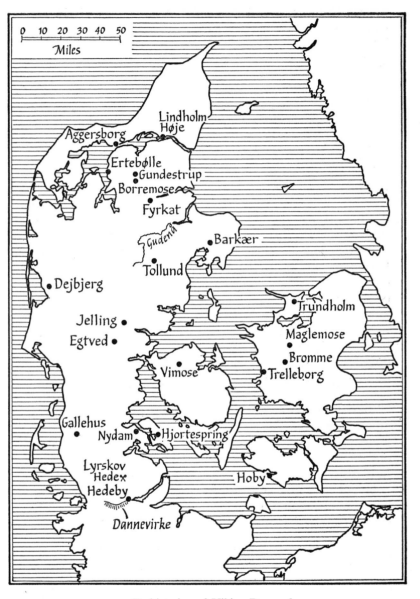

2. Prehistoric and Viking Denmark

approached through stone-lined passage-ways and, in some cases, capable of holding up to over a hundred bodies at a time. The great care with which these passage-graves (*jættestuer* or 'giant's rooms' in Danish) were constructed, so that they have survived under the mounds of earth which covered them to the present day, and the objects buried in them and at the entrances to them—all suggest a highly developed cult of the dead. A rich settlement-site of the period at Troldebjerg on the island of Langeland was thoroughly excavated before the Second World War.

The passage-graves seem to have developed naturally from the dolmens and were certainly built by the same peoples. But about 2100 B.C. a new wave of immigrants practising a quite distinct culture arrived in Jutland. These drove both the megalithic farmers and such Gudenå hunters as survived on to the islands to join the Ertebølle fishermen. The newcomers belonged to a branch of the Boat-Axe People, so named because of their characteristic stone implements. Unlike their predecessors, they buried their dead in simple shallow graves covered with low mounds of earth (hence their alternative name of Single-Grave People). And they appear to have been more interested in cattle-raising than in growing crops. They may have introduced the horse into the country. In time they penetrated on to the islands, and a fusion of cultures took place. A specifically Danish culture emerged which was distinguished by the practice of burial in simple stone cists and by beautiful flint tools, especially a form of dagger, which is the reason why the period is often referred to as the Dagger Age; the finest known example of these daggers is that discovered at Hindsgavl on Fyn and now in the National Museum.

Long before this, however, objects of copper and bronze had begun to make their appearance in Denmark; the forms taken by the daggers just alluded to and by the axes of the Single-Grave People suggest metal prototypes. And about 1500 B.C. bronze was being worked in Denmark itself. The Bronze Age, which in northern Europe lasted about a millennium, was the high-water mark of prehistoric culture in Denmark. Thanks to a lively trade along the rivers which debouch into the Baltic and the North Sea, the inhabitants of Jutland and the islands could obtain many foreign treasures like bronze swords, axe-heads and daggers and vessels and ornaments of gold, for which they exchanged furs, slaves and the much-prized amber washed up on their beaches. But some of the most beautiful objects they possessed were made by native craftsmen, who often employed spiral decorations derived ultimately from Mycenean Greece. Their skill can be judged from the exquisite model found at Trundholm in north-west Zealand and consisting of a horse and gilded disc set on a six-wheeled framework. Its purpose is a mystery, but it was probably associated with sun-worship, of which there is much other evidence from this period. This may also have been the case with the most interesting of the home-made products—the six-foot-long curved horns known as *lurs*, familiar to the British housewife from the wrappings on Danish butter. About thirty-five of these have been found in Danish bogs, nearly always in pairs spiralling in opposite directions and cast in three sections. Quite a number can still be played today and sound rather like a trombone.

Nowhere else in northern Europe is there evidence of such a high standard of material culture in this period, although it is likely that it was enjoyed by only a comparatively small upper class, possibly made up of the descendants of the Single-Grave People. There is no copper or tin under the soil of Denmark, and bronze was expensive even where supplies of its two ingredients were more accessible. Flint continued to be the material out of which most everyday tools were made, and even bone was still widely used.

In the early centuries of the Bronze Age, inhumation was still practised, and the tannic acid from the oak coffins in which corpses were sometimes buried has preserved not only the nails and hair but also the clothing in which they were dressed at the time of burial. The most intriguing of the seven outfits which have survived in this way belonged to a young girl who was interred at Egtved near Kolding in eastern Jutland. It consists of a short skirt of woollen cords wound twice round the hips, a short-sleeved jacket and a woollen belt decorated with a large bronze disc (see Plate 1). The girl's hair and nails had been carefully groomed. Male costume includes kilts with shoulder straps, oval-shaped cloaks and tall woollen caps. The earth mounds over the bodies were often arranged along main lines of communication and can still be seen on many a Danish skyline.

In the late Bronze Age inhumation gave way to cremation, suggesting a change in religious beliefs. The ashes were at first placed in stone cists, but in time earthenware urns were used and deposited in existing mounds or in the ground without any external evidence of their existence. Grave goods from this period are much poorer, most of the dead man's possessions having been consumed by the flames of the funeral pyre; the treasures which we now possess all come from bogs, into which they had presumably been thrown in sacrifice.

About 500 B.C. several developments occurred which profoundly affected life in Denmark and indeed throughout Scandinavia, of which it formed the gateway. The spread of the Celts across central Europe from France and southern Germany cut the trade routes with the rich Mediterranean world on which Denmark had previously been so dependent for the development of its culture. But commerce was no longer so important because of the growing use of iron, which, unlike copper and tin, was available in the country's bogs. And since it was so easily obtainable, it not only replaced bronze in the making of weapons but also flint and bone for common tools. At the same time came a considerable worsening of the climate. The weather became much colder and damper than in the Bronze Age. This led to the abandonment of the less fertile soils and men had to pay more attention to building substantial shelters for themselves and their livestock, which had to be wintered under cover; a considerable number of long houses with thick earth walls, roofs supported on a central row of wooden posts and accommodation for animals at one end has been traced in northern Jutland. Clothing also had to be modified; the scanty dress of the Egtved girl would no longer have been sufficient even in the summer months, and the wearing of trousers was learned from the Celts. The graves of the period suggest a cultural poverty which can be attributed to these factors, and the population may well have declined.

Yet the bogs tell a rather different story. Those in Jutland especially have yielded a rich harvest of objects which were, as in the Late Bronze Age, probably deposited in the course of religious ceremonies. Most outstanding of these are the great silver cauldron of Celtic design found at Gundestrup in north Jutland and the remains of two handsome wooden carts with gilded mountings from Dejbjerg in the west of the peninsula, very reminiscent of the wagons mentioned by the Roman historian Tacitus in his account of Germany as having been used to transport a fertility goddess round the fields before being sunk in a sacred lake with the unfortunate slaves who had attended the deity. Even more interesting in view of the importance of seafaring in Danish history is the earliest known Scandinavian boat, found, together with a large collection of iron swords, spearheads and shirts of mail, in a bog at Hjortspring on the island of Als. It is a very simple affair made of planks sewn together with twine. It lacks mast, keel and rudder and is similar to the vessels depicted on rock carvings of the Bronze Age.

Some fifty bodies, a number of them in a remarkable state of preservation, have also been recovered from bogs in various parts of the country. These appear to have been thrown in either as sacrifices to the gods or after execution for crimes against the moral code of the time; of the two most famous, the Grauballe Man (now to be seen in the Århus Museum of Prehistory) and the Tolland Man (whose head is on display in Silkeborg), the first had had his throat cut, and the second had been strangled. That these were troubled times is suggested by the great earthwork surrounded by a ditch which has been traced at Borremose near Gundestrup and dated to this period. It protected a village and stood on an island linked to the mainland by a stone causeway. Roman sources record the mass migration of Germanic peoples southwards in this age; the Cimbri and Teutons who defeated Roman armies in the second century B.C. and penetrated as far as Spain and Italy may have come from northern Jutland, from the areas known as Himmerland and Thy respectively.

The barbarian tide, however, ebbed, and the Romans themselves began to expand northwards and westwards. About the beginning of the Christian era, objects which had their origin within the borders of their empire began to appear in Denmark. These goods reached the Baltic via the German tribes who had replaced the Celts as the dominant element in central Europe. They were exchanged for the familiar Scandinavian exports of fur, slaves and amber as well as for cattle and dairy produce. Ornaments and household objects of silver, bronze and glass, often of a very high quality, have come to light especially in well-stocked graves on the Danish islands; a particularly rich find, including two exquisite silver beakers decorated with scenes from Homer's *Iliad,* was made in 1920 at Hoby on Lolland. Many home-made articles show strong Roman influence. Altogether this seems to have been a peaceful and prosperous epoch. The climate began to improve, and rye, which was to become Denmark's most important cereal, was cultivated for the first time.

From the third century the wares which were imported came less and less from Italy by way of the rivers Elbe, Oder and Vistula and more and more from the western regions of the Empire, above all from Gaul; they were generally of inferior quality. Rival cultural influences were now reaching Denmark from the Goths, a people who had settled near the Black Sea after wandering from the Baltic area. It was possibly from them that the Scandinavians learnt the art of writing the characters known as runes, adapted from Mediterranean alphabets, but examples of Danish runes before the Viking Age are confined to a few brief inscriptions in primitive Scandinavian with a magical purpose. The impact of the Goths is also to be seen in artistic design, most readily on the booty which was cast by victorious armies into sacred lakes, which later dried out into bogs— shield bosses, swords, spearheads and harness. Again the islands are richer in remains than Jutland; one of the most famous sites is at Vimose on Fyn, the discoveries at which, including a fine coat of mail, may be seen in the provincial museum in Odense. A further advance in shipbuilding technique is demonstrated by the three ships found among one of these hordes at Nydam in Slesvig. The best preserved is now displayed in Gottorp Castle. Iron has been used in its construction, and it has a rudder, but, like the Hjortspring boat, it lacks mast and keel and could hardly have been used in the open sea. Some historians believe that the conflicts reflected in these bog finds may have resulted from an invasion of the islands by a tribe referred to by the sixth-century Gothic historian Jordanes as Danes, who, he claimed, came from Sweden and drove out the Heruli, peoples mentioned in much earlier sources. In time the Danes probably conquered the whole country which bears their name.

The fifth and sixth centuries have been called the Scandinavian Age of Gold because of the great number of gold objects which have been found in the area and dates to the period. Among them were the two gold horns discovered at Gallehus near Tønder in Slesvig in the seventeenth and eighteenth centuries. These were unfortunately stolen from the royal collection in 1802 and melted down by the thief, and the most accurate drawings made of them were lost at sea, but rough copies of these enabled the reproductions in the National Museum to be made. One of them has on it one of the rare runic inscriptions —'I Lægæst, son of Holte, made the horn' (see Plate 2a). Many other articles are of great beauty and are often decorated with the intertwined animal ornament associated with the Goths. Some of this gold, which is never found in graves, was doubtless offered to the gods, but much of it was probably hidden in the ground until some danger should pass and then misfortune overtook the owner. For the peoples of northern and eastern Europe were again on the move, causing great unrest. Inhabitants of Denmark undoubtedly took part in this second great migration, which caused the break-up of the Roman Empire in the West; it has been argued that the Vandals and the Burgundiand came originally from Vendel in northern Jutland and the island of Bornholm respectively, while the Jutes and Angles who came to Britain with the Saxons after the withdrawal of the Roman garrison in the fifth century may well have had their homelands in Jutland and Slesvig, the Danes having moved down into the territory they evacuated.

With the seventh century more settled conditions returned, although Frankish records speak of Danish raids on Frisia, probably aimed at securing a share in the new trade opened up by the Franks with the wealthy Arab world. Finds in Denmark are rather meagre for this and the following century, the last one before the Viking period, and for the first time Norway and Sweden provide evidence of a richer culture. This was doubtless connected with the advance of the Slavs along the southern shore of the Baltic which diverted trade routes away from Jutland. The population seems, however, to have been growing fast at this time, and much fresh land was being cleared. The majority of Danish settlement names have been traced back to the Late German Iron Age, as this time is called: those, for example, ending in *-inge*, *-lev* and *-sted*. And many of the tales recorded by the twelfth-century historian Saxo Grammaticus[1] may have their origin at this time. Though all such legends must, of course, be treated by the modern historian with great caution, some of the characters mentioned in them, like Harald Hildetand ('Wartooth'), who is said to have united the country and to have been killed fighting the Swedes at the battle of Brávellir, may have actually lived in the late sixth or early seventh century; while the story of Amled (Hamlet), first told by Saxo, may enshrine memories of the early days of Danish settlement.

[1] See below, p. 65.

# CHAPTER II

## *The Viking Age (c. 800-1047)*

---

IN spite of the records of raids on the Frisian coast in the sixth century, Danish contacts with western Europe between the end of the Migration Period and the middle of the eighth century appear to have been largely of a peaceful nature. Considerable trade was conducted with Dorestad and other Frisian ports near the mouth of the Rhine and on the coast north and south of it, and there is even evidence of extensive Danish settlement in this area, which the Jutes had probably used as a staging-post on their way to Britain. It was the northward advance of the Franks that transformed the situation.

About 770, the great Frankish king Charlemagne began his conquest of the Saxons, the next-door neighbours of the Danes in north-west Germany. The Danes felt themselves seriously menaced, and Frankish annals, on which we must rely for much of Denmark's early political history, speak not only of this granting asylum to Saxon refugees by a Danish king named Sigfrid but also of Danish warriors fighting side by side with the Saxons against the Franks. Thus the Danish expansion of the Viking period began as a defensive reaction to the threat of absorption by a great power to the south, and it was distinguished throughout from that of the Norwegians and the Swedes by its more highly organized character, a reflection to a large extent of the more highly organized state of the country.

The extent of Sigfrid's dominions is very uncertain; they may have been limited to southern Jutland, or he may have been a 'high king' to whom lesser rulers in Jutland and the islands owed a vague allegiance and whom they recognized as leader in time of war. Of the power of his successor Godfred there can, however, be little doubt. He countered the penetration of Hol-

29

stein by the Franks by striking at their Slav allies to the south-east, whose capital he destroyed, and by beginning the construction of a great defensive wall across the southern neck of the Jutish peninsula—the ancestor of the *Dannevirke*.[1] About 810 he went on to launch a successful raid further afield, in Frisia, which was now part of the Carolingian Empire. Soon after this raid Godfred was murdered, and his nephew and successor Hemming concluded a peace with the Franks which fixed the southern border of the Danish dominions on the river Ejder. But he reigned for only two years, and after his death his kingdom disintegrated in the midst of a civil war between rival claimants for his throne. Finally, in 827, his son Horik brought this to an end by expelling his rival Harald 'Klak', who had become a Christian in order to secure Frankish support for his claims. Horik reunited his father's lands, and by 845 was strong enough to send a large fleet to sack the already considerable town of Hamburg. Meanwhile, Danish bands, possibly with royal encouragement, had been penetrating Frankish territory much further away from their homeland.

Charlemagne had eventually been able so to strengthen the coastal defences of his empire as to make sea-borne attacks on it unprofitable. But the civil war which broke out between his son Louis the Pious and his grandsons in 833 had led to neglect of those defences. Large-scale Scandinavian raids on Frisia were resumed almost immediately, and when, after Louis's death in 840, the quarrels between his sons threatened to dissolve the Frankish dominions in a welter of anarchy, the raids spread down the North Sea coast to the Channel and even as far as Spain. Viking fleets (the records do not distinguish clearly between Danes and Norwegians any more than they probably did themselves) used the river systems of the Seine and the Loire to penetrate far inland; Paris had to withstand constant attack.

Early eighth-century Britain also offered a tempting bait to marauders. The death of king Offa in 796 had been followed by the rapid dissolution of the great Mercian kingdom covering most of England which he had created. Serious Scandinavian raids recorded in the Anglo-Saxon Chronicle began around 835 and grew in intensity during the next three decades. In 850 parties of Vikings for the first time adopted the practice of

[1] See below, p. 56.

spending the winter on an island near the mouth of the Thames and using it as a base for attacks on both sides of the Channel. About the same time a Danish army penetrated as far as Ireland, captured Dublin and for a brief period established a supremacy over the Norwegians already there. And in 865 the so-called Grand Army, probably about a thousand strong, landed in eastern England and began to occupy permanently Yorkshire, Lincolnshire, East Anglia and a large part of the Midlands, an area later referred to as the Danelaw, which in 878 Alfred of Wessex, having with great difficulty repulsed an attack on his own kingdom, recognized as independent by the Treaty of Wedmore.

The extent of Scandinavian settlement in England has long been the subject of considerable controversy, but in the region of the 'five boroughs' of Stamford, Leicester, Nottingham, Derby and Lincoln in particular it appears to have been considerable and certainly left long-lasting linguistic and administrative legacies, as in the description of the divisions of Yorkshire as ridings (*thridings* = third parts) and wapentakes, and in local dialects and place-names ending in *-by*, *-thwaite*, *-thorp* etc. down to the present day. The frequent mention on Swedish rune stones of journeys to England shows that by no means all the Scandinavians who went there were Danes, but the vast majority of the actual settlers almost certainly came from Jutland or the Danish islands.

After Wedmore, the attention of the Viking armies was diverted back to the continent for a period. The valley of the Rhine was devastated by them until 882, when their leader Godfred was granted Frisia as a fief by the Frankish king Charles the Fat. Godfred was, however, murdered soon afterwards at Charles's instigation, and northern France became the main field of operations. In 885–6 Paris had to endure an eleven-month-long siege, and for several years after this a Scandinavian army under a new leader named Sigfrid appears to have had the country at its mercy. Then, after a defeat near Louvain in 891 and weakened by sickness and famine, it left for England. There, however, it encountered stiff resistance from Alfred, who in the meantime had developed a defence system based on a fleet and fortified boroughs, and in 896 the host broke up, a large part of it returning to France. Already many of Sigfrid's followers had settled on the devastated land at the mouth of the Seine, and the grant of the area to Rollo (possibly a Norwegian) in 911 as a fief for which he owed allegiance to the king of the West Franks was little more than a recognition of a *fait accompli* and a means of keeping it under some sort of royal control. This area formed the nucleus of the Duchy of Normandy which rapidly adopted Frankish customs and ceased to be a part of the Scandinavian world.

Little is known of political conditions in Denmark for a long time after the death of Horik in 854, so that it is impossible to trace the connection between internal developments and the raids and settlements just described. Horik's work of unification does not, however, appear to have long survived him. Some of the accounts of contemporary travellers in the Baltic which Alfred the Great appended to his translation of Orosius's *History of the World* at the end of the ninth century suggest that Denmark was then divided into several princedoms. And a passage in Adam of Bremen's history of the archbishops of Hamburg–Bremen from the late eleventh century, together with the inscriptions on two rune stones found in the area concerned, indicate that, from the beginning of the tenth century to the 930s at least, the region round the port of Hedeby at the base of the Jutish peninsula (now part of German Schleswig) was in Swedish hands. With Baltic trade at its height, this area, which formed its hub, was a rich prize.[1]

The veil is not again lifted until 936, when a Saxon chronicle makes mention of a king Gorm. With him the continuous political history of Denmark begins. Little certain is known about him beyond what is recorded on the famous stone which he caused to be set up at his chief seat at Jelling in the middle of Jutland, and this is brief enough: 'King Gorm erected this memorial to Tyra his wife, glory (or saviour) of Denmark.' But he appears to have united the country once more, and this time for good. He died before 950, and was succeeded by his son Harald, nicknamed Bluetooth by a twelfth-century scribe. Harald raised the second of the Jelling stones in memory of his father and mother. He had during his reign to cope with a serious threat from the Ottonian emperors of Germany; the second of them in 974, having been provoked by Danish incur-

---

[1] See below, pp. 37–8.

1. Young woman's clothing from Early Bronze Age burial at Egtved, eastern Jutland (see p. 23). *National Museum, Copenhagen*

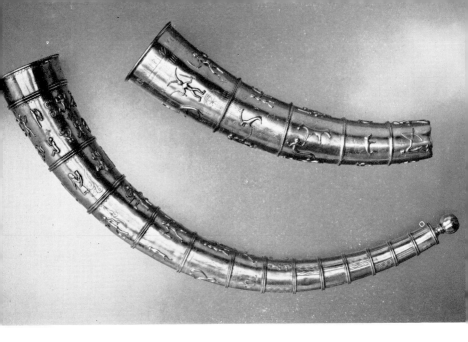

2. (a) Reconstruction of Late Iron Age gold horns from Gallehus, southern Jutland (see p. 27). The larger horn was discovered in 1639, the smaller (with runic inscription) nearby in 1734. *National Museum, Copenhagen*

2. (b) Tenth-century gold brooches and gold bracelet from Hornelund in Jutland. *National Museum, Copenhagen*

sions into Holstein, occupied parts of southern Jutland. But in 983 Harald's son Svend (Forkbeard) reconquered the territory for his father while Otto was fighting the Saracens in Italy. And Harald had already succeeded in extending his dominions northwards. In 961 he had defeated and killed King Håkon the Good of Norway in alliance with the latter's nephews, and about 970, after the fall of Harald Greycloak, the most successful of these, divided the country with the jarls of Trøndelag, Harald himself taking the rich area around Oslo Fjord. But his most momentous act was to allow himself to be baptized.

Denmark was the first Scandinavian country where serious attempts were made at conversion to Christianity. Frankish annals mention the visit there of Willibrord, the Northumbrian bishop of Utrecht, as early as the 730's, when he preached before a mysterious Danish prince whose name is given in Latin as Ongendus. But after this nothing further is heard of Christian activity for nearly a century. And, when it was resumed, the results were not encouraging. In the case of Harald Klak, as has been seen, the Church backed the wrong horse in the dynastic struggle. Harald had, however, been accompanied on his last campaign against Horik by a Frankish monk named Ansgar, who was shortly after it appointed to the new archbishopric of Hamburg with responsibility for missionary work throughout Scandinavia. He re-established a foothold for Christianity in Denmark by helping Horik, about the middle of the century, to make peace with the Emperor and was given permission by a grateful king to preach and to build the first church on Danish soil in Slesvig. Horik's successors allowed another church to be set up in Ribe, and even after Ansgar's death in 865 his assistant and biographer Rimbert appears to have been left to work in peace. But after Rimbert's death in 888 Christian activity slackened until Unni, a successor of Ansgar as archbishop of Hamburg–Bremen, visited King Gorm in 936. This visit marks the beginning of the systematic conversion of Denmark, but it was a slow business. Harald Bluetooth was not baptized until about 965, and there was no guarantee that his heirs would follow his example. According to tradition, a priest named Poppo converted him by successfully acquitting himself in the ordeal by fire, but a more telling reason for the king's decision was the need to deprive the German emperor of the excuse to invade his realm in the guise of a crusader against the heathen. Still, the inscription which Harald caused to be put on his Jelling stone—'the Harald, who . . . made the Danes Christians' —suggests that he took a genuine pride in his achievement; and on one side of the stone is a large figure of Christ.

To reconstruct a credible picture of Nordic paganism is a very difficult task. For one thing it lacked both a recorded body of doctrine to which the orthodox could appeal and an organized priesthood, so that, as with all such primitive systems of belief, its form changed from generation to generation and from one part of Scandinavia to another; gods and goddesses rose into favour and fell out of it again, acquired new attributes and lost them, divided and coalesced. The oldest written accounts of it flow from the pens of Christians living in a period when Scandinavia had for some time been subjected to strong western European influence. The main source, the *Elder Edda* of the Icelander Snorri Sturluson, while undoubtedly containing some ancient elements from the Viking Age, was not composed until the thirteenth century, and the beliefs which are there described cannot have been seriously professed anywhere for well over a century. Some of the stories in it can be found illustrated in Viking works of art, but others undoubtedly owe their origin to Mediterranean mythology and to Christian ideas; the parallels between the story of Baldur and of Christ seem too close to be coincidental. It is anyway highly unlikely that any pagan Viking's view of the world corresponded at all closely with that given by Snorri in *Gylfaginning* (The Deluding of Gylfi).

Place-names fill out the picture to a certain extent; no proven traces of heathen temples have been found anywhere in Scandinavia, but there were sacred sites at which sacrifices were performed by the local chieftain, and these are associated with, for example, the suffixes -*ve* and -*lund*, while the popularity of a god or goddess in a district can be judged from the prevalence of his or her name there. The frequency of the names of gods in areas which are known to have been settled early also enables us to trace, though unfortunately only in the vaguest outlines, the rise and fall of deities. The most familiar *Æsir* gods, led by Thor, Odin and Frey, seem to have been comparatively recent arrivals in the Viking period and to have succeeded in popularity older fertility gods like Tyr, who was particularly well liked in Denmark and may have been descended from those worshipped in the early Iron Age.

Harald Bluetooth's son Svend (*Anglice* Sweyn) was a pagan, but he does not appear to have been a fierce opponent of Christianity as such. What he did object to were the attempts by the archbishops of Hamburg–Bremen and their servants to interfere in secular affairs which, in his eyes, were none of their business; he seems to have been able to oust his father from power about 985 partly due to the support he received from those Danes who resented Harald's encouragement of German influences as well as his attempts to extend royal power. Svend welcomed to his kingdom English priests who constituted no threat to its independence, and behaved towards them and their activities with considerable tolerance.

In the last decade of the tenth century, Svend joined the great Norwegian king Olav Tryggvason in a major raid on England, and, after securing control of most of Norway by the defeat and death of his former comrade-in-arms at the naval battle of Svolder in or around the year 1000, he could turn his attention once more to the glittering prize across the North Sea. After the dissolution of the Grand Army, England had been untroubled by Viking activity for some eighty years. Alfred's sons had been able gradually to gain control of the disunited southern Danelaw and in 954 had been able finally to add to it the kingdom of York, which had been under Norwegian control for some forty years. But with the accession of the weak Ethelred (the Unready) in 978, Scandinavian raids were resumed, and in the 990's were conducted on an increasingly large scale, encouraged by the English king's attempts to buy off the attackers with vast 'danegelds', very welcome to them at a time when other supplies of silver from the East were drying up. Svend himself came again in 1003 to wreak vengeance for the massacre of his Danish subjects which had been organized by Ethelred the previous year, and ten years after this he finally set out to conquer the country. It is this period that have been dated the four great circular military camps of *Aggersborg* in north Jutland, *Trelleborg* in western Zealand, *Fyrkat* in east Jutland and the still-to-be-excavated *Nonnebakken* in the middle of Odense, together capable of housing some 4,000 warriors and possibly inspired by Eastern models. The most remarkable feature of them is the mathematical accuracy with which they were built, using a common unit of measurement—the 'Roman foot' (29·5 cm.). Their precise purpose is not known, but some historians have linked them with Svend's English enterprise.

Svend did not live to see his task completed; he died early in 1014. But his teenage son Knud (Canute) was chosen king by the English two years later, after the death of Ethelred's able warrior-son Edmund, and Knud proceeded to consolidate his position by marrying King Ethelred's widow Emma. Two years after this, he succeeded his elder brother Harald as king of Denmark also. The final defeat and death in 1030 of (St.) Olav Haraldsson, who had seized Norway in 1015, gave him control of a great North Sea empire, held together by sea-power and based on England; it was there that Knud spent most of his time, leaving Denmark to be ruled on his behalf, by a *jarl*[1] or viceroy. The marriage of his daughter Gunhild to the German emperor was a recognition of his European status. With his death in 1035, however, and the accession of his weaker son Hardeknud, this empire rapidly fell to pieces. St. Olav's son Magnus immediately regained Norway, and in 1042 Ethelred's son Edward (the Confessor) was chosen king of England on the death of Hardeknud. For five years after this Norway and Denmark were reunited under Magnus Olavsson, who even managed to assert temporary control over the Wends, Slavic tribes who inhabited the later German territories bordering on the Baltic; he inflicted a crushing defeat on them at Lyrskov Heath in south Jutland in 1043. But Scandinavia was now drawing in on itself, and the Viking Age was rapidly coming to a close. The main European trade routes had shifted away from the Baltic; the exploitation of silver mines in southern Germany was helping to create a strong political bloc in central Europe, which, as has been seen, was already a threat to Denmark in the tenth century; while the population of Scandinavia continued to grow, the pressure on land which led to the large-scale emigration was slackening; and the emergence of national monarchies in Denmark, Norway and Sweden considerably limited the scope of private raiding.

The expansion of the Viking period does not appear to have been accompanied by any fundamental changes in the way of

---

[1] The term is cognate with the English 'earl'.

life followed by the majority of the inhabitants of the Scandinavian homelands, who took no part in it. As far as can be judged on the basis of rather scanty evidence—archaeological finds, brief runic inscriptions, references in written sources, often, like the Icelandic Sagas, dating from a much later period —the social structure, legal systems and economies of Norway, Sweden and Denmark were basically little different in the ninth and tenth centuries from what they had been in the German Iron Age preceding. Even the modifications wrought by the closer contact with the more advanced countries of Europe in the period, above all by the adoption of Christianity and the development of royal power, only slowly altered the pattern to any appreciable extent.

The extent of Viking overseas settlement—from the Norwegians in Greenland to the Swedes in Russia—together with the study of place-names in Scandinavia itself suggests a continuation of the growth of population which had been in progress for several centuries; much new land was brought under the plough, and new villages grew out of colonies sent out by older ones. The remains of one of the latter has been unearthed in recent years at Lindholm Høje on the north side of Limfjorden. After having been inhabited for some five centuries, it was abandoned about the year 1100 and fossilized under a thick layer of sand; which has preserved even the furrows made by heavy ploughs and cart-tracks. Lindholm appears to have served as a trading and manufacturing as well as an agricultural centre, so that it is difficult to know how typical were its plan and its buildings, of which at least four different types have been identified.

But in some parts of Scandinavia settlements both larger than the village and different in kind from it were emerging for the first time in the Viking Age. The town, distinguishable in this period for its dependence on commerce, was to play a much more important role in the economic and social development of Denmark than of the other Scandinavian countries, and it is therefore appropriate that the most important of these early urban centres should be located at the base of the Jutish peninsula—at Hedeby. In spite of many years of patient investigation by German archaeologists, the sixty-acre site circumscribed by an earth rampart has still not been fully investigated, although a

# The Viking Age

considerable amount is known about it. First mentioned in a Frankish annal in 804, it was from the beginning of the Viking period until its destruction in the middle of the eleventh century,[1] the main centre of Baltic trade, at a time when the Baltic was one of the main trade routes of Europe. In Hedeby met merchants of many different nationalities bringing goods from as far afield as the Arab world (silver coins, glassware, silks and spices) and the far north of Scandinavia (furs and ivory) as well as from western Europe (cloth, pottery and weapons). The sea lane into the Baltic round the north of Jutland was a dangerous route for the ships of the period, especially as it was a favourite hunting-ground for pirates, and it was often quicker as well as safer to transport merchandise overland from the North Sea coast of Slesvig to the river Sli on which Hedeby stood and down this into the Baltic, or vice versa. New light has recently been thrown on the types of ship used by Viking Age merchants by the discovery in 1957 of six vessels dating from about 1000 at Skuldelev on Roskilde Fjord, for the carefully preserved remains of which a special museum has been built in Roskilde itself. At least two of these appear to have been intended for the conveyance of bulk cargoes; they are appreciably broader and deeper than the familiar 'long ships' used in Viking raids, though basically similar in construction.

Towns are traditionally associated in particular with the middle classes of society, and the merchants and craftsmen of Hedeby and of other smaller places like Århus and Roskilde which were emerging in the tenth century may be described as belonging to such. It must, however, be remembered that the basis of the economy was farming, that town and countryside were very closely bound together, and that while most town dwellers probably did some growing of crops, many farmers combined trade and handicrafts (and occasional participation in a Viking raid) with the raising of cattle and planting of corn. Rural society was already complex, the only clear line being that which divided freemen from unfree thralls. The number of the latter, who were at the full disposal of their masters, probably increased as a result of the conflicts of the Viking period, though they were not drawn exclusively from the ranks of prisoners-of-war; servitude might, for example, be a conse-

[1] See below, p. 42.

quence of indebtedness. Even a modest landowner might be expected to own a number of thralls to do his bidding. But while no thrall could own land, by no means all freemen did so either, and with the rise in the population, the proportion of freeman who had either little land or no land at all to work or who could only rent land from another almost certainly grew; it may have been such men as these who inhabited the small rectangular huts with sunken floors found at Lindholm. At the other end of the scale came men with great landed wealth and many retainers—the Viking aristocracy from which royal councillors and officials were chosen. Some of its members might aspire to a jarldom with vice-regal powers or, if they were related to the present or to a past king, even to the crown itself. But the nobility was still an ill-defined class, merging at its lower end with the upper reaches of the peasantry.

Large landowners could undoubtedly exercise considerable influence in local affairs, but in theory all decisions affecting the welfare of the immediate community were taken collectively by the freemen of the district (*herred*) meeting regularly in the *thing*. The *thing* was both a political assembly and a court of law, where those accused of offences against the unwritten law of the area were given the opportunity of clearing themselves by means of a judicial duel, compurgation (the swearing by an agreed number of one's fellows that one was innocent) or the ordeal. The latter usually took the form of holding a red-hot iron, the burns from which had to heal up within a certain time to secure acquittal. The duel, an institutionalized version of the blood-feud, had disappeared with the blood-feud itself before the end of the Viking period and had been replaced by compurgation or the ordeal, both of which were preferred by the Church and may indeed have been introduced under its auspices. The punishment for most crimes, even those involving death, was a fine payable to the offended party or his family, but in certain serious cases temporary or permanent exile could be imposed, and the common thief usually suffered an ignominious death by hanging.

Above the district *things* lay the provincial *things*. Exactly how many of these there were in Denmark in the Viking period is not known, but there were undoubtedly at least four—one each for Jutland, Fyn, Zealand and the territory ruled by the king of Denmark on the eastern side of the Sound (Halland, Blekinge and Skåne). In theory the king had to be elected by each of the provincial *things* before he could claim authority in the country as a whole, and this was indeed no formality when any member of the royal house could claim the crown on the death of its wearer and disputed successions were common. Such a system imposed considerable limitations on the king's powers. As will be seen, the Church, by hedging him with a degree of divinity, was able to enhance his prestige considerably, and even in late Viking times his officials seem to have been interfering more and more in the work of the *things*. But the extent of his authority, like that of any of his nobles, rested finally on the strength of his own personality and his wealth in land and followers.

Of the so-called fine arts—painting, sculpture and architecture—the Danes of the Viking period have left little trace. Buildings were all of wood and have consequently long since disappeared, but what can be gathered about them from later written descriptions in Saga literature and from excavations such as those at Lindholm Høje suggests that they were simple but solidly constructed like the ships which were capable of withstanding voyages as far afield as North America. Paint was used only to enhance the effect of carvings in wood and stone; the designs on the Jelling and many other rune stones were originally coloured. And it can only be surmised that the small metal and wood figurines of gods and goddesses which have come down to us were models of larger idols. But in the field of applied and 'minor' arts—metal-work, wood-carving and weaving etc.—the Danes of the period were able to produce work as fine as that to be found anywhere else in Europe in the ninth, tenth and eleventh centuries (see Plate 2b), due acknowledgement being paid to their debt to outside influences, such as those from the Celtic, Frankish and Anglo-Saxon worlds; the lion and the figure of Christ on the larger of the Jelling stones raised by Harald Gormsson may even have been carved by an Englishman. Like their fellow Scandinavians, they remained in their ornamentation firmly attached to the stylized animal motifs of earlier ages, to which the so-called 'gripping beast' was a delightful addition. As during the Bronze Age, design tended to become more elaborate and varied as time went on.

This can be seen by comparing the so-called Jelling and Mammen styles of the tenth century with older work such as that on the Oseberg ship in Norway. The former is named after the pattern on a silver goblet found in 'King Gorm's mound' at Jelling, although it is now generally believed to have been first developed among Scandinavians in northern England, who were in close contact with the Irish Celts. The second is named after a gold-inlaid axe from a horde at Mammen in central Jutland, but, like the Jelling style, is found widely outside Denmark.

# CHAPTER III

# The Early Middle Ages (1047-1157)

TOWARDS the end of the reign of Magnus Olavsson (Magnus the Good), his claim to Denmark was disputed by Svend Estridsen, the son of Canute the Great's sister and an English nobleman named Ulf, and when Magnus died in a riding accident, in 1047, Svend was elected his successor. He was, however, challenged in his turn by the new King of Norway, Harald Hardradi, Magnus's uncle and the last of the great Vikings. Harald embarked on a number of raids on Svend's territories (including one on which he finally destroyed Hedeby), and he generally seems to have had the better of his rival in battle. But he could not drive Svend permanently from the Danish throne, and finally turned his attentions to England. In 1066 he died at Stamford Bridge trying to win the crown of that country from Harold Godwinsson, less than a month before the latter lost it at Hastings to the descendant of another Viking warrior. For the next century relations between the Scandinavian rulers were comparatively peaceful. About 1070 Svend and King Emund of Sweden agreed on a frontier between their two realms which was largely respected until the seventeenth century. The whole of what is now the southernmost and westernmost area of Sweden south of the river Göta, consisting of the three provinces of Halland, Skåne and Blekinge, was recognized as owning allegiance to the wearer of the Danish crown, and stones were set up to mark the boundary along its northerly and easterly sections, Skåne being sufficiently cut off from Sweden by a deep belt of largely uninhabited forest.

While the rulers of Denmark were long to be spared threats from their neighbours, this does not mean that they were to be secure on their thrones. The hundred years following Svend

Estridsen's accession were indeed a time of great internal strife, during which the crown was constantly in dispute. But such struggles were motivated not only by a lust for power. Behind them can also be discerned ideological differences between the contestants and their supporters, different concepts in particular of royal authority. And these usually involved different views of the Crown's relations with the Church. For the Church was growing increasingly powerful as it became more highly organized and its missionary period in Denmark came to an end. Finally, out of such strife was to emerge a much more sophisticated type of government, similar to that in England and France in the same period and far removed from that of the Viking Age. The late eleventh and early twelfth centuries therefore constituted, for all its apparent confusion, a formative period of considerable importance.

As far as Europe as a whole was concerned, the Viking Age may have come to an end in the middle of the eleventh century. But how much the Viking spirit remained alive in Denmark after this can be judged from the invaluable account of the country in the late eleventh century given in Adam of Bremen's *History of the Archbishops of Hamburg–Bremen*. Composed in the 1070's, this is the first really important contemporary source for Danish history. Adam was head of the cathedral school in Bremen and visited Denmark frequently to gather material for his work. Though much of his information must have been obtained at second hand, the picture he draws is a reasonably convincing one. And it is not very complimentary to the Danes. Their courage is acknowledged, but they are castigated for their arrogance and addiction to food, strong drink and women (Adam points out, however, with equal distaste, that unfaithful wives ran the risk of being sold into slavery). Piracy seems to have made all travel between the islands extremely perilous. The close relations which Adam established with King Svend mean that what is said in the book about the monarch himself must be treated with caution, but while stress is laid on the latter's piety and learning, it is obvious that he shared a number of his countrymen's vices; it is admitted that he indulged in much feasting, had at least fifteen illegitimate children by various mistresses, and permitted a nest of sea-robbers to establish themselves on an island between Fyn and Zealand. And though other sources confirm Adam's account of the support which Svend gave to the Church, the King was not willing to submit meekly to the dictates of its servants. When Archbishop Adalbert of Bremen called on him to dissolve his marriage to a Swedish princess to whom by Canon Law he was too closely related, Svend threatened the interfering prelate with the devastation of his province. He did give way after an appeal from the Pope, but Adalbert's strictures strengthened his resolve to free the Danish Church from the control of a foreign archbishop, and at the end of his reign he was engaged in negotiations with Rome with the object of having Scandinavia declared a separate archdiocese.

Svend Estridsen died in 1074 or 1076 after what must be accounted a successful reign, in which the power of the Crown, still based largely on the king's body of retainers (*hird*), was strengthened and a close relationship, valuable to both parties, established with the Church. He was buried in Roskilde, where lay his principal residence. In spite of his four marriages, he left no legitimate children behind him, and the throne was disputed between two of his bastard sons—Harald and Knud. The mild and introspective Harald was supported by the peasantry, who regarded him as the less likely leader of the two to try to encroach further on the autonomy of local groups, and by the Church which appreciated his piety. Knud, on the other hand, was a tough warrior, who had played a prominent part in a raid on England under Svend's brother and was championed by his own kind among the nobles. Harald in fact won the crown without bloodshed. Knud admitted temporary defeat and sailed off on what proved to be the last Danish attack on England, but he later returned to attempt to unseat his half-brother. The enemies of the new king accused him of being weak-willed and consequently nicknamed him *Hén* or 'whetstone', but he seems to have had some gifts as a ruler. He is credited with a thoroughgoing reform of the currency which gave the country a uniform and reliable coinage, and he managed to resist Knud's threats until his death in 1080. Knud then managed to secure the crown with surprising ease.

In the fourth Knud Denmark secured a native saint to match Olav of Norway. But this was not because of any fundamental change in his character after he came to the throne. He made generous provision for the Church in the shape of grants of royal land and allowed the bishops a prominent place in his Court. But he remained the passionate, power-hungry Viking of his younger days, who resumed his father's efforts to strengthen royal power with considerably less tact than Svend seems to have shown; he claimed all unoccupied land for the Crown, imposed heavy fines on all those who had transgressed what he adjudged to be his rights, and demanded large contributions in kind for the upkeep of his Court as it travelled round the country. All this caused growing unrest among the farmers who had supported his predecessor. In 1085 he formed a large fleet in the Limfjorden with which to attack England and perhaps attempt to revive the empire of his great namesake. For reasons which remain obscure, this armada never sailed, and in the spring of the following year the common people of northern Jutland, where the King was staying, finally rose in revolt. The movement soon spread, and Knud was forced to flee to Odense. The rebels pursued him there and slew him before the very altar of St. Alban's Church.

The circumstances of Knud's death were in the eleventh century enough in themselves to give him a strong claim to martyrdom, but his case was strengthened by the events which followed it. His brother Oluf, whom he had arrested and sent off to his father-in-law in Flanders for safe custody, was chosen to succeed him. And Oluf's ten-year reign was marked by a series of disastrous harvests, which earned him the nickname of 'hunger' and were claimed by Knud's champions to be signs of divine wrath after the murder. Yet another of Svend Estridsen's sons, Erik, who had stood by Knud during the revolt and had been with him at the end in St. Alban's, came home from Sweden to be elected king on Oluf's death. Erik was to enjoy the nickname of *ejegod* ( = Always Good), and Saxo Grammaticus, writing at the end of the following century, pictures him as a popular monarch, but another source gives the impression that he asserted his prerogatives as harshly as Knud had done. And his sympathy for the aims of the latter led him to put all his weight behind the campaign for Knud's canonization which had been begun by the priests of Odense, one of whom was already recording the miracles which were supposed to have taken place at the dead king's tomb.

# THE DESCENDANTS OF SVEND ESTRIDSEN

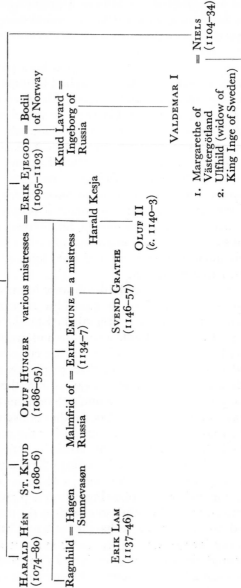

Thanks to such evidence and the close relations which Erik established with the Pope during a pilgrimage he made to Italy in 1098 (and doubtless helped also by the series of exceptionally good harvests which had succeeded the poor ones of Oluf's time), the campaign was successful. In 1101 Knud's remains were solemnly reinterred under the high altar before which he had been slain, and a richly endowed Benedictine monastery, staffed by English monks from Evesham, was established in Odense to perpetuate his memory. Knud was, however, never a popular saint in Denmark; memories of his rule among the common people defied all the efforts of the hagiographers to expunge them. Erik further exploited his good relations with the Papacy, as well as the latter's bad relations with the Archbishop of Hamburg–Bremen, who was supporting an anti-pope, to revive his father's attempts to secure the independence of the Scandinavian Church under its own archbishop. And in this also he triumphed. Before his death in 1103, Bishop Asser of Lund, a member of the great Thrugotsen family of Jutland and closely related to the Crown, was made primate of all Scandinavia.

As has been suggested, heathen morality died hard in Denmark. And in Adam of Bremen's time heathen rites were still being practised there; indeed parts of north Jutland and the whole of the island of Bornholm appear still not to have been converted. Nevertheless, by 1100 Christianity was becoming firmly rooted in most parts of the country, even at the cost of some compromise by the clergy with old customs. Adam himself, for all his strictures, was impressed by the progress which had been made:

> Behold the fearsome land, whose idolatry hitherto made it inaccessible. Now is its former savagery put off, and everywhere its inhabitants compete to bid welcome to the preachers of the truth. Heathen altars are destroyed, churches rise on every hand, and all praise together the name of Christ.

In the 1050's, while the two men were still on relatively good terms, Svend Estridsen and the Archbishop of Hamburg-Bremen agreed on the organization of regular dioceses in Denmark. Jutland, which was described by Adam as bleak and barren, was nevertheless given three new sees at Århus, Viborg and Vestervig (transferred to Bøglum in 1135) to add to those of Slesvig and Ribe. And the territories on the eastern side of the Sound were taken from the Bishop of Roskilde and divided into two dioceses based on Lund and the nearby Dalby, though the latter was soon suppressed.

Most parishes had by this time acquired simple buildings, consisting of vertical oak planking set on a framework of posts, within which masses could be said. These were often erected by the local large landowners near the meeting-place of the *thing*. Adam noted no fewer than 300 such churches in Skåne, though this fertile and thickly populated province was apparently more highly organized than the rest of the country, for in the following hundred years few new churches appeared there, while on Fyn and Zealand the number given by Adam trebled. None of these wooden 'stave' churches have survived in Denmark, but traces of them have often been found under their more substantial stone successors, which began to appear in the middle of the eleventh century. Still very simple in design, they often followed the groundplan of their wooden forebears: a rectangular nave and a lower and narrower square chancel with sometimes a rounded apse at the east end. The stone was usually left in a rough state, and towers of any kind were as yet rare. But in the sees more impressive buildings in the sturdy Romanesque style, with its solid walls and rounded arches, the style of the vast majority of Danish medieval churches, were beginning to rise by the early twelfth century. The most ambitious was the sandstone cathedral in Lund. Its foundations were laid during the incumbency of Archbishop Asser, who soon after his elevation invited builders from Speyer to start work on a structure similar to that in their city. Lund has unfortunately been considerably altered over the years, but in Ribe may still be seen a cathedral of the same period much as it was when first built, of tufa stone imported from the Rhineland for the purpose.

Exterior decoration on these buildings was largely confined to geometrical patterns or simple naturalistic motifs on pillars and arches and to carvings over doorways, but the execution of the latter was often extremely powerful, especially when carried out in Jutland granite, as can be seen in the Crucifixion scene on the tympanum over the 'Cathead Door' of Ribe Cathedral.

3. 'Golden altar' of the mid twelfth century from Lisbjerg, northern Jutland (see p. 49). *National Museum, Copenhagen*

4. Carmelite Abbey Church (St. Mary's) in Elsinore. Mid fifteenth century (see p. 88). *National Museum, Copenhagen*

The same skill is found on twelfth-century fonts, in particular the 'Lion fonts' peculiar to eastern Jutland. But the most spectacular of early medieval Danish ecclesiastical furnishings are undoubtedly the magnificent 'golden altars', in fact sheets of gilded copper beaten into elaborate representations and set on wooden mountings before and above the stone altars of Jutish churches. A number of these are to be seen in the National Museum in Copenhagen, including one of the oldest, the Lisbjerg Altar from about 1150 which may have stood originally in the first Århus Cathedral (see Plate 3).

Erik Ejegod died, appropriately enough, in Cyprus while on a pilgrimage to the Holy Land. His queen continued the journey with their young son Knud, and in Denmark Erik's brother Niels, the last of Svend Estridsen's sons, was elected to succeed him as the only mature candidate. Niels was a peace-loving man who continued his predecessor's good relations with the Church. He also made generous gifts to it, especially to St. Knud's monastery in Odense, and its organization made considerable strides during his reign; the tithe finally replaced the payments exacted by the clergy for individual services which had scandalized Adam of Bremen, and ecclesiastical matters were withdrawn from lay to separate clerical courts. Niels does not seem to have been quite so spineless as he was later pictured by Saxo Grammaticus; his reign saw the evolution of a central administration under a chancellor (always a priest, since he had to be able to read and write), which replaced the inchoate *hird* of royal retainers, and closer contacts were established between Denmark and the rest of western Europe. But he was not able himself to deal effectively with renewed threats from the Wends, who invaded southern Jutland and whose fleets made the whole of the southern Baltic unsafe for trade. And the temporary solution which Niels adopted for this problem only sowed the seeds of future trouble. In 1115, possibly also in an attempt to reconcile a potential rival, he appointed his able and vigorous young nephew Knud, called *Lavard* (= Bread-giver), *jarl* or duke of southern Jutland, and granted him the extensive powers of a marcher lord. Knud not only conducted a brilliant campaign against the Wends but in 1129 even got himself elected their prince. His success and his arrogant behaviour aroused the fears of Niels's son Magnus, who saw in Knud a threat to his

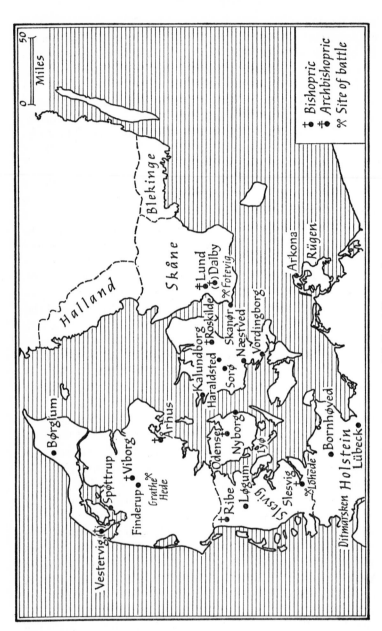

Miles
0
50

† Bishopric
‡ Archbishopric
✗ Site of battle

Blekinge

Halland

Skåne

‡Lund
†Dalby
✗Fotevig

Arkona

Rügen

Bbörglum

Vestervig
Spøttrup
†Viborg
Finderup
✗Grathe Hede

†Arhus
Kalundborg
Haraldsted
Roskilde†
Sorø
Skanør
Næstved
Vordingborg

Odense
Nyborg
Lyø

†Ribe
Løgum
Slesvig
✗Lohede
†g

Bornhøved
Lübeck

Ditmarsken Holstein

3. Medieval Denmark

own position as heir. Finally, in 1131, Magnus lured the Duke into Haraldsted Wood near Ringsted and murdered him. This deed led to a civil war which lasted on and off for a quarter of a century.

Knud Lavard's cause was taken up by his half-brother Erik *Emune* (= memorable), who was joined by a large number of nobles. The Church and the common people backed the King. Niels appears to have had the best of the fighting during the three confused years which followed and finally forced Erik to flee to Norway. But in the spring of 1134 the latter reappeared in Skåne, where he secured the support of the Archbishop and decisively defeated Niels and Magnus at Fotevig. This bloody battle is of considerable long-term significance, for Erik owed his victory largely to a body of 300 German armoured knights, for whom the old-style popular levy on which his opponents had to rely was no match. A new type of warfare which was to have far-reaching social and political consequences had arrived in Denmark.

Magnus fell at Fotevig, together with no fewer than five Danish bishops, and his father was slain soon afterwards by the citizens of Slesvig, whither he had fled for refuge. The throne was occupied by the victor. But Erik Emune proved as brutal and reckless in peace as he had been during the war. He managed to repress a serious uprising against him in Zealand, but in September 1137 was struck down by one of his aggrieved subjects while attending a *thing* in Ribe. He was succeeded by his nephew, also named Erik. It was the nephew who had led the German knights at Fotevig, and he had shown considerable physical courage on the occasion of his uncle's murder, but he was essentially a peace-loving man lacking in firmness of purpose—hence his nickname of *lam* (= the Meek). And his reign was dominated by a man of much stronger character: Eskil, who succeeded his uncle Asser as Archbishop of Lund just before Erik Emune's death. Although not a particularly subtle politician, Eskil combined genuine piety with a moral vigour which his predecessor apparently lacked, and his long period of forty years in office provided an invaluable element of stability in a very unstable political situation. While studying in Germany, he had become imbued with the tenets of the great Gregorian reform movement within the Church with its call above all for the Church's independence in its relations with the State. He had been a vigorous opponent of Erik Emune in defence of such freedom when he had been Bishop of Roskilde and seems to have been implicated in the unsuccessful rebellion against that king in his own diocese. His views were probably reflected in the important *Roskilde Chronicle*, a history of Denmark written by an anonymous clerk about this time, which praises King Niels while picturing Erik Ejegod and other rulers who attempted to assert royal power as tyrants. Soon after his election to the primacy, Eskil held a great Scandinavian synod in Lund, attended by a papal legate, at which the implications of the reform movement were debated.

Fortunately for internal peace, Erik Lam was willing to work with Eskil, and indeed he appears to have relied heavily on the Archbishop in lay as well as in ecclesiastical affairs. The Church benefited greatly from this co-operation. Eskil was able to welcome to Denmark the new Cistercian Order of monks, who, by opening up new land, were to play an important role in the country's economic development, and also founded communities of Premonstratensians and Hospitallers. He pressed ahead with the building of his own cathedral, whose choir was ready for consecration in 1145. Paradoxically the increase in the power of the Church during these years, while it was yet to bring about serious clashes between the clerical and lay powers, ultimately benefited the latter.

For much of his reign Erik Lam had to face a serious threat from Erik Emune's nephew Oluf, who launched a series of attacks on him from Sweden in support of a claim to the throne. Oluf was finally killed in 1143, but only three years later Erik himself fell mortally sick, abdicated and retired to die in St. Knud's monastery in Odense. The freemen of Jutland, gathered at the provincial *thing* in Viborg, thereupon chose Magnus's son Knud to be king, but those of Zealand and Skåne opted for Erik Emune's son Svend Grathe. The result was a renewal of the civil war. Svend was joined by Valdemar, Knud Lavard's posthumous son by a Russian princess (his name is a version of the Slavonic Vladimir), and in 1151 Knud Magnusson suffered what appeared to be decisive defeat near Viborg. Svend was crowned by the Emperor Frederick Barbarossa himself in Merseberg, but he promised on this occasion to grant Zealand to Knud as a fief. He had already made an enemy of the Arch-bishop, and when, on his return to Denmark, he failed to honour his promise to Knud, Valdemar changed sides. Svend now showed himself to be his father's son, and as act of tyranny was heaped on act of tyranny, his support fell away, until he found it wisest to flee to Germany and seek help from the Emperor who had crowned him and to whom he had sworn allegiance.

In 1155 Archbishop Eskil was arrested as a rebel as he passed through the Emperor's territories on his way back to Denmark after a visit to Rome, and two years later Valdemar and Knud finally agreed on a division of the kingdom with Svend. During a meeting between the three men in Roskilde, however, the latter caused his fellow kings to be treacherously attacked. Knud was slain, but Valdemar, though wounded, managed to escape by dousing the candles in the hall and roused the peasants of Jutland against Svend. In October the armies of the two rivals met on Grathe Heath, south of Viborg, and Svend was killed. The conflict which had begun with the murder of Knud Lavard ended with the triumph of his son, whom he had never seen, and the dawning of the golden age of Danish medieval history.

# CHAPTER IV

# *The Age of the Valdemars (1157-1241)*

---

THE year after the victory at Grathe Heath which gave Valdemar Knudsson the Danish crown, the new king caused a man who was to become one of the greatest figures in Danish medieval history to be appointed Bishop of Roskilde. Absalon was a member of the Hvide family, the most powerful in Zealand. We know a great deal about him from the history written by Saxo Grammaticus, for Absalon was the writer's patron. Because of this relationship, what Saxo says about the Bishop must be treated with caution; we can expect him to be pictured in the best possible light. But his stature has been little diminished by later research. Absalon was only thirty years old at the time of his election and thus only a few years older than Valdemar, whom he had known well since childhood and whom he had stood by during the civil war. He realized that, while the Church might be able to make considerable gains during a period of political confusion, as had happened in the England of Stephen's day, it stood to benefit even more from a strong lay power which was willing to co-operate with it, recognize its rights and offer it physical and legal protection. In this spirit, therefore, he set out to work closely with Valdemar, who also appreciated the profits which might accrue from the support of the Church. He in fact succeeded so well that it is difficult for the historian to decide how many of the achievements of the reign to attribute to the Bishop and how many to the King.

Even Saxo's account, while it gives the impression that Absalon dominated the partnership, makes it clear that Valdemar was also a powerful personality. And the remarkable harmony which characterized his relations with Absalon was notably absent from his dealings with the elderly Archbishop. Eskil was not only opposed to the kind of strong royal government for which Valdemar stood and which Absalon supported, but he was also soon at loggerheads with the King over relations with the Emperor Frederick Barbarossa. In the latter's great struggle with Pope Alexander III, Valdemar, who swore allegiance to him soon after attaining the Danish throne, took his overlord's side and recognized the anti-pope Victor IV, while the Archbishop backed Alexander, to whom he owed his release from captivity in Germany after Valdemar's victory. Finally, in 1161, Eskil found it wisest to leave Denmark for France, where he took up residence in the great monastery of Clairvaux. As the Emperor's position weakened, however, Valdemar became anxious for a reconciliation with the prelate, and, with Absalon's aid, he achieved it in 1170. In that year, at an impressive ceremony in St. Mary's (later St. Benedict's) Church in Ringsted, not only was the canonization of Valdemar's father, for which the Lavard party had long been working, affirmed, but Knud, the King's eldest son, was crowned by Eskil himself as the acknowledged heir to the throne. This latter move, undertaken by Valdemar in an attempt to prevent a repetition of the civil war of all too recent memory, seemed to many nobles to threaten the replacement of an elective by an hereditary monarchy, which would mean a considerable reduction of their power, and a number of them, including members of the Archbishop's family, became involved in a series of revolts. While there is no evidence that Eskil himself was implicated in these, he was undoubtedly embarrassed by them, and his resolve to retire from office was strengthened. In 1177 he left Denmark for good, to die in Clairvaux only four years later.

Like Eskil in his younger days, Absalon was not averse to aiding the Crown in military enterprises. The most serious external problem which Valdemar had to face at the beginning of his reign was that of the Wends. Under pressure from German settlers, who throughout the twelfth century were pushing steadily eastward across the Elbe, these had turned increasingly to a life of piracy, which the growing amount of trade through the waters around Denmark made extremely profitable. Their depredations became especially serious during the civil war, when no firm, united action could be taken against them, and in the first year of the new reign Århus was attacked by them. Absalon joined Valdemar in operations against their bases in alliance with Henry the Lion, Duke of Saxony and the mightiest prince in northern Germany. Since paganism still survived in Wendish territory, these expeditions could also be given the colour of crusades. Finally, in 1169, an exceptionally large-scale Danish enterprise succeeded in capturing and destroying the main enemy fortress of Arkona on the island of Rügen at the mouth of the river Oder, and the great heathen temple which was found there was burnt to the ground. Rügen became a fief of the Danish king, and its inhabitants were compelled to accept Christianity.

Valdemar the Great (as he came to be called) refused at first to share the booty which he had won from the Wends, and Henry revenged himself by stirring up the latter against his former ally. The two rulers soon, however, became reconciled, Prince Knud becoming engaged to the Duke's daughter in 1171, and the Wends ceased to be a serious menace to the Danish coasts. Valdemar had already begun to strengthen the defences of his realm by means of an additional brick rampart on the *Dannevirke* and a number of fortresses, of which Vordingborg on the southern coast of Zealand became a favourite royal residence. And he was joined in this work by some of his leading nobles. His nephew constructed the castle of Nyborg protecting the western end of the crossing from Zealand to Fyn, and on an island on the Sound which formed part of the episcopal estates, Absalon built a castle overlooking the settlement of Havn (Danish for 'harbour'), which was destined to grow into the city of Copenhagen.

On Eskil's retirement, Absalon's succession to his dignity was almost a foregone conclusion, even though the new incumbent did protest against his elevation; by an unusual papal dispensation, he was allowed to continue to enjoy the see of Roskilde in plurality with Lund. The inhabitants of Skåne soon came to regret the change. Absalon was a man who expected strict obedience to his commands and also seems to have made himself unpopular by his insistence on clerical celibacy and his appointment of Zealanders to important positions. So bitter indeed did feelings become that open revolt broke out, and the Archbishop was forced to flee from his see. Valdemar attempted

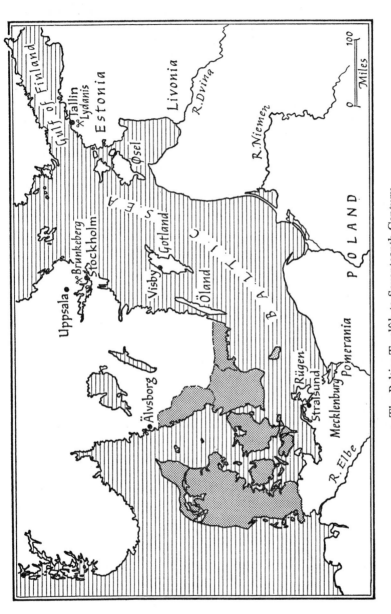

4. The Baltic: Twelfth to Seventeenth Century

in vain to bring about a reconciliation and had in the end to go over to Skåne with an army. Even then he could restore some kind of order only by making concessions over Absalon's head, and the province was still restless when the King died in Vordingborg in 1182.

With the accession of the nineteen-year-old Knud, Absalon became the real ruler of the realm. It was he who determined to seize the opportunity presented by an attack on the Danish protectorate of Rügen by the Prince of Pomerania finally to put an end to the power of the Wends, and in so doing launched the kingdom on a process of territorial expansion to south and east which was to continue into the following century. In 1184 he secured a decisive victory over the Prince at sea, and not only the latter but also his fellow rulers in Mecklenburg were compelled to acknowledge Danish suzerainty. This and the further gains which followed were possible to a large extent because at the end of Valdemar's reign the Emperor had crushed the might of Henry the Lion, thus leaving something of a power vacuum in northern Germany, and had turned from the Baltic to the Mediterranean in pursuit of his Italian ambitions, which were to lead eventually to the virtual collapse of his authority in central Europe. Absalon took further advantage of the Emperor's preoccupations to abjure the allegiance which successive Danish kings had sworn to his predecessors since the beginning of the twelfth century.

The great Archbishop died in 1201 in the rich monastery of Sorø in the middle of Zealand and was buried in its church. The 'father of his country', as Saxo described him, was succeeded by his cousin Anders Sunesøn, a scholar with a European reputation who had studied in both Paris and Bologna and who had served the King as chancellor. King Knud himself, who remains a rather shadowy figure beside Absalon, followed him to the grave two years later.

During the reign of Knud IV a quarrel broke out between his brother Valdemar, who was made Duke of Slesvig (i.e. southern Jutland) in 1187, and the local bishop of the same name, a bastard son of King Knud III with an eye on the throne. This had encouraged the aggressive Adolf of Schauenberg, count of Holstein on the south side of the river Ejder, to intervene in Danish affairs. Just before he came to the throne in succession to Knud, Valdemar Duke of Slesvig struck back, occupied Adolf's lands and went on to force the cities of Hamburg and Lübeck to submit. At his accession Denmark was well on its way to securing control of the whole southern coastline of the Baltic west of the Oder and of the North Sea east of the Elbe. The princes of Germany were too busy fighting among themselves on behalf of pope or emperor (Guelf or Ghibelline) to resist the Danish advance, and in 1215 Emperor Frederick II recognized Valdemar's conquests. The latter was consequently able to turn his attention to the eastern Baltic. In 1219 he undertook a crusade against the still heathen Estonians, already the object of a campaign by Knud IV, a good cover for an attempt to gain control of the southern shore of the Gulf of Finland and with it of the Russian trade route from Novgorod into the Baltic, a route in which German traders also were much interested. It was before the defeat of the Estonians at the battle of Lydanis that *Dannebrog*, the flag consisting of a white cross on a red ground which is now Denmark's own, is reputed to have descended from heaven to assure the Danish troops of victory; the tradition is in fact a late one, and the real origin of the device remains a mystery. Valdemar built a fortress at Tallin (= Danestown), but Danish rule of the area was little more than nominal.

Denmark's Baltic empire was short-lived. In 1223 Valdemar and his eldest son, while on a hunting expedition on the small island of Lyø, off the southern coast of Fyn, were kidnapped by Count Henry of Schwerin, a Danish vassal, and carried off to captivity in Mecklenburg. The princes of Pomerania and Mecklenburg immediately renounced their allegiances, and, after Count Henry's army had defeated one raised to free the King by force, Valdemar was compelled to submit to his enemies' demands and surrender all his acquisitions except Estonia and Rügen as well as pay a large sum of money before being released; Denmark's southern boundary ran once more along the Ejder. Valdemar attempted to regain Holstein in 1227, but his army was soundly beaten by that of the German princes at Bornhøved, and he lost an eye in the battle. The victories of Valdemar the Victorious (an appellation he was given in the sixteenth century) were at an end, and the remaining fourteen years of his reign, apparently to the immense relief

# THE DESCENDANTS OF VALDEMAR THE GREAT

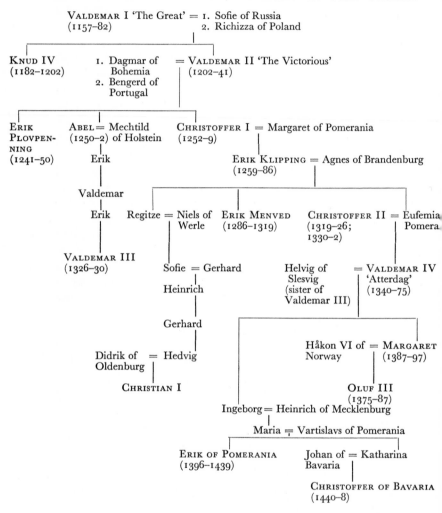

of most of his subjects, who had reaped little benefit from his conquests, were passed in peaceful progress.

The Age of the Valdemars has generally been considered to be the high-water mark of Danish medieval history. It was a period, if a brief one, when the country counted as a power of some significance and when her culture won respect far beyond her borders. It was also certainly a time of economic prosperity. During it the population seems to have risen to a peak of some million souls, more than lived at the same time in Norway and Sweden combined and more than were to live in Denmark again until the nineteenth century. New land was broken on the common 'outfields' of the villages or taken from the forests which still covered a large part of both the islands and eastern Jutland. New settlements sprang up, many of them still to be identified by the ending *-torp*, *-rup* or *-tolpe* (all originally *-thorp*), *-rød*, *-bøl* or *-bølle*, until they reached roughly their present number. This expansion was not, however, accompanied by any great changes in methods of food production; the average yield per acre was still very low by modern standards, and it is by no means certain that the average peasant lived any better than he had done earlier. Except in the less fertile western Jutland, where isolated farmsteads were the rule, he would live in a village, whose lands were worked to a common pattern by all the inhabitants. In west Jutland a two-field rotation, with half the land left fallow every year, was still practised, but elsewhere a threefold rotation of rye or wheat, barley or oats and pasture may have begun to appear during the twelfth century. The arrangement of the strips which each peasant was granted by his fellows in these common fields followed a variety of customs. The best known is perhaps the so-called *solskifte*, whereby they ran strictly in accordance with the order of houses along the village street. Beyond the cultivated lands lay the meadows for grazing cattle in common herds and beyond these again the village woods, valuable sources of firewood and game as well as of mast for the pigs, for which the village swineherd was responsible. There was little room for individual initiative but a strong feeling of community and the much-needed sense of security which goes with it.

The rise of population during the early Middle Ages was a feature which Denmark shared with the rest of western Europe.

Together with the suppression of the most damaging piratical activities in Danish waters and the eastward expansion of the Germans, it encouraged a great increase in north European trade, in which Danish agricultural produce (principally grain and butter) played a considerable part. This in its turn led to the foundation of new towns, especially (like Elsinore or, to give it its Danish name, Helsingør) on the now safer coasts of Denmark. All were very small by later standards—a few thousand inhabitants at most—but many of them were, nevertheless, large enough to support a new class of burghers—independent merchants and craftsmen, often working for the Church and the local nobility. These were organizing themselves increasingly in gilds, which helped their members in case of need and often vouched for them in the town court of law, where a special town code, often harsher in its terms than that of the country-side, was applied. At the end of Valdemar II's reign there were some eighty recognized towns in Denmark, most of them on royal land and under the special protection of the Crown. They included nearly all those which exist today and amounted to more than twice as many as could then be found in the whole of Norway and Sweden put together. The progress which had been made can be judged to a certain extent from the fact that a mere dozen towns are mentioned by Adam of Bremen but, even more significantly, half those existing in the early thirteenth century had been founded since the middle of the twelfth. In order of size, Roskilde appears to have been over-taken since Adam's day by Ribe, which owed its importance largely to the trade which was conducted through Jutland with the Rhineland and the rest of western Europe. Roskilde was still, however, the most important administrative centre, as far as there was one when the King and Court spent most of their time at one or other of the royal castles.

Copenhagen owed its growing importance in the thirteenth century to its situation on the Sound, to the protection afforded by Absalon's fortress and to its excellent harbour (its Danish name of København means 'merchants' harbour' and originally it was in fact known as Havn), but even more perhaps to its proximity to the great herring-fishing grounds which lay off the coast of Skåne. Every autumn the sands off the south-west tip of the province—Skanør—were covered with the temporary wooden booths which housed the fisherfolk who had come there to sell their catches and the merchants who had come to buy them and forward them to many different parts of Europe; the consumption of fish in the Middle Ages was particularly great because of the Church's ban on meat-eating on Fridays, throughout Lent and on many other fast-days in its year. A large proportion of the merchants who gathered at Skanør came from the North German Baltic ports, in particular from Henry the Lion's foundation of Lübeck. These were favoured by easy access to the silver mines of the Harz Mountains, which provided them with ready funds, and to the extensive salt deposits of Lüneburg, needed both for preserving the herring on their often lengthy journeys to the consumers and, throughout Scandinavia, for keeping food from putrefying during the long winter months when nothing fresh was available. For, while the herring was the most important article dealt with at Skanør, much general trading was also conducted there; each of the larger Danish towns was assigned an area of the beach on which its merchants could, on payment of dues to the Crown, sell their goods and buy others, like fine textiles and metal articles, from abroad.

The income from the grant of privileges at Skanør was doubtless very welcome to the Crown at a time when its warlike activities were making great demands on its financial resources. The old popular levies, untrained and poorly armed, were of little use against the knights on whom the German princes like the Count of Holstein now relied, and to restore the balance the King had to increase the size of the *hird*, the core of his army, by the addition of armoured cavalry drawn from among his richer subjects, who were rewarded with exemption from the payment of taxes, and to replace the peasants' military obligations with a tax, usually paid in kind. In an attempt to assess the resources available to him, the second Valdemar in 1231 ordered the institution of a great land survey, in particular of his own holdings throughout Denmark. Although only part of this has survived and this part is difficult to interpret, *Valdemar's Land Book* has proved almost as useful for historians of early medieval Denmark as has *Domesday Book* for those of Anglo-Saxon and Norman England.

That such a survey could be undertaken at all suggests a considerable degree of administrative sophistication and governmental centralization. At this time the king's officials, besides looking after the royal estates scattered about the country, were indeed taking over more and more of the functions previously performed by the popular assemblies and their elected officers. At Court, the great officers of state were emerging. The chancellor (always a bishop after the end of the twelfth century), who looked after the increasing amount of correspondence and record-keeping in the Chancery, was joined by the marshal, who acted as head of the Crown's armed forces under the monarch, and, most important of all, the steward, who combined the functions of treasurer and home secretary.

The extent and nature of royal power in the early thirteenth century was perhaps most graphically demonstrated by the promulgation by Valdemar II, at a great assembly of his nobles at Vordingborg in 1241, only a few weeks before his death, of a law code for Jutland, with its famous opening lines: 'With Law shall the Land be built.' Codes for Zealand and Skåne had already been written down by private individuals earlier in the century, and, like them, what was contained in Valdemar's Jutish Code (which also covered Fyn) was basically the old law which had been observed in the *things* of the province for many years in accordance with oral tradition. But the very fact that it was now fixed on parchment and at the instigation of the monarch himself is an indication of the considerable changes which were in progress in this field, changes which were to some extent reflected in the provisions of the Code themselves. Earlier in his reign, Valdemar had ordered, without any reference to the *things*, the abolition of trial by ordeal, which had been condemned by the Lateran Council of 1215. The law was gradually ceasing to be the law of the people and becoming the law of the king, whose officials rather than, as had formerly been the case, the plaintiff was responsible for the execution of the decisions made by the Court, even if they did not themselves preside over it, and who were entitled to claim for the Crown a proportion of the fines imposed on wrongdoers.

Growing contacts with the rest of Europe encouraged in Denmark a flourishing of its spiritual and cultural life at this time. Here the most important agent was the Church, a great international organization, many of whose leading members in Denmark had, like Eskil and Absalon, studied abroad, in Germany or, increasingly, in France, where a Danish College for Scandinavian students at the University of Paris was established in 1170. Monastic and cathedral schools were the only ones in existence, though important new centres of learning appeared in the thirteenth century in the shape of the town houses of the friars. The Dominicans, who were particularly interested in the acquisition of knowledge as a weapon in the fight against heresy, settled in Lund as early as 1223, only seven years after the foundation of the order, and the Franciscans followed them ten years later.

Whether the author of the most important piece of literature of the age—the *Gesta Danorum* (Deeds of the Danes) of Saxo Grammaticus—was a cleric or a layman we do not know, though the former seems the more likely. In fact we know hardly anything about him, apart from the statement given in his work that around the year 1200 he was encouraged by his patron Absalon to record in Latin the history of Denmark. He completed his account as far as the year 1185 in no less than sixteen large books, now known almost solely from the printed version of the early sixteenth century. The first nine deal with legendary times and introduced the rest of the European world for the first time to such figures as Hamlet and Rolf Krake. But even those which treat of periods nearer to the writer's own have often been drawn on too uncritically by historians, who have assumed Saxo to have been both better informed and more objective than he is now believed to have been. For he undoubtedly sought to glorify not only Absalon, the hero of the last three books, which deal with the reigns of Valdemar I and Knud IV, but all the Archbishop's predecessors who had sought to bolster royal power, and consequently he seems to have been biased against these kings who had worked within an older tradition, the heroes, for example, of the composer of the *Roskilde Chronicle*.[1] The work also reveals a strong anti-German prejudice, understandable enough in the circumstances of the period when it was composed. In spite of such shortcomings, Saxo's work, written in a vigorous, compelling style, was a truly remarkable achievement with few parallels in any other country. The only other important source for the period—and a much lesser one—is the *Short Chronicle of Denmark's Kings,*

[1] See above, p. 52.

written by Archbishop Eskil's nephew Svend Aggesen about 1185. Svend does something to counterbalance Saxo by making Valdemar rather than Absalon the hero of his account of the late twelfth century, but the bulk of his work is concerned with mythical times, and it is strongly influenced by the chivalric romance just coming into fashion at the Danish Court.

As far as the plastic arts are concerned, survivals of lay architecture from the period are very rare. Most buildings were still of wood, and even where they were not, as with royal castles, subsequent rebuilding has generally left only the foundations intact, like those of Absalon's fort at Havn which can be seen under the present *Christiansborg Palace* in Copenhagen. Once it had established itself, however, the Church built to last, and its monuments have withstood the ravages of time more successfully. Church-building reached its height in the Valdemar Age, to which most of Denmark's 2,000 or so parish churches belong. Of these, the most unusual are the round churches constructed on Bornholm which could serve not only as places of worship but also as refuges during Wendish raids. New cathedrals of more generous proportions than the old were rising in addition to that at Lund. Stone was the commonest building material, but at the beginning of the Age an entirely new substance—brick—was introduced, probably from northern Italy, whose masons left a strong influence on Danish architectural style. Among the earliest examples of its use are the monastic buildings at Ringsted and Sorø. To a rather later stage belongs the unique fortress-church at Kalundborg, built by Absalon's brother in the form of a Greek cross with a tower at each extremity, for which the nearest parallels have been traced to Russia. And a new style, that of the Gothic from northern France, began to exert its influence. Pure Gothic, with its slender pillars and large pointed windows allowing much light to penetrate to the interior of the building, came to Denmark rather later,[1] but both Absalon's new cathedral at Roskilde and the Cistercian monastery at Løgum in Slesvig look forward to it.

The furnishings of these churches provide the most impressive examples of artistic production on a smaller scale. Most of the 'golden altars'[2] seem to belong to the period, as do those

---

[1] See below, p. 77.    [2] See above, p. 49.

fine Romanesque frescoes in bold, clear colours usually against a sky-blue background which still adorn the interior walls of many churches in Zealand and eastern Jutland. Intended to impress upon the congregations the majesty of Christ and the lessons of the Scriptures, their strong Byzantine overtones suggest, like Kalundborg and the round churches of Bornholm, the powerful influences from the East which were acting on Denmark at this time.

Against all these achievements, however, must be set the evidence of troubles which lay ahead. Class differences were growing. As the population increased and the burden of royal taxation became heavier, the proportion of freehold peasants within Danish society was decreasing and the proportion of tenants paying rent and labour services for the right to work their plots to noble and ecclesiastical landlords or to the Crown was rising, particularly on Zealand and the islands to the south of it; according to *Valdemar's Land Book*, less than half the farmers on Falster owned their own land. The class of thralls finally disappeared at this time, partly as a result of pressure from the Church, but its former members found themselves almost as dependent as before on their masters, to whom they owed what little property they enjoyed. And a new class of nobles or *herremænd*, sharply distinguished from those beneath them by their exemption from taxation in exchange for military service on horseback, and often possessed of very considerable landed wealth, was resisting more and more effectively any attempt to extend royal power any further. The speedy collapse of Valdemar II's empire in itself demonstrated the limitations of Denmark's power in a turbulent world, and the apportioning at the end of his reign, to his sons, of large areas of the country to be ruled as semi-independent princedoms, bore in it the seeds of feudal dissolution such as made of Germany little more than a geographical expression. But although a centralized German monarchy was no longer a serious menace to Scandinavia, German economic and cultural expansion was to become increasingly threatening. Not only the Skåne herring trade, but all Danish commerce was falling more and more into the hands of German merchants from the cities along the southern shore of the Baltic which were forming the mighty Hanseatic League.

# CHAPTER V

## Decay and Renewal (1241-1380)

THE peace which had prevailed during the last fourteen years of the reign of Valdemar the Victorious was rudely shattered after the accession of his twenty-five-year-old son Erik. Indeed the event heralded a century of political confusion and the near-dissolution of the kingdom. It must have seemed to many contemporaries that the Valdemar Era had been no more than an interlude and that its monarchs and their ministers had worked in vain. The nature of the problem which faced Valdemar II's successors was, however, in several respects different from that which had faced those kings of the late eleventh and early twelfth centuries who had worked to unite the country under their control. The elective nature of the monarchy still proved a serious weakness, but the main challenge to centralizing authority was no longer a free land-owning peasantry jealously protecting local autonomy but an organized nobility, influenced by the feudal pretensions of its equals in other parts of western Europe, who sought to control both national policy and provincial government in its own interests. And both a general economic decline and the growth of German infiltration into all aspects of Danish life now made the task of even a vigorous and able king, such as finally emerged in the person of the third Valdemar, yet more difficult.

Erik's nine-year reign was filled with a series of struggles with his brother Abel, peasant revolts and the beginning of a fresh phase of the conflict between Church and State, which had been only temporarily muted after Valdemar II's reconciliation with Archbishop Eskil. Abel had, before his father's death, been invested with the Duchy of Slesvig in the form of a fief, which he proceeded to rule almost as an independent principality.

68

When Erik attempted to restrict his powers, Abel secured the support of the Count of Holstein, whose daughter he had married, and a bitter civil war broke out. After some three years, the brothers agreed to a truce, but the bishops, led by the headstrong chancellor, Niels Stigsen of Roskilde, accused the King of having infringed the rights of the Church in the course of the fighting. Erik replied by charging Niels with having plotted against his life and forced the Bishop to flee abroad. Whereupon war broke out again, Abel now being backed by the Church as well as by his brother Christoffer, Duke of Lolland-Falster, and his half-brother Knud, Duke of Blekinge, both of whom had been granted their fiefs on the same terms as Abel and both of whom also felt their autonomy threatened. A new truce was patched up in 1249, and Erik turned to the task of attempting to improve his very shaky financial situation. He imposed a tax on ploughs, which earned him the nickname of *Plovpenning* (Ploughpenny). The peasants of Skåne rose in protest, and no sooner had they been cowed than fresh trouble arose between Erik and Abel. The former's seizure of the town of Slesvig persuaded the latter to submit, but his German relations still constituted a serious threat to the kingdom. On his way through Slesvig to counter this, Erik, apparently under the impression that the quarrel between the two men had finally been resolved, turned aside to visit Abel. Too late he found that he had put his head into the lion's mouth; Abel had him seized, murdered and his body cast into the river Sli.[1]

Abel then ascended his victim's throne, but, doubtless to the great satisfaction of the chronicler who described him as 'Abel by name, but Cain by nature', he enjoyed the briefest reign of any Danish king on record. In 1252, after only two years, he fell in a battle with the semi-independent Frisian peasants of western Slesvig, upon whom he had attempted to impose a tax.

Christoffer, the last of the sons of Valdemar the Victorious and the one by all accounts most like his father in temperament, now was proclaimed king. But Abel's widow, supported by the Holstein nobility, vigorously championed the claims of her son and had to be bought off by the grant to him of Slesvig as a fief

---

[1] It has recently been pointed out that this version of Erik's death dates from later in the century and that there is consequently some doubt about Abel's responsibility for his brother's fate.

on terms which meant in practice the removal of the duchy from royal control. And the nobles also demanded their price for continuing support: Christoffer had to give them guarantees that the Crown's judicial powers, which had been strongly developed under the Valdemars, would not be used arbitrarily against them. From such concessions the Church took heart. In 1256 the fiery archbishop Jakob Erlandsen called an ecclesiastical council at Vejle and secured there an agreement to threaten the King with an interdict should he attempt in any way to interfere with the privileges enjoyed by the episcopate. In the King's eyes this constituted a serious threat to his authority, and in 1259, after the prelate had refused to crown his son as heir to the throne as Erik Ploughpenny had been crowned in the lifetime of Valdemar II, he had Jakob arrested and borne off to prison on Fyn.

In this quarrel the King had the support of most of his nobles, also jealous of the wealth and power enjoyed by the Church. And the bishops were divided. One of them, Niels of Viborg, was Christoffer's trusted chancellor and headed the party which, in the tradition of Absalon, saw in royal power and in co-operation with the Crown the best conditions under which the Church could perform its functions. Only in the dioceses of Lund and Roskilde was news of the Archbishop's fate followed by the enforcement of an interdict, and even there royal pressure soon brought about the resumption of services. But Christoffer also had external enemies to deal with. Jaromar, Prince of Rügen, egged on by the Duke of Slesvig, took up Jakob's cause. After occupying Bornholm, he landed in Zealand and entered Copenhagen with an army. Christoffer retired to Ribe, where he suddenly died.

His son Erik was only ten years old in 1259, and the problems left behind by his father had consequently to be dealt with by his mother Margaret, a Wendish princess, who was recognized as regent. She was a woman of energy and ability, but after Jarimar had defeated her army in Zealand she had to agree to release the Archbishop. And soon afterwards her attempts to rescind the grant of Slesvig to Erik Abelsen led to a crushing defeat of the royal army at the battle of Lohede. Margaret and her son fell into the hands of their enemies, but they were released after Albert of Brandenburg, Margaret's relative, had marched into Holstein and she had consented to add Langeland to Duke Erik's fiefs. She then appointed Albert her steward and gave him a free hand to deal with the Crown's internal enemies. Erlandsen sought safety in flight. But the Steward's brutality made him so unpopular with the Danes that he was soon compelled to withdraw again to his duchy. An uneasy peace settled on the country. Meanwhile the Archbishop was pleading his cause in Rome, and in 1266 a papal legate arrived demanding compensation for maltreatment of a servant of the Church. When his terms were rejected, Denmark was placed under an interdict. This was not lifted until 1272, when a settlement was reached between the Crown and a new pope, but Erlandsen died on Rügen on his way back to take up his duties again.

Erik was now of age, and the methods of government which he adopted, especially his reliance on a large bodyguard of German mercenaries to enforce his will and his failure to consult his nobles as they felt he should, rapidly worsened his relations with the latter. The situation was in many ways similar to that faced by King John in England earlier in the same century. And the outcome was a Danish Magna Carta. At a meeting in Nyborg in July 1282, a 'constitutional party', headed by Stig Andersen Hvide, forced Erik to limit his powers in a far-reaching *håndfæstning* or charter. He had to promise, among other things, that his judgements would be made strictly in accordance with the laws of the various provinces of the realm and even, like John, to accept the principle of *habeas corpus*. Shortly before this, he had agreed to meet the leading men of the kingdom once each year in a *danehof* or parliament, an institution which had emerged since the middle of the century but which had been called only infrequently, and the victorious 'constitutionalists' went on to fill the leading offices of state with their own adherents; Stig Andersen became marshal. So ended the first round in what was to prove a centuries-long struggle between the Crown and the Danish nobility for control of Denmark's destinies.

For a short time all went well, and co-operation between the King and his nobles produced a series of measures which went far to defining the rights and duties of all classes of society. But at the end of 1286 Erik, known to later ages as *Klipping* (probably an allusion to his 'clipping' the coinage), was murdered while on a hunting-trip at Finderup near Viborg. Who was responsible will never be known, but the 'king's men' who had suffered at the hands of the constitutional party seized the opportunity to accuse eight of their leading opponents, including Marshal Stig, of complicity. They gained the ear of the Queen-mother, who was acting as regent for her twelve-year-old son Erik, already recognized as his father's heir when only two. A special court was set up to try the defendants, and, though no evidence of any worth was ever produced, they were condemned to outlawry.

Stig and his companions fled to Norway, whose king willingly helped them to make raids into Halland and Skåne and against the coastal districts of Jutland and the Danish islands. They also gained the support of the new archbishop of Lund, Jens Grand. Jens was a fiery idealist who modelled himself on Jakob Erlendsen and had already come into conflict with Erik Klipping when he had been Bishop of Roskilde. Jens was also closely related to a number of the exiles. After he had excommunicated the royal steward, he was in 1294 arrested, like his hero, on the King's orders and imprisoned in the castle of Søborg in north Zealand where he suffered humiliating treatment. He managed to escape after a few months with the help of the castle's cook and fled to Rome. Erik was excommunicated and yet another interdict laid on his kingdom. But the Pope was at this time involved in a quarrel with the King of France which led to the Babylonish Captivity, and in 1303, by submitting humbly and promising to pay a large sum in compensation, Erik *Menved* (= Bird of Ill Omen!) managed to make his peace with the Church. He gained also Jens Grand's translation to the see of Riga in the eastern Baltic. The King had already come to terms with the ruler of Norway while the Archbishop was in prison and had granted an amnesty to the exiles. Of these, Andersen was dead, and, while some of his companions chose to continue the struggle, they became less and less effective as time wore on.

The memory of the Exiles and the deed of which they had been accused was, however, kept alive in a number of ballads which were composed soon after the events they celebrate. Of such ballads, which constitute Denmark's greatest contribution to medieval literature, only one has survived in a manuscript older than the sixteenth century. But this is from the late thirteenth, and they appear to have been cultivated in Court circles during the Valdemar Age under the influence of French ideals of chivalry reflected in the contemporary *chansons de geste* and poems of the troubadours and *trouvères*. In such a spirit are the ballads in praise of Valdemar II's first queen Dagmar of Bohemia, who obviously made a deep impression by her goodness and beauty (which qualities were perhaps accentuated in the poet's mind in comparison with her highly unpopular successor). Only gradually were these ballads adopted by the lower classes of society, who seem to have changed their basic form very little, often over several centuries. The subjects with which they deal are many and varied, ranging from the heroic deeds of legendary kings to tragic love stories; the earliest historical event mentioned in any of them is the death of King Erik Klipping.

After 1305, Erik Menved, his peace made with the Church and his position within his realm apparently secure, was free to devote all his attention to attempts to revive the empire of his great grandfather, Valdemar the Victorious. He first persuaded the city of Lübeck to acknowledge Danish overlordship and then joined in the Swedish civil war on behalf of his brother-in-law King Birger against Birger's brothers. He formed shifting alliances with various German princes against cities of the Hansa League and the Margrave of Brandenburg. But all that he had to show for his ambitions after fifteen years was an enormous bill for the hire of German mercenary troops. This could be paid only by mortgaging a large number of his estates, including the whole of the island of Fyn, to German and Danish nobles and by imposing heavier taxes on the freehold peasantry. The latter led to a series of large-scale revolts, of which that in Jutland in 1313, in which some nobles also took part, was the most serious. And these revolts could be put down only with the help of yet more expensive mercenaries and wholesale executions, which increased the number of the King's enemies.

At the time of Erik's death in 1319 the Crown's position was again extremely weak. And at the meeting to elect a new king held, as usual, at Viborg, his brother Christoffer could win the votes of those present only by putting his hand to a strict *hånd fæstning*. This was the first occasion on which such a charter was

73

imposed on a candidate for the throne as the price of his being chosen. There were to be many more. The nobles and bishops secured a confirmation of their exemption from taxation, and Christoffer had to bind himself not only to consult annually with the *danehof* but also to discuss day-to-day policy with a permanent noble council or *råd*, without whose consent he was not to wage war. In addition, he promised to redeem all the estates which had been mortgaged by his brother but at the same time to impose taxes no heavier than those imposed in the time of Valdemar the Victorious—and this in spite of the constantly rising costs of government in the fourteenth century. It is hardly surprising to find him almost immediately trying to wriggle out of such onerous obligations. He secretly sought to revive a 'forward' policy in Germany in alliance with the Emperor and his son, the Margrave of Brandenburg, who was promised the hand of Christoffer's daughter, and he began to impose new taxes in order to pay for it. This led to the creation of a formidable opposition to him within and without the country, an opposition headed by the rough warrior Count Gert of Holstein-Rendsborg, to whom a large part of the Crown's revenue was pledged. In 1326 Gert and his allies forced the King to flee to Mecklenburg and set up the twelve-year-old Valdemar, Duke of Slesvig, as puppet king in his place.

The nobles' victory seemed complete, and they proceeded to carve up the country into a number of extensive fiefs for themselves. Their government, however, especially that of the Holsteiners, grew increasingly unpopular with both the common people and a large number of the lesser nobles. Christoffer determined to take advantage of the reaction, and in 1329 he returned to Denmark. Gert, threatened also by divisions within his own party, agreed to restore the crown to him and to bundle Valdemar off to his duchy. But Christoffer found himself to be little less of a puppet than Valdemar had been, and when he tried to free himself he was decisively defeated in battle by Count Gert. Peace between the two men was not restored until Gert was granted Jutland and Fyn in pledge and his cousin Count Johan of Plön, who had changed sides more than once during the struggle, received Skåne, Zealand and Lolland-Falster. Christopher, just before his death in 1332, had to face one final humiliation. The inhabitants of Skåne, the richest province of the Danish realm, rose in revolt against Count Johan and offered their allegiance to King Magnus of Sweden. In exchange for a large sum of money, the Count was persuaded to agree to the arrangement.

In the disturbed conditions which were characteristic of the late thirteenth and early fourteenth centuries in Denmark it was the peasantry who suffered most, and more and more small independent proprietors were driven to seek the protection of the local noble. In order to obtain this, they had to surrender their land to him and become his tenant, paying him rent and often performing labour services on his demesne. But the latter was usually only a small part of his estate, and such service did not at this time constitute a heavy burden. And the tenant, by a concession to his nobles made by Erik Klipping, was exempt from regular (though not from extraordinary) royal taxes. As the proportion of non-noble freeholders sank, the peasantry ceased to be an important political factor in Danish history. It did not become so again until the nineteenth century.

For eight years after Christoffer's death Denmark was ruled by the two Counts of Holstein, or rather by their German followers, to whom they mortgaged a large part of the land they had won. While the country appears to have prospered economically during this period, German control was deeply resented and there were frequent revolts such as that which had lost Skåne to the Danish crown. It was on his way to put down one of these in Jutland in April 1340 that Count Gert was slain, in Randers, by Niels Ebbesen, a petty noble who had managed to smuggle some of his men into the town. The feelings of the common people at this time are reflected in the ballads composed in praise of Niels, who became a folk hero. Although he was killed a few months after his deed while besieging Skanderborg, which was being held by the Count's men, Gert's death deprived the Holsteiners of what little unity they had possessed, and Gert's sons agreed to allow Christoffer's only surviving son, the twenty-year-old Valdemar, to ascend the throne at last.

The Holsteiners continued to control the estates which had been mortgaged to them. But they soon found that Valdemar had no intention of leaving them in possession for longer than he could help. And, raised at the Courts of the Emperor and of his brother-in-law, the Margrave of Brandenburg, he was as ruthless and as unscrupulous as they and considerably more astute. In the task of rebuilding national unity and royal power, Valdemar could count on the support of the bulk of his subjects as well as of the Church, which longed for the peace which firm government brought. Over a period of twenty years, he succeeded in winning back all the alienated lands either by paying off the debts for which they had acted as security or by subtle diplomacy, chicanery and even naked force. Money was raised in a variety of ways—the sale of Danish claims in northern Estonia to the Teutonic Knights, new taxes and the efficient exploitation of the royal estates which were resumed. By such means Valdemar even managed to acquire a surplus from which to pay for the rebuilding or construction of forts, garrisoned by Danish troops and placed under the command of trusted nobles, who administered the area of the castle in the King's name.

By 1360, with his debts paid, the Holsteiners gone and opposition to him from nobles who feared his growing power crushed, Valdemar's prospects looked bright. He had certainly earned his appellation of *Atterdag* (= again day). But during the preceding years of political progress Denmark had been struck by a disaster against which large armies, well-filled treasuries and diplomatic acumen were of no avail. At the end of the 1340's the Black Death reached her shores. The evidence is too slender for historians to be able to assess its effects in any detail, but there can be no doubt that it carried off a large proportion (possibly 25 per cent or more) of the population. It appears, however, to have reinforced a decline in agricultural production and an associated decline in population which had set in already earlier in the century and from which there was little recovery until the fifteenth. The reasons for this development, which is found throughout western Europe, are obscure, but a deterioration in the climate may have played some part. Its results were the abandonment of less fertile soils, the disappearance of many settlements and a sharp drop in landowners' incomes. Further groups of smaller proprietors, including members of the nobility, were forced down into the ranks of the tenantry. The richer landlords were better able to weather the storm, but shortage of labour often forced them to offer favourable terms to tenants and higher wages to labourers in order to get their estates worked at all. And while the number of freehold peasants declined even more sharply than hitherto, the number of landless men also probably went down.

At the same time as Denmark's internal economy was weakening, her external economic contacts were falling more and more into foreign—and specifically German—hands, though the merchants of the Hansa never gained such a stranglehold in Denmark as in Norway, which came to rely on them even for supplies of grain. Many Germans settled in the larger Danish towns, and by the 1370's about one-quarter of Copenhagen's burghers had German names.

Economic decline and political unrest undoubtedly had a deleterious effect on artistic and intellectual life. It is evident that in the course of the fourteenth century Denmark was being drawn more and more into the German cultural as much as economic sphere. While her scholars tended to confine their foreign experience to German universities, her artists, if not themselves of German origin, tended to look to north Germany for their models. Her world was contracting. Comparatively little new church-building took place after the end of the thirteenth century, with the result that the Gothic style is rather poorly represented in the country. The earliest and in some ways the most important construction for which it was employed was the new church of St. Knud in Odense of around 1300. But if completely Gothic buildings are rare, a number of older ones were remodelled with Gothic additions. Among them were parish churches, which often now gained towers for the first time. And many interiors were decorated or redecorated. Stylized Romanesque frescoes gave way to more realistic portrayals of both religious and secular subjects in watercolours on dry walls. These form in many cases valuable historical evidence for costume and customs.

In 1360 Valdemar Atterdag took advantage of internal dissension in Sweden to complete his work of reconstruction by reconquering Skåne, Halland and Blekinge. The following year, he went on to increase his dominions by seizing the Swedish island of Gotland. But this act of aggression brought about a breach between Denmark and the Hanseatic League, whose members had generally welcomed the restoration of stable government under Valdemar, even though he had not confirmed their privileges. For on Gotland lay the city of Visby, one of the League's most valuable bases in the Baltic, in particular for trade with Russia. Valdemar forced the inhabitants of the city to pay a large ransom after crushing a peasant army under its walls. The Hansa agreed to a truce after the defeat of a Lübeck fleet, but used the breathing-space this provided to form a formidable anti-Danish coalition, including Sweden, her troubles temporarily settled, the Duke of Slesvig and the counts of Holstein. In 1367 Valdemar left his kingdom to seek help in Germany. One after another Denmark's towns were seized and plundered by his enemies until in 1370 the council which ruled in his absence secured peace on onerous terms. By the Treaty of Stralsund, the League was granted what amounted to control of the Skanør market, guaranteed for fifteen years by possession of the castles along the western coast of Skåne. Valdemar at last returned home and took charge of operations against his only remaining enemies—the nobles of Holstein. Not only were these cowed, but the death of the Duke of Slesvig in 1375 opened up the prospect of a resumption of his lands by the Crown. Valdemar, however, himself died before he could take any action.

He left behind him only a twenty-three-year-old daughter, Margaret, married to King Håkon VI of Norway, and the Danish nobles seized the opportunity to impose on her five-year-old son Olof a *håndfæstning* which undid much of his grandfather's work and threatened to introduce a new period of unrest. But Margaret proved her ability as regent by slowly building up royal authority, and in 1380 Olof became king of Norway on the death of his father, thus initiating a connection between the two countries which was to last for over 400 years and also the process which led to the formation of the Kalmar Union.

# CHAPTER VI

## *Scandinavian Union (1380-1523)*

---

THE origin and character of the union which was formed between all three Scandinavian monarchies at the end of the fourteenth century has been subjected to a variety of interpretations. Some historians have represented it as largely the fortuitous result of the marriage of Erik, son of Magnus Ladulås of Sweden, to the heiress of Håkon V of Norway, followed by that of their grandson to the daughter of Valdemar Atterdag. As a result the destinies of both Norway and Denmark were placed in her hands when her father and her husband died within five years of each other, and she was in a good position to exploit the failure of King Albert of Mecklenburg to maintain himself in Sweden. Others, especially Swedish historians of the nineteenth century, have regarded the Union as the successful conclusion of long-sustained efforts by the rulers of Denmark, the richest and most populous of the three powers, to unite them all under their sceptre. Yet another explanation has been that it was the outcome of a plot hatched by the closely related noble families of Scandinavia with the object of forming a united front against the increasingly restive peasant masses (who, some claim, were imbued with a national feeling absent from the minds of their selfish betters) and of ensuring peace on the frontiers of the kingdoms in more than one of which many had estates.

What is certain is that the extinction of the lines of Sverre in Norway and the Valdemars in Denmark paved the way for dynastic union between these two countries; that the wealth and cultural maturity of Denmark determined that it should be she who would dominate any partnership; and that, while there is little evidence of patriotic sentiment among the lower classes at this period, the Scandinavian aristocracy paid relatively little attention to national boundaries when making their economic plans. But another factor of considerable significance must also be considered in this connection. The whole of Scandinavian society was in the fourteenth century being increasingly threatened by German cultural and economic domination. As has been seen, Denmark was for some time during it partitioned among nobles from Holstein, and Valdemar Atterdag's council was compelled by the Treaty of Stralsund[1] to grant the merchants of the Hanseatic League some say in the election of his successor. These same merchants completely dominated Norway's overseas trade, and the election of Albert of Mecklenburg to the throne of Sweden in 1364 resulted in the granting to his countrymen of many castles and fiefs there; he could count on considerable help from north Germany in the struggles which ensued between himself and the Swedish nobility. The Union can therefore be seen also as, at least partly, the result of a common realization on the part of Margaret of Denmark and the leading men in the three countries of the need for a defence against further German encroachment, which only political federation could provide.

In 1386 Margaret reached an agreement with the discontented Swedish nobility by which they bound themselves to expel King Albert and elect her son Olof, already king of Denmark and Norway, in his place. Olof died the following year when only seventeen, but Margaret was made regent in Denmark–Norway until a new king should be chosen, and the leaders of the rebellion which broke out in Sweden in 1389 offered her a similar status there. In 1396, Albert having been defeated and taken prisoner, the nobles of both Sweden and Denmark agreed to recognize Margaret's fourteen-year-old great-nephew Erik of Pomerania, who had assumed the Norwegian crown in 1388, as their king also. In 1397 he was crowned in the Swedish city of Kalmar by the archbishops of both Lund and Uppsala in the presence of a large number of the leading men of his future realms. At the same time a document was composed which detailed the character of the Union thus formed: while all three kingdoms were in future to be ruled by one king, each of them was to continue to be governed in

[1] See above, p. 78.

accordance with its own laws and, under the monarch, by its own nationals headed by a council of magnates. This charter appears never to have been given a definitive form or to have been properly ratified, possibly because Margaret objected to having her hands tied so tightly, but it undoubtedly expressed the views of the Swedes, who reacted with vigour when it seemed that these views were being ignored.

In its early years, while Margaret lived and was in effective control of policy, the Kalmar Union worked reasonably well and ostensibly fulfilled all the functions expected of it. External threats diminished. Albert of Mecklenburg did not surrender his claim to the Swedish crown, but he soon ceased to be a serious menace. The danger to Denmark from the south had been temporarily exorcized in 1386 by forcing the Count of Holstein to do homage to the Danish Crown for the Duchy of Slesvig, which he had ruled effectively since the death of Valdemar Atterdag. And when he died in 1404 Margaret began gradually to absorb the duchy into the kingdom by taking over estates within it as pledges for loans made to the Count's widow. This policy eventually led to a brief war, but an armistice signed in 1410 left the key town of Flensborg in Danish hands.

Internal peace was also ensured, largely by the firm rule which Margaret exercised, though the extent of the power which the Crown acquired under her and some aspects of the policy which she initiated led eventually to the first of the Union's many crises. While her son Olof was still alive she had begun to strengthen the throne's position in Denmark; she ordered the destruction of the private castles which the nobles had been allowed to build by the terms of Olof's *håndæstning*, forbade private warfare and attempted to protect such peasant freeholders as remained by forbidding nobles to purchase their land. She also passed legislation through local *things*, now largely under royal control, without consulting her council or the *danehof*, and left the great offices of steward and marshal vacant. She strengthened her financial position by using the royal court to resume estates which had been alienated by her father and by compelling the Hansa under threat of war to return the castles they controlled in Skåne. She was generally respected if not loved in all three realms and her piety won her the support of the Church, to which she made generous donations.

F                                          81

There were, however, some rumblings of discontent in Sweden when she granted some fiefs and castles there to Danes and Germans, not because they were Danes or Germans but because they were men whom she knew and trusted, whereas she knew few Swedes. And when Erik came into his own after her death in 1412, the situation began to deteriorate appreciably. The thirty-year-old monarch was handsome and debonair and not without ability and foresight; he indeed emerges from the records as in many ways a more attractive personality than his tough patroness. But he continued her general lines of policy with far less caution and diplomatic finesse. In July 1413 he persuaded a meeting of the *danehof* (the last as it turned out) to declare the whole of Slesvig forfeit to the Crown, and three years later war broke out again with the increasingly Germanized nobility of the duchy. Soon afterwards Erik also came into conflict with the Hansa. The League had hitherto backed his Slesvig policy as the best means of ensuring peaceful trading, which was being seriously interfered with by Holstein privateers. But he was keenly aware of the benefits which could be gained from encouraging Danish commerce and favoured the growth of Danish towns. He granted extensive privileges to Malmö and Copenhagen, the most important of them, and took over control of the latter from the Bishop of Roskilde, an act which marks its beginnings as the realm's chief administrative centre. In 1422 he not only forbade all trading outside towns but granted their inhabitants first pick of the produce brought within their walls from the surrounding countryside. When the German merchants protested against these restrictions, Erik cancelled all the privileges which they had hitherto enjoyed in Denmark. In 1426 war broke out. It went badly for the League. Its fleet suffered a crushing defeat the following year, and in 1428 an attack on Copenhagen was repulsed with heavy losses. In 1429 Erik felt strong enough to begin imposing a toll on all ships passing through the Sound, whose northern entrance was dominated by his new fortress of 'Krogen' (= The Hook) near Elsinore.

But these conflicts drained his inadequate financial resources and compelled him to impose heavy additional taxes on both freeholders and tenants. These brought widespread peasant unrest. His appointment of German and Danish bailiffs and fief-holders in Sweden on a more lavish scale than heretofore and his interference in the election of Swedish bishops caused growing dissatisfaction among the country's nobles and led them to exploit the discontent among the inhabitants of the iron-mining regions of the central provinces, who were hard hit by the blockade imposed by the Hansa against export of iron. When the miners rose in rebellion, the Swedish magnates assumed the leadership of the movement and demanded that Erik should grant them what they regarded as their rightful place in government. Erik's war in Slesvig had been going badly; Flensborg had fallen to the Holsteiners in 1431. And the Danish nobility and Church leaders, headed by Archbishop Hans Laksmand, joined their Swedish equals in protesting against what they felt to be high-handed methods of government. Erik finally fled to Gotland, there to await an opportunity to regain his throne. But the opportunity never presented itself, though he held out on the island for eight years before returning to Pomerania. In 1439 the Danish and Swedish councils declared him deposed and agreed to elect in his place his nephew Christoffer of Bavaria. The Norwegians followed suit in 1440.

In Christoffer the Scandinavian nobles seemed to have found at last a king after their own hearts. He made no attempt to wriggle out of the obligations imposed on him by his *håndfæstning*, and the powerful families were given a free hand to rule their estates undisturbed. In view of the continuing agricultural crisis, their economic interests were of particular importance to them at this time. Labour was still difficult to come by, and in 1446 the nobles of Lolland agreed on a series of regulations by which cottagers could be compelled to take over a vacant tenancy and servants were to be allowed to change masters only twice each year. This marked the beginning of increasingly harsh conditions for the Danish peasantry, imposed on them by landlords who were strongly influenced by the knowledge that in Holstein and other parts of northern Germany, with which they had close contact, tenants had even fewer rights. Many nobles were finding it profitable to create or extend existing demesnes or large blocks of land by purchase or by exchanging isolated plots, and were working these directly with labour imposed as one of the conditions for enjoying a neighbouring tenancy. Such services had been demanded earlier, but they were now becoming more common and grew more onerous as the tenants' legal position deteriorated. Rather later, land-owners on the eastern Danish islands began to insist that a tenant's heir take over his father's holding on the latter's death whether he wished to or not. Even such a limited form of serf-dom, referred to as *vornedskab* (a term used with a more restricted meaning since the beginning of the fourteenth century), was unknown in the rest of Scandinavia, but it was to persist in Denmark until the beginning of the eighteenth century.[1]

It must not be imagined that the late-medieval Danish nobi-lity was a uniform class. The magnates who sat on the royal council and enjoyed the title of *herre*, which indicated the grant-ing of knighthood, had considerable estates scattered through-out the country, could afford many imported luxuries like fine cloth and were keen to follow the latest European fashions, which in the fifteenth century were often of quite extraordinary extravagance. Associated with them were a number of the bishops, like Queen Margaret's chancellor Peder Lodehat, who about 1400 had built the unique castle of Gjorslev on the east coast of Zealand, where it may still be seen much in its original form. But below them lay a much larger number of poorer men, who shared with them privileges like exemption from taxation as well as obligations like marrying only within their class, but who, especially in Jutland, sometimes had to work on the land themselves and lived side by side with peasants in simple houses of wood and clay.

Christoffer's reign gave the Scandinavian countries eight years of much-needed peace, broken only internally by a serious peasant uprising in Jutland in 1441. Erik had made peace with the Hanseatic League in 1435 by restoring to it its privileges, which included exemption from payment of the Sound Dues, and Christoffer had himself temporarily settled the Slesvig problem on his accession by granting to the Duke the small amount of land in the duchy which was still remaining to the Crown. But in 1448 Christoffer suddenly died.

The councils of the three kingdoms were caught off their guard, and out of the ensuing confusion two rival monarchs emerged. The Swedish marshal, Karl Knutsson, was elected king of his country under pressure from those of its leading men

---

[1] See below, p. 138.

who wished to counteract the growing power of the Oxen-
stierna family, while the influence of the Count of Holstein in
Denmark brought about the election there and in Norway of
his twenty-two-year-old nephew Christian of Oldenburg, a
handsome young warrior who promised to work closely with
his council and not to grant any offices or lands to foreigners.
That there was a strong desire on both sides to preserve the
Union is shown by the conclusion within two years of an agreement by which the first of the monarchs to die should be succeeded by the survivor. But unfortunately neither man was
prepared to wait for this eventuality, and war broke out.
Christian emerged victorious in 1457 after the Swedish nobles,
many of whom had grown jealous of the power Karl was arro-
gating to himself, had themselves expelled him from the country.

Karl had, however, considerably weakened the ties between
Denmark and Sweden by appealing against Christian to
national sentiments in the hearts of the Swedish lower classes,
and it was just these classes that suffered from the heavy taxes
which Christian began to impose on his territories. These were
necessitated to a large extent by his policy towards Slesvig and
Holstein. In 1459 his uncle the Count died without heirs, and
the nobles of the two lands, many of whom owned estates in
both, offered their allegiance to the King on condition that
county and duchy should always remain united. Such an
arrangement seemed to be the best guarantee against conflict
and the absorption of Slesvig into the Danish monarchy, which
Margaret and Erik had threatened. Christian agreed, and a
treaty on these lines, which also guaranteed extensive privileges
to the nobles, was concluded in Ribe in 1460. Slesvig and Holstein were thus bound together under the same ruler, but an
important difference in status continued to distinguish them: in
Slesvig the King was overlord as well as elected duke, but
Holstein remained a county of the Holy Roman Empire for
which he owed allegiance to the Emperor.

As part of the bargain reached at Ribe, Christian promised to
buy out the claims to Slesvig and Holstein enjoyed by other
members of his family. This involved a large sum of money,
which could be raised only by means of new taxes. And Karl
Knutsson was able to exploit both his popularity with the
Swedish commoners and their discontent with the King's

exactions to secure his re-election to the Swedish throne in 1464. He was soon expelled again, but returned for a third time in 1467.

Christian also recognized, as Erik had done before him, the usefulness to the Crown of the commoners as allies in limiting noble pretensions. In contrast to Sweden, peasant freeholders in Denmark were becoming so few as to be of little account, but the country's urban population, though small, was considerably larger than in either of the other Scandinavian powers. Christian called representatives of the burghers, as well as of the freehold peasants, clergy and nobility, to the first meeting of the Estates (*stændermøde*) held in Kalundborg in 1468, and during the 1470s he renewed the prohibitions against 'country trading' which had not been very strictly observed by German merchants since Erik's day. Towns had always been the special concern of the Crown. While some, like Copenhagen, had grown up on ecclesiastical property, most were situated on royal estates, and it was the king who granted them the privileges embodied in their charters. In the later Middle Ages urban government was generally in the hands of small circles of wealthy merchants who provided the members of the ruling councils headed by burgomasters and filled by co-option. Handicrafts were strictly regulated by the masters of the various gilds, who also determined who should practise a particular 'mystery'; competition was in this way reduced to a minimum. But townspeople were to a much greater extent than the bulk of the peasants the king's subjects. His bailiff presided over their courts and claimed for him a proportion of the fines imposed therein. On the other hand, in view of the revenue which the monarch could obtain from the trade conducted by the burghers, it was in his interest to foster their prosperity even at the risk of foreign complications.

Two years after the first *stændermøde*, Karl Knutsson died, and Christian prepared to reassert his authority in Sweden. But Karl's supporters and his policy were inherited by his nephew Sten Sture, and when the Danish king tried to impose his will by force he was decisively defeated by Sten's forces at the battle of Brunkeberg, just outside Stockholm, in October 1471. Christian did not surrender his claim to the Swedish throne; a large party of Swedes still wished to restore the Union. But for the time being he had to recognize Sten's position. At a meeting between the councils of Denmark and Sweden in Kalmar peace was re-established and a committee of Danes and Swedes set up to examine the differences between the two sides and attempt to reconcile them.

The emergence of a centralized monarchy based on the support of the common people and on an emergent national sentiment such as Karl Knutsson and Sten Sture attempted to create in Sweden presaged the end of the Kalmar Union. But there were other factors which were at this time weakening the ties between Sweden on the one hand and Denmark and Norway on the other. One was economic. The Hansa's position in the Baltic was being seriously threatened by Dutch (and to a lesser degree also by English and Scottish) merchants sailing through the Sound and diverting trade away from the old Lübeck–Hamburg route through Holstein. The newcomers could be used to counterbalance the economic threat to Scandinavia from Germany without the need for political unity. Secondly the decline in the power of the Teutonic Knights who controlled the lands bordering the south-eastern Baltic (the later Baltic States) created a vacuum into which Denmark and Sweden could expand. External menaces, such as that from Russia to Finland, still existed and occasionally helped the 'unionists', but they were neither serious nor sustained enough to give comfort to the latter for very long.

If, however, the German economic hold on Denmark was loosening in the course of the fifteenth century, German influence on the country's cultural life remained extremely strong into the sixteenth. In the plastic arts, the realism already noted in the High Gothic wall paintings,[1] reached its peak in the work of immigrant German sculptors headed by the Lübecker Bernt Notke, who in 1482 completed a new reredos for Århus Cathedral, and Claus Berg, responsible for the magnificent reredos now in St. Knud's Church in Odense but originally carved about 1520 for the Greyfriars Chapel in the same town. Church walls continued to be decorated with paintings, but these were less imaginatively conceived than earlier and often betray the strong influence of German pattern books. This was an age of renewed building activity, perhaps reflecting a re-

[1] See above, p. 77.

covery from the economic and political disasters of the fourteenth century. A fair number of smaller Danish towns gained
new brick churches. Of these St. Olav's in Elsinore is typical.
The church nearby, attached to the Carmelite monastery, was
rebuilt after a fire in 1450 and is one of the finest specimens of
Late Gothic architecture in the country (see Plate 4). Existing
structures were also added to. The most outstanding of these
additions is the Chapel of the Three Kings which Christian
ordered in 1459 for Roskilde Cathedral, to serve as a resting-
place for his descendants and a hall for members of the new
knightly order which he instituted in 1462. Secular architecture
was of a much more utilitarian character, as can be seen in the
simple keeps of Glimmingehus in Skåne, built for the noble
Jens Ulfstand in 1499, and of Spøttrup, commissioned by the
Bishop of Viborg about the same time.

Ballads were certainly still being composed, but the only piece
of Danish literature of any real significance from the Union
period is a rhymed history of Denmark, probably composed in
Sorø Monastery around 1478. In 1495 it became the first
Danish book to be printed. To provide a national home for
higher learning, Christian obtained the Pope's sanction for the
founding of a university in Copenhagen, which was inaugurated
in 1479, two years after Sweden had secured one at Uppsala.
The attraction of the German academies, however, remained
strong, and at the end of the century Christian's son Hans had
to insist that his subjects study for at least three years in
Copenhagen before attending a university abroad.

Christian had promised at the beginning of his reign to work
closely with his nobles, and his relations with the small number
of them who made up his council (*råd*) were generally good. He
consulted frequently with its individual members and exercised
his judicial functions at full sessions of it known as *herredage*. But
by his death in 1481 he had managed to build up royal power
in Denmark to a degree which to many of his more influential
subjects seemed to constitute a threat to themselves. Like rulers
in other parts of Europe in this era of the 'new monarchies', he
had often turned to commoners to execute his wishes, and he
had frequently appointed men who were entirely dependent on
the Crown to positions of authority in both central and local
government. His use of the *stændermøde* in place of the defunct

*danehof*, which had been made up entirely of nobles, is indicative of this trend.

It was therefore decided that his son and successor Hans should be bound by a strict *håndfæstning*, which emphasized the power of the councils of Denmark and Norway to make and unmake the two countries' rulers. Hans signed the document in 1483. He soon, however, resumed his father's policies, appointing commoners to control royal fiefs and using his influence over the Church to secure the election of bishops favourable to him. At the end of his reign he charged a number of magnates with treason. His increasingly suspicious mind may have believed them guilty, but the fact that, if they were convicted, their estates would escheat to the Crown may well have provided the main motive for his action.

Most of Hans's time was, however, occupied with affairs outside Denmark. On his accession he was compelled by his strong-willed mother, Dorothea of Brandenburg, to promise half Slesvig and Holstein to his younger brother Frederik. The division was carried out in 1490. This surrender in the south was more than offset, however, by a gain in the north seven years later. The Russian threat to Finland finally forced Sten Sture, after lengthy negotiations and under strong pressure from a large Danish army, to recognize Hans formally as king of Sweden and to agree to his coronation in Stockholm. But the latter's success proved to be short-lived. In 1500, he suffered a humiliating military defeat while aiding his brother and the nobles of Holstein in an attempt to reduce the independent republic of Ditmarsken to obedience. The enemy opened the dikes across the low-lying land and then cut off the retreat of the heavily armoured Danish and German knights on a narrow causeway. Many were drowned, and Hans himself barely escaped. A fresh rebellion broke out in Sweden almost immediately, and Sten Sture was restored to his old power.

Yet once more the pendulum swung back in Hans's favour. In 1510 he became involved in a war against both Sweden and Lübeck, the latter having been alienated by new restrictions which he had placed on the activities of German traders in Denmark, by alliances which he had concluded with England and Russia and which seemed directed against the town, and by the activities of Danish privateers against Hansa shipping.

# THE OLDENBURG DYNASTY

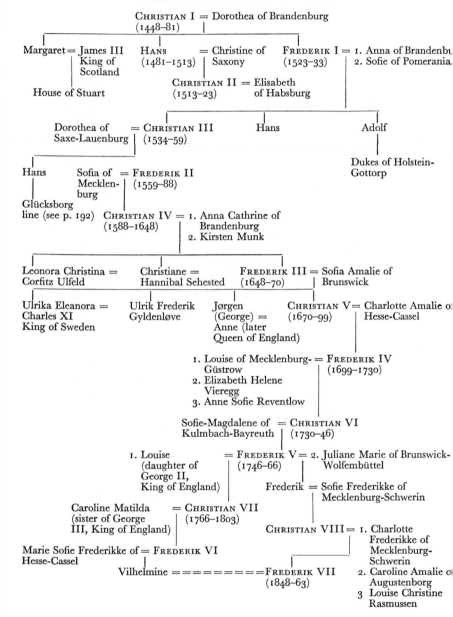

Hans scored a number of notable successes with the fleet he had created—the first real one possessed by any Danish king—and when peace was restored in 1512, the Swedes had to promise to pay an annual tribute and Lübeck to acknowledge the Danish monarch's right to regulate his realm's commerce.

A year later, Hans, the last ruler of Denmark up to the present time not to be named Christian or Frederik, died in Ålborg with his nobles in a considerable state of unrest. In view of the harsh way in which his son Christian had ruled Norway for his father for several years, it is not surprising that his new subjects regarded him with considerable suspicion. A group of Jutish nobles did indeed offer the crown to his uncle Frederik of Holstein, but on this occasion the cautious man rejected the idea. And while Christian II's *håndfæstning* did contain some new restrictions on his power, as on his right to create new nobles, it was in some respects less demanding that the one to which his father had had to subscribe. Christian was a man of undoubted ability and could exercise considerable charm when he chose to do so. But he was basically weak, liable to fly into uncontrollable rages when crossed, easily influenced by stronger personalities and inclined to lose his nerve in an emergency. He had also inherited Hans's pathologically suspicious nature.

His general policy was similar to that of his father—at home, to build up the power of the Crown with the help of non-noble servants and to encourage the prosperity of the towns; abroad, to re-establish the Kalmar Union and reduce the power of the Hanseatic League. He filled his Chancery, which he made the main organ of his government, with young commoners and granted fiefs to others. He turned for advice particularly to a Dutchwoman named Sigbrit Villoms, the mother of his young mistress Dyveke, whom he had met in Bergen and brought to Copenhagen with him. She was a coarse and sharp-tongued woman but a competent administrator especially in financial matters. Christian also looked to Hans Mikkelsen, the burgomaster of Malmö. When Dyveke died mysteriously in 1517, the King appointed a special judicial panel of peasants to try Torben Oxe, the custodian of Copenhagen Castle, for her murder. Torben was duly condemned and executed, and Sigbrit's influence grew even greater.

All this naturally exacerbated Christian's relations with the

Danish nobility, but he was able to keep control of the situation until his Union policy suffered shipwreck. After a number of unsuccessful attempts to regain control of Sweden by force, he took advantage of a quarrel between Gustav Trolle, the fiery archbishop of Uppsala, and the new Swedish regent, Sten Sture the Younger, to invade the country again in 1520 as a defender of the rights of the Church. Sten was defeated and mortally wounded, and Christian entered Stockholm in triumph to be proclaimed hereditary king of Sweden. Immediately after his coronation, however, he (probably on Sigbrit's advice) took a savage revenge on his defeated opponents. In the so-called Stockholm Bloodbath over eighty Swedes, including two bishops, were executed for heresy. This and the persecution which followed it in other parts of the country led to a rebellion under the young noble Gustav Vasa, whose father had been one of the Bloodbath's victims. Lübeck came to Gustav's aid. It had turned against Christian because of the close ties he established with its chief rivals, the Dutch, and had granted Gustav shelter after he had escaped from Denmark, where he had been held hostage. Soon most of Sweden had slipped from Christian's grasp.

Meanwhile he had returned to Denmark, where he proceeded to tighten his grip on fiefs, force through the Council a series of decrees to the benefit of the burghers and peasants and take a number of Lutheran preachers under his protection. When news came of the Swedish revolt, most of the Danish nobles and ecclesiastical leaders united against him and even some towns joined them. At the end of 1522 a group of Jutish nobles again offered the crown to Duke Frederik of Holstein-Gottorp. This time Frederik, who had come to fear that his nephew had designs on his duchy, accepted and marched northwards through Jutland with a large army under the command of Johan Rantzau. At Viborg in March 1523 he was formally elected. Christian still enjoyed a considerable measure of popular support, but his nerve seems to have failed him. With his devoted wife and the hated Sigbrit, he set sail from Copenhagen for the Netherlands, there to seek help from his brother-in-law, the Emperor Charles V. After holding out for some time in the hope of relief from this quarter, the capital opened its gates to Rantzau's troops.

# CHAPTER VII

# Religious Upheaval, Foreign Adventure and Economic Advance (1523-88)

FREDERIK I was already fifty-two years old when he became king, and to the end of his days he deeply resented the fact that the chance of birth alone had kept him so long from power. He was, however, an intelligent and cool-headed man who had learnt the value of patience and tact, qualities which stood him in good stead when dealing with the serious problems which faced him after his accession. The nobles expected a king whom they regarded as their nominee to respect their privileges and to allow them a large say in the government of the realm. Every concession made to them would, however, not only restrict royal initiative but also be likely to exacerbate the resentments of the commoners, among whom Christian II could count on considerable support whenever he should make a bid to regain his throne. Recent events had also left a bitter legacy to Dano–Swedish relations. And on top of all this there was a growing demand for religious reform. In 1517 Martin Luther had nailed his ninety-five theses to the door of the monastery church in Wittenberg, setting in train a series of events which eventually divided western Christendom into two irreconcilable religious camps. The close links between Denmark and north Germany meant that the progress of the Protestant movement was followed closely in the kingdom from the beginning and that Lutheran doctrine became influential there at an early stage. The whole question required very careful handling by the Crown both at home and in its relations with foreign powers, as their rulers took up sides. That civil disturbance was kept under control to such an extent and international peace maintained throughout Frederik's ten-year reign is handsome testimony to his abilities as a ruler.

In his *håndfæstning* Frederik had to promise that nobles alone would be appointed to important offices in central government and to the fiefs through which the countryside was largely controlled and that his council would be consulted on all important matters of policy, including the succession to the throne, the imposition of new taxes and the conclusion of treaties. In the main he remained faithful to these pledges. He had no wish to follow his nephew's policy of employing middle-class men in important positions. And, while beneath his cold exterior he was a man of a humane disposition, whose reign saw the peasants ensured lifelong tenure of their holdings, he made no attempt to revive the corpus of laws favouring the lower classes which had been promulgated by Christian II and burnt by the triumphant nobility after his flight. The Council, made up of the great officers of state, the seven bishops and up to thirty other members, was too large and unwieldy for frequent consultation; it met *in pleno* only in the comparatively rare *herredage*, where matters of particular moment were discussed. But the King always had a number of councillors in attendance on him to help with the day-to-day business of government, and he relied particularly on the advice of his chancellor Mogens Gøye.

But there was another reason why Frederik had so little trouble with his nobles. For most of his reign both he and they were faced with a common threat from Christian II; any serious dispute might open the door for the ex-king's return. Christian also menaced the new Swedish regime, but in spite of this relations between Gustav Vasa and Frederik were strained for several years at the beginning of the reign. The main bone of contention was the island of Gotland. This had been seized after Christian's departure from Denmark by his admiral, Søren Norby, who used it as a base from which to attack Danish, Swedish and Hansa shipping indiscriminately. When the Swedes launched an expedition against him, he secured his master's consent to offer the island to King Frederik on condition that he should be allowed to retain possession of it as a Danish fief. Frederik accepted, and Gustav, who regarded Gotland as part of his rightful inheritance, adopted a very threatening attitude. Both rulers, however, recognized that only Christian would benefit from a war between them, and the Swede consented to the temporary occupation of the island by Denmark once Norby had been removed. But Norby not only refused to surrender it, but in 1525 took a body of troops to Skåne and raised a peasant revolt in the province on behalf of Christian. Meanwhile an army from Lübeck had landed on Gotland, and the fear that it might become a Hansa possession drove Frederik to offer Norby Blekinge in exchange. The Admiral accepted, but proceeded to use his new possession as he had used Gotland, for launching piratical raids on Baltic commerce. Finally a joint Dano–Lübeck fleet defeated his, and he was forced to flee to Russia. He ended his eventful life fighting for the Emperor in Italy.

In 1531 Christian II at last made his long-awaited attempt to regain his throne. His relations with his brother-in-law the Emperor had become strained to breaking-point after a visit he had paid to Wittenberg in 1523, when he had declared himself won over to Lutheranism. And for much of the 1520's Charles V was in any case too occupied with threats from France and the Turks to pay much attention to Scandinavian affairs. In 1529, however, the Turks having been repulsed from Vienna and peace having been made with the French, he offered to help Christian if the Dane agreed to return to the Catholic faith. Christian did so and was consequently granted funds with which to raise an army and gather together a fleet in the Netherlands to transport it. This finally set sail, but it was badly damaged by storms in the North Sea, and Christian arrived in Norway in November 1531 with a much-depleted force. He was nevertheless acknowledged as king by the Norwegian council at the beginning of 1532 and was soon in control of a large part of the country. The castles, however, remained in the hands of custodians faithful to King Frederik, and a strong Dano–Lübeck fleet threatened his communications. In the circumstances he agreed with delegates sent by his rival to open negotiations in Copenhagen under the protection of a safe conduct which they promised him. But the offer was not ratified by Frederik or his council, and Christian found himself carried on from Copenhagen to imprisonment in the castle of Sønderborg on the island of Als. Frederik enjoyed his triumph for only a few months. He died in April 1533 in Gottorp, where he had spent a large part of his reign.

The long crisis over the succession to the throne which followed Frederik's death was to a considerable extent religious in character. The degree to which Luther's claims constituted a threat to the established order had not been appreciated for some time. The Carmelite monk Poul Helgesen, principal of his order's college in Copenhagen, at first greeted the Reformer as a fellow humanist who wished, like himself, to cleanse the Church of its impurities. In 1520, however, with the issuing of the papal bull condemning Luther, Helgesen became the most prominent Danish protagonist of orthodoxy. Christian II remained sympathetic to the movement. He not only refused to allow the publication of the bull in his kingdoms but invited the radical Lutheran Anders Karlstadt to visit him. This policy drove the bishops into the ranks of his enemies.

One of the promises which Frederik had to make in his *håndfæstning* was to extirpate heresy in Denmark and Norway. But his chancellor was already a convert to Lutheranism, and his eldest son Christian had been deeply impressed by Luther's defence before the Diet of Worms in 1521, at which the young man had himself been present. As soon as his father had given him control of part of Slesvig in 1524 he had founded a seminary at Haderslev for the training of Lutheran priests. A year later the monk Hans Tausen began preaching Lutheran doctrine in Viborg, and the King clarified his own attitude. Tausen, who had come under Luther's spell while studying at Wittenberg, rapidly won over the burghers of the Jutish town, and when he was threatened by its bishop, Frederik not only provided him with a letter of protection but made him a royal chaplain. Similar letters were subsequently drawn up for other reformers, and the King reacted strongly against the demands of his bishops, the Catholic majority on his council and the eloquent Helgesen to embark on a policy of persecution.

This does not mean that he had espoused the new faith. He feared that an exacerbation of religious strife might open the way for Christian II, and he seems at this stage to have hoped, as did many others, that the Church could be reunited after it had been purified through a General Council. But he also shared the desire of even fervent Catholic rulers for more con-

5. King Christian II. Portrait by Michel Sittow (or Michiel Zittos) painted in 1515.
*Royal Museum of Fine Arts, Copenhagen*

6. A sixteenth-centu[ry]
nobleman and his ho[use]
(a) Peder Oxe. Pain[ting]
of 1574. *National
Historical Museum at
Frederiksborg*
(b) Gisselfeld on Zea[-]
land. *National Museu[m],
Copenhagen*

trol over ecclesiastical affairs in his kingdom. In 1526 he went so far as to forbid bishops to seek confirmation of their election from Rome or to make payments to the Curia. Similar moves by Henry VIII in England began the movement which ended in the setting-up of an independent national church, but whether Frederik envisaged going as far as this is uncertain.

From such developments, however, the reformers naturally took heart, and in the late 1520's their numbers in Denmark grew rapidly, particularly in the towns. From Viborg, Tausen's message spread rapidly throughout Jutland; Lutheran congregations mushroomed. From Malmö, a large proportion of whose congregations had been won over by 1528, the 'infection' spread to the other centres east of the Sound. Copenhagen itself held out until 1529, when Tausen began to preach in St. Nicholas's Church there with great success. He himself was opposed to any excesses, but the words of other reforming preachers were often highly inflammatory and led to attacks on both persons and property. Friars were favourite targets. They were often driven from their houses, which were converted to secular use as 'hospitals' (i.e. refuges for poor as well as sick) or occasionally town halls. Other ecclesiastical buildings and their contents were destroyed. No fewer than twelve churches in Viborg were pulled down in 1529, and at the end of the following year a Copenhagen mob broke into the Church of Our Lady and destroyed or dispersed much of its contents; its priceless reredos was saved only by the courageous intervention of some of the church's servants. In spite of all appeals from the bishops and many of his lay advisers, Frederik refused to do anything to stem the tide.

When the Council met in Copenhagen in 1533 to decide on his successor, a division appeared within it between a Catholic majority, who wanted the election of his younger son Hans, who had remained within the old faith, and a Protestant minority who wanted his elder son Christian, who, as has been seen, had become an ardent Lutheran. In view of this disagreement and the absence of Norwegian representatives, it was decided to postpone a decision until the following year; the country was in the meantime to be governed by the Council. Before, however, the date in 1534 set by the meeting, Count Christoffer of Oldenburg, a grandson of Christian I's brother, landed in Zealand

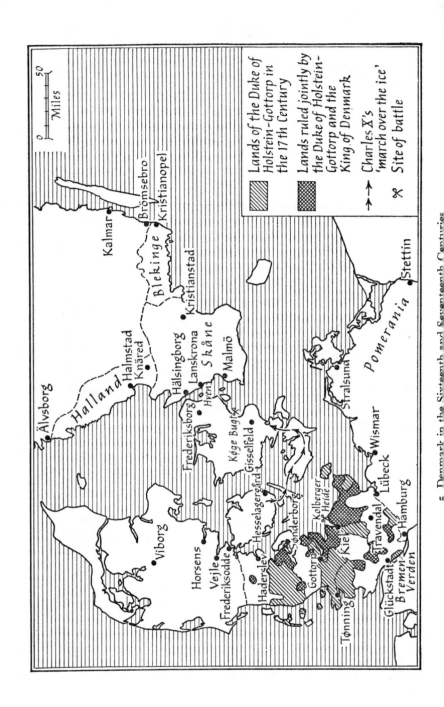

5 Denmark in the Sixteenth and Seventeenth Centuries

Älvsborg
Kalmar
Brömsebro
Kristianopel
Blekinge
Halmstad
Knäred
Halland
Hälsingborg
Lanskrona
Kristianstad
Skåne
Hven
Malmö
Frederiksborg
Køge Bugt
Gisselfeld
Viborg
Horsens
Vejle
Frederiksodde
Hesselagergård
Sønderborg
Haderslev
Kolberger
Heide
Gottorp
Kiel
Travendal
Tønning
Glückstadt
Bremen
Verden
Lübeck
Wismar
Hamburg
Stralsund
Pomerania
Stettin

Lands of the Duke of
Holstein-Gottorp in
the 17th Century

Lands ruled jointly by
the Duke of Holstein-
Gottorp and the
King of Denmark

→→ Charles X's
'march over the ice'

✕ Site of battle

0    50
Miles

with an army and demanded the release and restoration of Christian II. He was backed by a fleet from Lübeck, which had decided to support the enterprise after the Danish Council had concluded a ten-year alliance with the Dutch. He could also count on the sympathy of the burghers of Copenhagen and Malmö and a large proportion of the Danish peasantry, who still remembered the favours they had won from Christian, who had grown increasingly restive under the financial burdens imposed on them by Frederik I, and who feared that the failure to elect a new king was part of a plot to establish a permanent oligarchy which would leave them with no protection against the abuse of noble power.

The so-called Count's War which ensured therefore tended to assume the character of a class as well as a religious conflict. It is this that goes far to explain the savagery with which it was fought and the terrible destruction of lives and property which it caused. Christoffer's troops soon overran Skåne and the islands, and the nobles there agreed to recognize the former king once more. But in Jutland and the Duchies (Holstein had been raised to equal status with Slesvig in 1474) nobles and bishops rallied to Duke Christian, who marched north with an army of German mercenaries and was proclaimed king at Horsens. After crushing at Ålborg an army of Jutish peasants who had risen for Christian II, the new king's supporters went on to occupy Fyn and cross from there to Zealand, while Swedish troops, having subdued Halland, invaded Skåne. Gustav Vasa had seized the opportunity to throw off the yoke which Lübeck had imposed on him as its price for helping him against Christian II and had allied with Duke Christian. After suffering a heavy defeat at sea in 1535, the Lübeckers sued for peace. In spite of terrible privations, Copenhagen continued to hold out against the victor in the hope of being relieved by a fleet which was being fitted out in the Netherlands. But in the end the situation became unbearable, and in July 1536 the city surrendered. The last civil war in Danish history was over.

Christian III's triumphant entry into Copenhagen began the last brief phase in the Danish Reformation. The new king was a convinced Lutheran. But of perhaps even greater significance at this stage was the fact that he was the ruler of a country which had been devastated by war and whose people were quite incapable of providing the Crown through taxes with the means of paying off the German mercenaries who had helped him to achieve victory or the crushing debts which had been left behind by Frederik I. The temptation provided by the lands of the Church, which made up over one-third of the total cultivated area of the realm, would probably have been too great to resist even for one who was not already doctrinally committed to reform. Christian determined to strike at once. After carefully concerting plans with his German captains, he had all the bishops arrested on the grounds that they had been largely responsible for delaying the election of his father's successor and thus for the war and also that they had, in calling for the suppression of heresy, opposed the preaching of the word of God. The lay members of the Council were then forced to approve the action under threat of suffering the same fate and to agree both to a confiscation of all Church lands and the introduction of a Lutheran Church order. After they had themselves consented to these measures most of the bishops were released and were even granted lands on which to support themselves during their enforced retirement. But Bishop Krumpen of Børglum remained in prison until 1542, and the powerful Bishop Rønnow of Roskilde died there the same year. Helgesen had disappeared mysteriously during the war.

The new order was set out in detail in the *håndfæstning* agreed between the King and his councillors and in the 'recess' adopted by the Estates when they met in Copenhagen in October 1536. Christian, like Henry VIII, could claim popular sanction for his policy. But such an appeal to his subjects was not a sign of weakness. He was indeed, with his army at his back, in a very strong position at the beginning of his reign, and his *håndfæstning* was more favourable to the Crown than most previous charters; any hope that the nobles of Denmark might have entertained in 1533 of establishing a permanent oligarchy had been dashed. They retained their previous privileges, and after his position had been established Christian was generally content to leave details of policy to his councillors. But it is significant that, unlike the situation in England after the break with Rome, the Crown in Denmark retained nearly all the land which it had confiscated from the Church; very little went to the nobles.

The new Danish Church was further regulated by an ordinance of 1537 which was specifically approved by Luther himself. It was declared to be a national body governed by the monarch, and the office of archbishop was abolished. The old dioceses were placed under superintendents appointed and paid by the Crown; their duties were to be confined to religious matters alone. Parish priests, who were now allowed to marry, were to be elected by their congregations unless the living was in the gift of a noble. The tithe was retained, but the third which had previously been paid to the bishop was appropriated by the king. Part of this new income was used to establish seminaries for the training of Lutheran ministers, of whom there was for some time a serious shortage. For the same purpose the University of Copenhagen, which had been closed since 1530, was reopened. The Recess of 1536 had declared monks released from their vows, but monasteries were not dissolved and were allowed to keep a certain amount of their land. Many continued to function until their last inhabitants died.

The superintendents were soon being referred to as 'bishops'. But the Protestant bishop had none of the wealth or the political power of his Catholic predecessor, and the office no longer attracted the great Danish families; most of the new men came from the middle classes. Such was the worthy Peder Palladius, granted the see of Roskilde in 1537 after returning from a period of study in Wittenburg. He did much to establish Lutheranism on a firm foundation in Zealand by means of frequent visitations throughout the island; the records of these often illustrate vividly the manners and morals of the time. Tausen did not receive his reward until 1542, when he was created Bishop of Ribe.

The Church Ordinance of 1537 was first printed in Latin, and the whole Bible did not appear in a Danish translation until 1550. But services were from the beginning conducted in the vernacular, and the Reformation is undoubtedly of considerable importance for the development of Danish as a literary language. The beginning of such a development, however, preceded the Reformation. A number of remarkable religious poems in Danish appeared at the end of the fifteenth century, and in 1510 Christiern Pedersen, Canon of Lund and the greatest of the Danish Humanists, published a Danish–

Latin glossary in Paris. Five years later he had printed in the same city a translation of a Latin book of miracles, in the preface to which he vigorously defended the virtues of his native tongue. But his two great contributions to Danish culture were his edition of Saxo's *Gesta* in the original Latin, produced in 1514, and 'Christian III's Bible' itself, which was largely based on his translation of Luther's German version. Denmark began to develop in the sixteenth century a great tradition of Protestant hymn-writing; the first official *Salmebog* (in fact a hymn book) appeared in 1569.

In other respects the Reformation's effects on cultural life were less fortunate. Many priceless treasures were lost in the upheaval, and the greater simplicity of the Protestant church interior restricted the scope of the artist. In any case the Lutheran Church did not possess the wealth needed for effective patronage, and only gradually were the Crown and the nobility able to take over this role.

Denmark's international position after the Count's War was a strong one. But the danger from Christian II, whose claims were upheld by his daughters and their husbands, remained a real one. In 1538 therefore Christian III concluded alliances with the Schmalkaldic League of Lutheran German towns and princedoms and with the Lutheran Duke of Brunswick. Negotiations were also begun with Francis I of France, but an alliance with him was not concluded until 1541. The following year he and Charles V went to war again, and Danish troops were sent to Flanders in accordance with the terms of the alliance and the Sound was closed to the Emperor's Dutch subjects. This latter action undoubtedly helped to persuade Charles to make peace, in spite of the military successes he had enjoyed against the French. By the Treaty of Speyer in 1544 he promised that he would give no more aid to Christian II, and the Sound was reopened. In 1541 a fifteen-year alliance had been signed between Christian III and Gustav Vasa at Brömsebro, but relations between the two kings became strained when the latter, who had also concluded an alliance with Francis I, found that he had been excluded from the Peace of Speyer. But no further foreign complications ensued before Christian's reign came to an end in 1559.

Christian's son Frederik had already been recognized as heir to the throne in his father's lifetime, and the prospects for his reign seemed bright. There had been no serious upheavals either at home or abroad for over twenty years. Norway appeared to have acquiesced in the status of a Danish province to which she had been reduced in 1536. The economy was recovering from the devastation caused by the Count's War. The Crown's financial resources were considerable, thanks to the Church lands acquired in 1536 and to the reorganization of fiefs carried out by Christian's chancellor Johan Friis, who had converted many of them from *afgiftslen*, where the holder paid a fixed sum to the Crown and pocketed the remainder of the profits he had made, to *regnskabslen*, where he was permitted to retain only a fixed sum, the rest of the income having to be sent to the Royal Treasury. Christian II died soon after Christian III, and the new emperor showed no interest in the claims of his descendants.

Unfortunately Frederik II was, at twenty-four, a rash young man, over-eager for personal and national glory, and his ambitions seriously jeopardized his position during the early years of his reign. The temptation for overseas expansion was, it must be admitted, very strong. The break-up of the power of the Knights of the Sword and of Livonia (the Teutonic Knights) in the eastern Baltic had provided an opportunity for some ruler to seize control of the valuable trade routes which ran from Russia to the Baltic through Livonia. And the opposition of the Danish Council to military adventures was weakened by the success of one which was undertaken in the first year of Frederik's reign. Frederik's two uncles, with whom he shared Slesvig and Holstein, had been planning a campaign against the peasants of Ditmarsken to avenge the humiliating defeat suffered by their ancestors in 1500,[1] and they called on the new ruler for help. Frederik's councillors agreed to allow Danish troops to participate in the action, and the tiny republic was crushed by an army led by the elderly Johan Rantzau. To Frederik's credit, he did allow the defeated to retain a degree of autonomy under himself as duke and resisted the local nobles' demands for wholesale deportations.

The first step taken to establish Danish power in the eastern Baltic was the occupation of the island of Øsel and of parts of

[1] See above, p. 89.

Estonia. Soon, however, Danish ambitions came up against those of Erik XIV, the equally impetuous new King of Sweden, and after some preliminary sparring, war broke out between the two countries in 1563. It did not at first go well for Denmark either on land or sea, and very soon Frederik's treasury began to show signs of strain. The sharp rise in prices characteristic of the sixteenth century in Europe made war an increasingly expensive business, especially for a country like Denmark, which relied on hired mercenary troops to do most of her fighting. The best solution to the problem which the Council could suggest was the recall of Peder Oxe. Oxe (see Plate 6a), a member of one of the country's leading families, had shown outstanding administrative ability under Christian III, but had fallen from favour and had in 1558 left the country to avoid being brought to trial. He was now invited to return, cleared of all the charges which had been brought against him and in 1566 made steward of the realm with control of finances. He immediately began to put these in order. He reorganized the Sound Dues, which he based on the value of the cargoes carried instead of on the size of the ships which carried them, so tripling the yield, and persuaded the nobles to contribute a share of new taxes. The financial situation was still grave when, after the tide of the war had turned in Denmark's favour, peace was restored by the Treaty of Stettin in 1570 on the basis of the *status quo*, and there was considerable unrest in the countryside. But the end of the fighting brought about a general relaxation of tension, and, under Oxe's guidance, the economy began to recover.

In spite of the religious, political and social upheavals which marked it, the sixteenth century was a period of considerable economic progress throughout western Europe. Inflation, hastened by the great influx of precious metals from America, set in motion new enterprises, and a rise in population stimulated production. Serious grain shortages in southern Europe led to an increase in the demand for corn from the Baltic, where prices tended to lag behind those further west. And, while grain exports from Denmark were not of great significance, the development did lead to an appreciable rise in the value of land there and to the cultivation again of marginal areas which had often lain waste since the beginning of the late-medieval crisis. Rising profits also encouraged landlords to continue seeking to create larger units out of scattered holdings, a movement which was after the Reformation led by the king himself as the greatest landlord of them all. This was especially true of Frederik II. By purchase and exchange with his nobles, he gathered together large unified holdings on the islands and in eastern Jutland. Demesnes were also extended by taking in waste land and tenant-holdings, although the latter always made up the greater part of most estates.

It was in the middle of these demesnes that, after the end of the Count's War, began to arise those impressive brick manor-houses, with their characteristic curved or stepped gables, which make the later sixteenth century the first great age of secular architecture in the country. Some seventy of them dating from before 1600 have survived to bear witness, with their accent on comfort rather than defence, to both the growing wealth of the class for which they were built and to the more settled conditions under which their inhabitants were able to live. The earliest is Hesselagergård in south-east Fyn, which was built for the chancellor Johan Friis in 1538. Some ten years later Peder Oxe ordered the construction of one even larger at Gisselfeld (see Plate 6b), which was still unfinished when he fell into disgrace.[1] The interior walls of such great houses were often hung with portraits of the owner and members of his family, in some cases executed by foreign artists, while in the local church might now be found elaborate monuments or whole chapels in memory of those who had passed away. The nobles, many of whom were highly cultivated and widely travelled men, were beginning to play an important part in the cultural and intellectual life of the realm.

The late-sixteenth and early-seventeenth century is often referred to as their golden age. In every *håndfæstning* their privileges were confirmed. They enjoyed exemption from all ordinary taxes and, at least with respect to their demesne lands, from extraordinary ones also. They had the exclusive right to all important offices. They enjoyed extensive judicial powers over their tenants, and some of the larger estate owners might be granted *birkeret*, which allowed them to appoint the district judge. It is difficult to assess how far these rights were abused. The amalgamation of holdings enabled the landlord's steward

[1] See above, p. 104.

to exercise a greater degree of control over a larger number of tenants, and the extension of demesnes meant that a larger number of tenants not actually dispossessed were compelled to perform heavy labour services at the time of the year when they needed every hour of the day to tend their own plots. Even in good years they could usually produce only just enough for their needs after they had paid their rent, their tithes and any extra-ordinary taxes demanded by the Crown. Well-to-do tenants there certainly were, but the vast majority seem to have been able to benefit little or not at all from the improvement in the general economic situation. The peasant freeholder was very rare by the end of the sixteenth century. In Jutland, the only area in which this class had survived, many of its members had been deprived of their lands as a consequence of participation in rebellion during the Count's War.

The most important item of export from Denmark was cattle, fattened on noble estates or by Jutish burghers and then either shipped off to the Netherlands from Ribe on Dutch ships or driven south into northern Germany. Yet Denmark's inter-national economic importance lay more in her geographical position than in the comparatively few commodities she pro-duced for foreign markets. She was excellently placed as an *entrepôt*, and, although the Dutch, who had largely replaced the German merchants of the Hansa, dominated Baltic trade, an increasing amount of Danish commerce was in the later six-teenth century being carried in Danish ships, which sailed as far afield as the Mediterranean. And in spite of a relaxation of the ban on 'country trading' after the fall of Christian II, the Crown continued to take a great interest in the towns, which prospered. Some merchants, like Oluf Bager from Odense, who lit a fire of promissory notes while entertaining Frederik II, were extremely wealthy. They could afford to build for them-selves substantial half-timbered or brick houses such as that which can still be seen *in situ* on Stengade in Elsinore. At the other end of the urban social scale, however, lay the beggars. As in Elizabethan England, these posed a serious problem, especially after the disappearance of the charitable organiza-tions associated with the Catholic Church.

The later part of Frederik II's reign, from the end of the Northern Seven Years' War in 1570 until his death in 1588, was a much brighter one than the earlier. He had matured considerably under the sobering influence of the war and gave up foreign ambitions. He was not, however, more interested in the day-to-day business of government than his father or grandfather had been; routine quickly bored him, and he preferred the hunting-field and the festive board to the council chamber. He was prepared to leave affairs of state largely to his advisers. These were fortunately able men, led, until his death in 1575, by Oxe and thereafter by the chancellor Niels Kås and the treasurer Christoffer Valkendorf.

Nor was Frederik II a particularly cultured monarch. He did nevertheless perform useful services for Danish intellectual and cultural life in the capacity of patron. In 1576 he presented the young nobleman Tyge (Eng. Tycho) Brahe, brother of one of his councillors, with an annual grant and the small island of Hven (now Ven) in the Sound on which to build an observatory and scientific research centre. As *Uranienborg* this acquired a European fame. From it Brahe during the following twenty years mapped the heavens with an accuracy which made him one of the fathers of modern astronomy.[1] The King also took a certain interest in the work of Brahe's former tutor, Anders Sørensen Vedel, the son of a Vejle burgher who in 1575 published the first Danish version of Saxo's *Gesta*, a task he had been encouraged to undertake by Peder Oxe. In 1584 he was appointed historiographer royal and began the composition of a history of Denmark in twenty-two volumes.

Frederik created the first Danish court orchestra, in which English musicians were invited to perform. But his greatest artistic joy was his new castle of *Kronborg* at Elsinore. Begun in 1574, on the basis of Erik of Pomerania's *Krogen*, it became in the space of ten years the largest and most magnificent Renaissance palace in northern Europe. Its architects were Flemings, who provided their creation with the Dutch-style towers and gables which are associated so closely with the buildings of Frederik's son and successor Christian, the greatest of Denmark's architect-kings whose achievements and misfortunes were to throw his father's into the shades of history.

---

[1] See further below, p. 116.

# CHAPTER VIII

## *The Age of Christian IV (1588-1648)*

CHRISTIAN IV was only eleven years old when his father died, and until he came of age in 1596 affairs of state were conducted by a regency council headed by Niels Kås. With the same ministers in charge of policy these eight years in many ways constituted a continuation of the later part of Frederik II's reign. No new initiative was attempted in foreign policy, and the Crown's finances remained in the healthy state which Peder Oxe had done so much to restore; the rapidly growing trade between western Europe and the Baltic area brought a considerable increase in the income from the Sound Dues. This continuity also manifested itself in the cultural field. In 1591 Vedel, under the patronage of the Queen mother, published a collection of one hundred Danish folk-songs, the first of its kind in the world. Ever since the middle of the century it had been the fashion among noblewomen to record such ballads, which survive largely owing to their efforts. But Vedel was not able to get very far with his planned continuation of Saxo's history, and the task was taken up by the noble statesman Arild Huitfeldt, who in 1595 issued the first volume of *Danmark Riges Krønike* (Chronicle of the Kingdom of Denmark), a history of Denmark which eventually covered the early Middle Ages and a large part of the fifteenth and sixteenth centuries. It was strongly biassed in favour of the nobility, but made a critical use of original sources and remained the standard account until the eighteenth century.

In 1596 Christian was crowned in the midst of lavish festivities, in which the young monarch patently revelled. He was possessed of a number of admirable qualities. Energetic, hard working and physically brave, he was also easy of access and of a naturally generous and cheerful disposition, had a strong sense of justice and felt a genuine concern for the welfare of all his subjects. Such attributes made him perhaps the most popular of all Danish kings. Yet he suffered at the same time from serious deficiencies of character, which tended to be forgotten by later generations, in spite of the fact that they helped to bring his kingdom to the verge of ruin on more than one occasion. Most serious was his inability to match his soaring ambition to the resources at his disposal. And, while his stubborn egotism made him unwilling to listen to advice, it also prevented him from learning from his own mistakes and led him constantly to underestimate his opponents, especially those in foreign lands.

Such weaknesses first became apparent in the war against Sweden which broke out in 1611. Christian had been pressing for such a war for a number of years, confident in his ability to make substantial territorial gains from his neighbour and even, it seems, to reassert control over a country which had been ruled from Copenhagen less than a century before. His council, which had a juster appreciation of the difficulties involved in such an enterprise than he, had refused to give its consent (which was needed under the terms of Christian's *håndfæstning*) time and time again. But the King was as Duke of Schleswig–Holstein a free agent, and he at last forced the Council to give way by threatening to open a campaign in this capacity, an act which would inevitably draw Denmark into the struggle. The war opened promisingly with the seizure of Kalmar, whence the title of 'The Kalmar War' by which it is usually known. And in the subsequent struggle the Danes generally had the better of the fighting. But outright victory eluded them. When peace was concluded at Knäred in Halland in 1613 Christian obtained only the surrender of the enemy's claims to the far north of Norway and the promise of a large indemnity, with the fortress of Älvsborg, Sweden's vital window on the west at the mouth of the Göta River, as the pledge for its payment.

The war had, however, confirmed Denmark's position as the strongest power in the Baltic, and the twelve years of peace which followed it witnessed considerable progress in internal matters. Christian was very keen to develop the economy of his realm in order to increase both his subjects' well-being and his own income. He did so in accordance with the prevailing principles which later historians have christened 'mercantilist'. These involved close supervision of enterprise by the State with the object of producing a favourable balance of trade and lessening dependence on the foreigner; in a stream of ordinances the Crown attempted to stimulate the growth of industry and commerce. Tariff barriers were raised against competition from abroad, and foreign artisans and entrepreneurs were encouraged to settle in Denmark, in particular artisans possessing new skills and entrepreneurs with money to invest in 'manufactories' (i.e. centralized agencies) for the production of such things as silk cloth, weapons and refined sugar, which had previously had to be imported. Opposition from the handicraft gilds was overcome by first abolishing them altogether and then restoring them after a lapse of eight years with their privileges so reduced that newcomers could practise their calling with little difficulty.

To break the Dutch hold on overseas commerce and encourage the development of a merchant marine, monopoly companies supported by State capital were set up to trade with the Danish possessions of Iceland and The Faeroes, with the West Indies, with the Mediterranean and, most ambitiously, with the Far East. In 1618 the young nobleman Ove Gjedde set out with a squadron of four ships for India, where he established a trading-post at Trankebar south of Madras. And three years later Jens Munk was dispatched with two warships to reach the same destination round the north of Canada; the expedition wintered in Hudson Bay, but only Munk himself and and two others survived to return to their homeland. Nor was it only in the fortunes of Denmark proper that Christian took an interest. He paid much more attention to Norway than any of his predecessors had done, visited that country on some thirty separate occasions during his reign and did much to encourage the development of its mineral resources in particular.

The results of all this activity were not, it is true, very impressive, and financial returns were disappointing. Capital and expertise were in short supply, and Denmark lacked natural resources on which to base flourishing industrial development. Most of the royal enterprises were short-lived. While the needs of the army and navy kept the 'manufactory' for coarse cloth in production, that for silk could not compete either in quality or price with the material which continued to be smuggled into the country in large quantities. And Denmark remained dangerously reliant on the Dutch for her commercial links with the outside world. The Iceland trade alone flourished, and the Icelanders undoubtedly suffered from the exclusion of foreign merchants from their shores, being often, in spite of the government's attempts to prevent abuse, forced to pay high prices for shoddy imports. But Christian's realm did grow more prosperous at this time. Copenhagen, more and more the centre of Danish economic life, expanded rapidly as foreigners and peasants from the surrounding countryside sought their fortunes or at least better conditions there. And some of the larger provincial towns did likewise; the elaborate four-storied Dutch Renaissance house of the merchant Jens Bang on Østeragåde in Ålborg bears witness to this day to what wealth might be acquired there from cattle, salt and Norwegian timber in the 1620's. New towns, too, like Glückstadt on the east bank of the Elbe in Holstein, Kristianstad in Skåne and Kristianopel in Blekinge, while they did not become the great trading-centre anticipated (Glückstadt was intended to rival Hamburg), proved economically viable and also strengthened the defence of the country's frontiers.

Christian himself took a hand in planning these towns, which are still distinguished by the regular grid patterns of their street networks. He was indeed passionately interested in building projects of all kinds. He did much to beautify his capital and left some striking monuments both within it and in its immediate vicinity, most of them in the style, strongly influenced by contemporary Dutch models, which had been anticipated in the later sixteenth century but which has been named after him. As early as 1602 he gave orders for the pulling-down of his birthplace, his father's modest palace of *Frederiksborg* at Hillerød to the north-west of Copenhagen, and its replacement by a magnificent brick structure. This was completed in the early 1620's, and, after extensive damage by fire in the middle of the nineteenth century, was faithfully reconstructed in its original form to house the Danish Museum of National History. On a less lavish scale was the summer palace of *Rosenborg*. Reminiscent of a noble's manor house, it was begun on the northern outskirts of Copenhagen in 1610 and now also serves as an historical museum. In the capital itself, Christian was responsible for *Børsen* (the Exchange) with its distinctive copper spire of intertwining dragons' tails (see Plate 7); *Regensen*, a hall of residence built in 1623 for poor university students; *Tøjhuset* (the Arsenal), earlier than the others and more Italianate in style; and a number of other memorials since destroyed. The strong Dutch influence is also evident in sculpture, a field in which the most outstanding practitioners were the brothers Hans and Lorentz van Steenwinckel, who decorated *Frederiksborg*. But it was not only the plastic arts that attracted Christian. Music also flourished at his Court, which was for eight years at the beginning of the reign graced by the great English lutanist and composer of madrigals John Dowland; he attracted a number of his compatriots to Denmark.

Christian's building enterprises swallowed up a considerable proportion of the royal revenue. A large part of the rest was devoted to defence; a fair-sized standing army was built up and a formidable fleet, in which the King took a special interest. And as time went on the temptation grew stronger to employ these resources to extend Denmark's influence in northern Europe, where her position was being increasingly threatened by Sweden under the great warrior-king Gustavus Adolphus. The very next year after the end of the Kalmar War, Gustavus had concluded a potentially dangerous alliance with the Dutch, and in 1617 began a war between Poland and Sweden which resulted in the rapid Swedish occupation of Livonia. Christian sought to counterbalance his rival's gains by the acquisition for his sons of the secularized bishoprics of Bremen–Verden, Osnabrück, Halberstadt and Paderborn in north-west Germany. The pursuit of such ambitions was likely to be looked at askance not only by the princes of the area, organized in the so-called Lower Saxon Circle, but also by the Dutch, who were interested in uninterrupted trade down the rivers Elbe and Weser. But relations between the latter and Denmark had improved after 1618, when Prince Maurice of Orange–Nassau gained firm control of the United Provinces from the merchant-oligarchs of Amsterdam; Maurice was interested in Denmark as an ally against Spain, which had not yet recognized Dutch independence. And in the same year the nobles of Bohemia rose in revolt

7. Acknowledgement of Frederik III as hereditary monarch in 1660. Painting by Wolfgang Heimbach of 1666, now in Rosenborg Castle. The artist has portrayed himself, hat in hand, in the extreme left-hand corner. Christian IV's *Exchange* stands in the centre background. *National Historical Museum at Frederiksborg*

8. (a) Johan Friedrich Struensee. Portrait by G. A. Lorentzen of 1771. *National Historical Museum at Frederiksborg*

8. (b) The first Palace Christiansborg. Eighteenth-century print. Frederik IV's *Chancery Building*, which still stands, can be seen on the extreme left of the picture. *Royal Library, Copenhagen*

against their Catholic Habsburg king and offered the crown of their kingdom to the Calvinist Elector Palatine, who was married to Christian IV's niece. The Thirty Years' War had begun.

The Bohemian revolt was crushed by the Emperor in 1620 with the help of troops provided by his Spanish cousin and the league of Catholic German princes, and the lands of the Elector Palatine on the Rhine were declared forfeit. These Catholic successes alarmed many German Protestant rulers, who naturally looked to the Lutheran Scandinavian kingdoms for support. Christian would have liked to offer active assistance, but his council insisted on waiting until the confused situation had become clearer. The following year, with the resumption of fighting between the Spaniards and the Dutch in the Low Countries, Maurice of Nassau sent a personal envoy to Copenhagen to try to obtain Danish aid. Again the Council urged caution, although, in view of the threatening situation, it did go so far as to authorize the raising of more troops and the conclusion of treaties of friendship with the United Provinces and England, whose King James I was both Christian's brother-in-law (he had married Frederik II's daughter Anna the year after Christian's accession) and the father-in-law of the Elector Palatine. Christian also managed at this time to get his second son Frederik elected heir to the bishopric of Bremen–Verden and bullied the great port of Hamburg into acknowledging his overlordship. In 1624 an English embassy arrived in Copenhagen to seek help for the Elector, but the Council knew that James was negotiating with Spain and feared that if Denmark committed herself she might be left in the lurch by her allies.

Christian was finally given his chance in 1625. The princes of the Lower Saxon Circle voted to invite him, who in his capacity of Duke of Holstein was one of their number, to lead their troops against the army of the Catholic League which was steadily approaching their part of Germany. Christian agreed. He had thus once more exploited his dual role to outwit his advisers, who were powerless to oppose the use of Danish troops in the enterprise. In June he crossed the Elbe with 20,000 men and advanced to the Weser. A new danger, however, now appeared from the east in the shape of a large Imperial army under the command of the Czech adventurer Wallenstein. In face of this, Christian ordered general mobilization and appealed to the

Protestant powers for support. The Dutch did call a conference in The Hague to consider the request, but only England sent a representative, and the King received merely a little money and a few troops.

In 1626 at Lutter-am-Barenberg near Wolfenbüttel, the army of the Catholic League inflicted a crushing defeat on the Danes and their allies. The latter hurried to make their peace with the victors, and Christian retired behind the Elbe. In 1627 the Catholics crossed the river into Holstein and were there joined by Wallenstein, who took over supreme command. Christian tried to stem the advancing tide at Rendsborg, but in vain; Jutland had to be abandoned to the enemy. By the spring of the following year Wallenstein was in control of the whole Baltic coastline of Germany with the exception of the city of Stralsund, which he closely besieged, and at Wismar he began to form a fleet with which to start an assault on the Danish islands.

By this time the Catholic successes had begun to alarm Gustavus of Sweden, who threw troops into Stralsund. But it was largely the operations of the Danish fleet off the coast of Pomerania that compelled Wallenstein eventually to raise the siege of the city, and a Danish squadron also managed to destroy his young fleet in Wismar. But, in spite of these successes, Christian's position seemed desperate, and he agreed to open peace negotiations in Lübeck. Gustavus tried to prevent Denmark from leaving the war by offering an alliance, and the two kings met at Halmstad to discuss its terms. But mutual suspicions led to a violent quarrel, as a result of which relations between the two men were worse than ever. In Lübeck Wallenstein, anticipating the intervention of Sweden in full force in the near future, made it known that he would not insist on his original humiliating demands on Christian, which included the cession of Jutland and Schleswig–Holstein, and when peace was finally concluded in May 1629 the Danes got away with a small indemnity, the surrender of all claims to north German bishoprics and an undertaking not to meddle any more in German affairs.

The war had a shattering effect on Denmark. For three years Jutland and Slesvig had had to suffer occupation by a hostile army of some 50,000 men and a largely Catholic army to boot; a large part of the population had taken to the woods while its cattle and crops were requisitioned by the enemy. The 'happy period' of Christian's reign was at an end. During the remaining twenty-three years of his life his difficulties mounted. He was, with justification, widely blamed for the effects of the war which he had undertaken with so little military or diplomatic preparation, and his relations with his council deteriorated still further. And the reputation of the royal family as a whole had been besmirched by the incompetence shown by the King's eldest son Christian while his father was away on campaign. The return of peace further revealed social antagonisms which had been exacerbated by the war; in 1629 the Crown was petitioned by a number of burghers, who bitterly attacked the privileges enjoyed by the nobility, especially its tax exemptions. As will be seen, when similar social conflicts broke out in 1660 after another unsuccessful war, Christian's successor used them to establish royal supremacy. But Christian himself refused to make any approaches to the commoners which might antagonize their betters.

His finances were now in a parlous state; income no longer kept pace with expenditure. And the expedients which were adopted in an attempt to remedy the situation only made it worse. Debasement of the coinage caused sharp inflation. Loans which were raised had to be serviced and eventually repaid. Attempts to raise the Sound Dues brought protests from foreign merchants and complications with their governments, especially that of the United Provinces. And heavy taxes kept social unrest alive. At a meeting of the Estates (to which peasants were no longer summoned) in Odense in 1638 the burghers again criticized the nobility and also called for the formation of a national militia to replace the expensive professional army on which Christian had hitherto relied. The nobles defended their privileges all the more stubbornly because their economic circumstances were now deteriorating. The price rise was coming to an end, and the unsettled conditions which succeeded it threw many landowners deeply into debt. They did agree to new financial contributions and to the organization of a militia but only on condition that military arrangements in the provinces should be under the control of commissioners drawn from their own ranks, and these men came in time to exercise considerable power at the expense of the influence of the central government. Not only this, but the standing army was retained. Christian's attempts to relieve the sorry plight of the peasants on the eastern islands by securing the abolition of *vornedskab*[1] were made in vain.

He was undoubtedly deeply affected by the war. After it he was no longer the bluff, pleasure-loving monarch of his earlier years and popular legend. He had always had a quick temper, but he now became notably more irritable and capricious, characteristics which were intensified by personal tragedy. In 1612 his first wife, a dowdy Brandenburg princess, had died, and three years later he contracted a form of marriage with a pretty and lively seventeen-year-old noblewoman named Kirsten Munk. She was never given the title of queen, but for more than a decade the couple appeared to have been happy together; she bore the King seven daughters and two sons. But in 1630 Christian suddenly accused her of infidelity and banished her from the Court. His private life was thereafter embittered by constant quarrels with her and a number of their children who took their mother's part.

In the midst of all these difficulties Christian did manage to retain his intellectual curiosity and his interest in cultural pursuits. Two years after the beginning of the reign, Tyge Brahe had fled the kingdom after charges had been brought against him in connection with his administration of Hven, and he had died in 1601 in Bohemia, where he had taken up residence at the invitation of Emperor Rudolf. But in 1637 Christian approved the design of a striking tower 118 feet high to serve as an observatory for the University of Copenhagen; a familiar landmark in the capital today, its simple outline contrasts with the elaborate buildings of the earlier part of the reign and may be seen as a symbol of the sobering time when it was constructed. And in 1643, the year after the inauguration of the Round Tower, appeared one of the most remarkable works of seventeenth-century antiquarian scholarship—*Monumenta Danica* (Memorials of Denmark), a description in six volumes of all runic inscriptions then known, including that on the longest of the Gallehus horns[2] discovered shortly before. Its author was a doctor from Århus named Ole Worm, who had begun in 1623

[1] See above, p. 84.
[2] See above, p. 27, and below, p. 168.

a collection of curios in his house which was to form the basis of the later National Museum. Foreign artists were also still attracted to the Danish Court in the 1630's and 1640's. The Dutch painters Karel van Mander and Abraham Wuchters established themselves there at this time and produced portraits of Christian in his old age, while Heinrich Schütz, the greatest of Bach's German predecessors, was for a time director of the royal orchestra.

In 1643 disaster again struck Denmark. Gustavus Adolphus had finally joined in the war in Germany in 1630, and until his death in battle in 1632 had gone from success to success. Even after he had left the scene the regents for his daughter Christina had continued the struggle. Christian had meanwhile tried to persuade the Emperor to accept him as mediator in any peace negotiations which might be arranged. In such a capacity he hoped to be able to limit Sweden's territorial gains in Germany. Neither side was prepared to consider a compromise peace in the 1630's, but Danish foreign policy did score some successes in the decade. In 1633 the Emperor granted Christian the right to collect tolls at Glückstadt for five years, and in the following year Prince Frederik, Christian's younger son, became Bishop of Bremen. Unfortunately each of these successes alienated both the Swedes and the Dutch. The latter in particular were further alarmed when in 1640 a Danish embassy was sent to Madrid. Its ostensible purpose was to conclude a commercial agreement, but it was feared in The Hague that political questions were also being discussed. Christian might have been able to exploit Dutch jealousy of Sweden's power, but, already antagonized by his tariff policy, the Netherlanders decided to renew their alliance with his rival. Dano–Swedish relations were worsened still more by the behaviour of the Danish mediator at the peace negotiations when they finally began in Osnabrück in 1642; he was obviously using all his influence to counter Swedish demands for the cession of Pomerania. At the end of the following year Swedish patience finally gave out, and orders were sent to Marshal Torstensson, then commanding a Swedish army in Moravia, to hurry north and attack Denmark.

In spite of warnings which the Danish envoy in Stockholm had been sending home for some time, no troops had been stationed in Holstein to reinforce the regular garrison there by the time

Torstensson arrived at the border, and by the end of January 1644 the Swedes had occupied the whole of Jutland. Another Swedish army then swept through Skåne, only Malmö managing to hold out against it. A Danish fleet under Christian's personal command managed to drive back a Dutch fleet which had been sent to help transport Torstensson's troops to the islands, and in July he met the main Swedish fleet off Kolberger Heide in Holstein and forced it to take refuge in Kiel Sound. The battle is commemorated in the Danish national anthem:

> *King Christian stood by lofty mast*
> *In mist and smoke.*
> *His sword was hammering so fast*
> *Through helm and brain of Goth it passed . . .*

He lost an eye in the process. And in vain, for the next month the Swedes not only broke out but joined up with Dutch ships which had forced the Sound and practically annihilated the Danish fleet between the islands of Lolland and Falster. Christian decided to sue for peace. As in 1629, the terms he was finally offered were more favourable than his position seemed to warrant. This was because France wished to limit Sweden's gains in the Baltic so as to maintain a balance of power in the region and mediated a separate agreement between Denmark and the Dutch. The Swedes consequently had to moderate their demands. By the Peace of Brömsebro in August 1645 they secured exemption from the Sound Tolls together with the Norwegian provinces of Jämtland and Härjedalen and the islands of Gotland and Øsel, but of the Danish possessions to the east of the Sound which they had hoped for, they were given only Halland, and that for only thirty years.

Christian was nevertheless a broken man. Before the Swedish war he had tried to counter the opposition from the Council by building up his own party within it. His principal instrument in this policy had been Corfitz Ulfeld, a gifted, ambitious but impoverished nobleman, who in 1636 had married Leonora Christine, Christian's favourite daughter by Kirsten Munk, and had been appointed governor of Copenhagen with a seat on the Council. After Brömsebro, however, Ulfeld, now royal steward, turned against his father-in-law and provided the Council with the leadership it had hitherto lacked. Christian's plot had back-fired. He turned to Hannibal Sehested, another nobleman married to one of Kirsten's daughters. Hannibal had led the embassy to Spain in 1640 and two years later been created viceroy in Norway, which he had defended with great skill against the Swedes. He was widely known to favour a strengthening of royal authority. But the jealous councillors, under Ulfeld's guidance, managed to whittle away his power, and the death of Christian's eldest son in 1647 placed them in a very strong position. They could use the fact that Denmark was still constitutionally an elective monarchy to bargain with the King about the terms on which they would accept his second son Frederik as his successor. Christian had to give up all his plans for reform, including one to improve his finances by farming out royal fiefs to the highest bidder. But he had still not concluded any definite agreement about the succession when he died at the age of seventy-one in February 1648. He had lost his last battle.

# CHAPTER IX

# *Frederik III and the Introduction of*
# *Absolute Monarchy (1648-70)*

As a condition for succeeding his father, Frederik III was compelled by the Council to agree to the terms of a *håndfæstning* which appeared to leave his hands more tightly bound than those of any previous Danish monarch; any vacancy created in the Council by the death of one of its members was to be filled from candidates put forward by the nobles of the deceased's province, and its powers were so extended as to leave the King in theory with hardly any initiative at all. The new ruler was nearly forty years old and, in contrast to his extrovert father, was a scholarly, introspective, patient and, at least outwardly, even rather lethargic man, whose innermost thoughts were rarely revealed to anyone. He had not been educated as heir to the throne, and for some time after his accession he seemed to take little interest in State affairs, spending many hours in the hunting-field. But there can be little doubt that, encouraged by his lively and ambitious young Brunswick wife, he was on the lookout for every opportunity which might present itself to assert his authority. He did not have long to wait.

Ulfeld continued to provide leadership for the Council, now increased to twenty-three members, but he was beginning to overreach himself. His arrogance and the considerable wealth which he had amassed during the recent war aroused the bitter jealousy of his equals, especially after a diplomatic mission to the United Provinces on which he behaved more like a ruling prince than a minister. On his return in October 1649, though he had managed to conclude both an alliance and a commercial treaty with the Dutch Republic, he was received coolly and found that in his absence his powers had been restricted and that several of his nominees had been replaced by those of the Crown. Vigorous attempts were now made to collect evidence to prove that he had abused his position, and, though this turned out to be extremely difficult to do, Ulfeld realized that he could expect little sympathy in any trial which might be staged, and to avoid arrest he fled to Sweden in the late summer of 1651. In 1653 he issued there a document defending his conduct and at the same time accusing the King of having broken his word. This enabled Frederik to have him deprived of all his lands and offices.

Ulfeld's fall brought with it that of Sehested, the other member of the so-called 'Son-in-Law-Party'. He had made himself very popular in Norway and had done much to create a separate administration for that country. He seemed indeed to his fellow councillors to be aiming at a dangerous degree of independence, and, as has been seen, moves against him had already been initiated at the end of the previous reign. His wealth, like Ulfeld's, also caused jealousy, and it was not too difficult to discover irregularities in his handling of the taxes with which he had been entrusted. While Ulfeld saved himself by flight, Sehested chose to stay and throw himself on the King's mercy. He resigned all his offices voluntarily and surrendered his Norwegian estates to the Crown. In return he was granted a pension and a stop to the investigations into his conduct, for, although he appeared to be a broken man, his personal relations with Frederik remained friendly, and the most important period of his public life was yet to come.

For the time being the Council lacked leadership. Ulfeld's successor as steward of the realm was Joakim Gersdorff, a widely travelled, intelligent and extremely rich man. He made tentative moves towards the centralization of financial administration and organized the Admiralty, a department set up under Frederik II, as a 'college' or administrative committee of a type first evolved in Sweden earlier in the century whose members were jointly responsible for the advice they gave the King and Council. But Gersdorff was a 'king's man', and political initiative lay with the Crown. And it cannot be said that Frederik used this initiative at first with great wisdom. For he must take much of the blame for the war which broke out with Sweden in

1657, a war for which Denmark was if anything worse prepared both militarily and diplomatically than she had been when Christian IV had marched into Germany some thirty years previously.

Denmark had been drawn into the first Anglo-Dutch War of 1652–4 by virtue of the alliance which had been concluded with the United Provinces by Ulfeld, but she was called on to do little fighting. The year after this struggle ended, however, Charles X, the new King of Sweden, invaded Poland and, after initial successes, found himself in difficulties when the Poles rallied round their King. This appeared to Frederik, a number of his younger councillors and in particular to the influential circle of Holsteiners round the Queen, to provide Denmark with a good opportunity to revenge herself on her neighbour for the Peace of Brömsebro and to gain compensation for the territories in north Germany which Sweden had won at the Peace of Westphalia which had ended the Thirty Years' War in 1648. And the representatives of the Estates, who were called to grant taxes for an offensive war, appeared, to judge by their generosity, to agree. But, although both the Emperor and the Elector of Brandenburg promised assistance, no definite agreement had been reached with any foreign power when the Council supinely approved the decision to attack, and the Dutch had recently concluded an alliance with the Swedes. The Danish army was, in addition, small, largely untrained and incompetently led. Frederik was taking a dangerous gamble.

After receiving news of the initial Danish moves, which included the occupation of Frederik's old bishopric of Bremen–Verden, now a Swedish possession, Charles rapidly withdrew from Poland, marched his armies through the lands of his father-in-law the Duke of Holstein–Gottorp, to whom he offered independence from Denmark, and occupied most of Jutland. The western Danish army withdrew to the half-finished fortress of Frederiksodde (now Fredericia), from which it was hoped to prevent the invasion of the islands. But Frederiksodde fell to a Swedish assault, and its surviving garrison of 4,000 surrendered. Then at the beginning of 1658 even the weather came to Charles's aid. The winter proved so severe that the Belts froze to a depth sufficient to enable him to march a force of 12,000 men across the ice to Zealand, via Fyn, Langeland, Lolland and Falster. Frederik and his council resolved that further resistance would be pointless and sued for peace. Terms were agreed at the end of February under English and French mediation and ratifications exchanged at Roskilde. The coming of the thaw had driven Charles to reduce his original demands in order to gain a swift settlement, but Denmark still had to pay a heavy price. She was compelled to surrender the whole of central Norway and Bohuslän, the island of Bornholm and all remaining territory on the eastern side of the Sound, as well as to grant to the Duke of Holstein–Gottorp full sovereignty over his part of Slesvig and Holstein. The greatest humiliation was perhaps a promise to restore all his property to Corfitz Ulfeld, who had acted as one of the Swedish negotiators.

Less than six months later, at the beginning of August, Charles, whose troops had remained in Jutland awaiting Denmark's fulfilment of all the treaty terms, landed again on Zealand and marched towards Copenhagen. Faced with an alliance of Poland, Brandenburg and the Emperor, he had determined to crush Denmark once and for all and to make the country a Swedish dependency. But this time Frederik decided to fight to the bitter end, and his appeals to the burghers of Copenhagen to defend their city against an enemy who had behaved so treacherously struck many a responsive chord. An initial Swedish assault on the walls was thrown back, and Charles was forced to mount a regular siege, for which he was not adequately prepared. Sweden's other enemies now came to Denmark's aid. In October a large Dutch fleet broke through the line of Swedish warships in the Sound, and by the end of 1658 an army of Poles, Brandenburgers and Imperialists had cleared Jutland of Swedes. And in Skåne the Swedish occupation forces were constantly harassed by pro-Danish peasant guerillas (*snaphaner*). A desperate full-scale assault on Copenhagen in February 1659 cost the attackers very heavy losses and failed in its objective, and in May, soon after a fresh Dutch fleet had set sail for the Sound, France, England and the United Provinces agreed to reimpose peace in the Baltic, where their trade had been seriously disrupted and where Swedish hegemony was in the interests of none of them.

Charles refused to be coerced and in February 1660 opened a new campaign in Norway. But the scene was suddenly transformed by his death of a stroke. The regents who now ruled Sweden for his four-year-old son Charles XI agreed to open peace negotiations in earnest. The final terms agreed on in Copenhagen in May proved to be slight recompense for the efforts Denmark had made since Roskilde. This was largely because the mediators considered it in their best interests to maintain a balance of power in the Baltic and in particular judged that its entrance should be shared between the two Scandinavian powers. Danish hopes of regaining Skåne were consequently dashed, and the only modifications made in the Roskilde settlement were the return of Bornholm, whose inhabitants had in fact already freed themselves at the end of 1658, and of central Norway, which was also cleared of Swedish troops before the peace was signed.

The war had made havoc of the Danish economy. Towns and villages had been burnt, crops destroyed, cattle commandeered by friend and foe alike, and the population had been decimated into the bargain by plague introduced by troops from the east. It was Jutland's third experience of enemy occupation within thirty years. Trade had been brought to a standstill, and the Royal Treasury was drained. Ever since the beginning of the reign, the Crown had been attempting to reduce the burden of debt incurred under Christian IV by disposing of its landed property. Now this debt was many times heavier, and the loss of Skåne in particular had enormously reduced the kingdom's potential resources. The Estates were summoned to meet in Copenhagen in September 1660 to discuss ways and means of relieving the alarming situation.

The two commoner Estates had already under Christian IV expressed their discontent with the privileges enjoyed by the nobles, and in 1648 there had been protests from the burghers when the former had been exempted from payment of a new excise duty on beer and spirits. Now, under the firm leadership of Hans Nansen, chief burgomaster of Copenhagen, and Hans Svane, the scholarly but ambitious Bishop of Zealand, they launched a full-scale attack. Not only were the nobles accused of failing to bear a fair share of the country's financial burdens but also of cowardice and even of treachery in the war. Particular reference was made to the surrender of Frederiksodde. There was in fact little substance in these latter charges, but the behaviour of some Jutish and Scanian nobles, concerned for the fate of their estates, did not compare favourably with that of the burghers of Copenhagen, whose self-confidence had been enormously boosted by the successful defence of their city and who had at the beginning of the siege been granted a charter of privileges by which they had gained the same rights of office- and land-holding as the nobles. The latter class had been steadily weakened by economic difficulties, by the policy which it had adopted in the late sixteenth century of excluding fresh blood and by divisions within it between the richer and poorer members and between families of Danish and German origin. It was thrown on to the defensive and finally agreed to make some concessions, including participation in a new excise. But to the commoners' demands for full tax equality, the equal right of all classes to enjoy royal fiefs and even the abolition of labour services on noble lands, they returned an adamant refusal.

Hannibal Sehested had reappeared on the scene during the peace negotiations and had thereafter risen rapidly into royal favour. He had always desired strong monarchy and was close to Bishop Svane, who held similar views. And he appears to have been largely responsible for the initiation of negotiations soon after the *stændermøde* opened between representatives of the clergy and burghers on one side and on the other the Treasury official Christoffer Gabel, whom Frederik had brought with him from Holstein to look after his personal finances and who was acquiring considerable power. During these talks the commoners were given to understand that the Crown sympathized with their demands, and the outcome was the presentation to the Council of a resolution by the two lower Estates in favour of making the Danish crown hereditary like all the other European crowns except that of Poland. Hereditary monarchy would mean that no king would in future have to agree to a *handfæstning* at his accession and the power of the noble Council would consequently be considerably reduced. The Council, realizing this, rejected the suggestion, and Frederik was approached directly. How far he had been involved in the preliminary moves and how genuine was his apparent hesitation to accept the plan have never been satisfactorily determined; modern historians tend to discount earlier theories of a plot to assume absolute power concocted between the King and his favourites even before the Estates were called. But he did accept, and the Council gave way. The citizen militia was called out in Copenhagen, the gates of the city were barred to prevent the nobles leaving, and they were then cowed into giving their assent to the reform. Frederik, having been freed from his oath to abide by the *håndfæstning*, received the allegiance of his subjects (including a body of the Crown's peasants) as hereditary king at an impressive ceremony before the walls of his palace (see Plate 7), and after a few more weeks the members of the *stændermøde* dispersed to their homes.

But this was the end of only the first stage in what proved to be a bloodless revolution in Denmark. Since the *håndfæstning* had been declared invalid, the royal powers had to be redefined. A committee chosen by the King from the three Estates had discussed with the Council what form the new constitution should take, but no agreement could be reached, and, largely on Svane's prompting, it had been decided to allow the matter to rest in the hands of the monarch. Perhaps if Frederik had been left to himself he would have allowed the Estates to continue to play a part in the political life of his realm, as most of the nobles and burghers at least hoped they would. But Gabel, the Queen, who had great influence with her devoted husband, and others around him favoured the removal of all restrictions on his freedom of action. Absolutism was the fashionable political doctrine in the late seventeenth century, the most popular solution to that threat of anarchy and social upheaval which thinking men, especially of the rising middle classes, feared more than anything else in the period, and a type of government which commoners regarded as preferable to noble oligarchy.

At the beginning of 1661 therefore a document granting the King absolute power was sent round the country for signature by all the leading members of Danish society. There was no opposition. The Estates were never called to a national meeting again. At the same time Svane was rewarded for his work with the title of archbishop, the first and last time the dignity was conferred on a Lutheran in Denmark. And Nansen was made president of the new governing body of Copenhagen. Both men received seats on the *statskollegium*, an advisory 'college' of eleven members presided over by the steward which was intended to replace to a certain extent the now defunct Council. For the introduction of hereditary and absolute monarchy provided an opportunity for a radical reorganization of central and local administration, and in the course of the following few years this was given a structure which it retained for nearly two centuries.

The main driving force behind this reform seems to have been Sehested, who was made treasurer of the realm at the end of 1660. At the same time the Treasury was made a college of a president and eight 'assessors' independent of the old Danish Chancery, which was also given a collegiate structure. And a College of War joined the Admiralty. A new supreme court (*højesteret*), which may be regarded as a sixth college, took over the Council's judicial functions. Foreign affairs (including those of the Duchies) remained largely the concern of the so-called German Chancery. In the provinces the fiefs were abolished and replaced by *amter* or counties under the direction of salaried *amtmænd* (intendants). Unlike the fief-holders these men had no military powers and no say in the collection of taxes. The latter were the responsibility of officials known as *amtskrivere* (county secretaries). The *amtmand* was closely controlled by the Crown, which was also to appoint not only mayors but all members of urban councils. The remodelling of the Treasury enabled Sehested to keep a closer watch on the financial position, and during the early 1660's this did improve, although the huge debt could be reduced only by granting away many of the remaining royal estates, with a consequent long-term diminution of revenue. And, as will be seen, the debt was soon again on the increase.

The new order brought the burghers most of the benefits which they had asked for specifically in 1660 and had hoped for in supporting the revolution. They were granted equal rights with the nobles to hold public office; half the Treasury assessors and half the members of the *højesteret* were to be commoners. And they could henceforth acquire land which had been reserved previously for the nobility. While most of the *amtmænd* were drawn from the local aristocracy, the *amtskrivere* were usually of lowlier birth. The nobles lost their exemption from the regular land tax, and much of the alienated royal demesne came into burgher hands. The greatest sufferers from the change of system were the old noble families. A number of their members were prominent in State service under the early absolute monarchs, but as a group they were regarded with suspicion, and they found themselves pushed more and more into the background by new men, often foreigners, who were wholly dependent on royal favour. Some of the latter were able to acquire great wealth and to take over the often heavily mortgaged estates of the more ancient lines, who now also paid for an exclusiveness which had considerably reduced their numbers.

The most prominent individual victim of the coup was Corfitz Ulfeld, although for his ultimate fate he really had only himself to blame. He was received back into the King's grace at the cost of half his lands. But then, while in Germany, he became involved in a conspiracy against Frederik and was condemned to death for high treason *in absentia*. He himself escaped arrest and was drowned in the Rhine in 1664, but his wife, the beautiful Leonora Christine, against whom the Queen had long waged a personal vendetta, was seized in England at the request of the Danish government, taken back to Denmark and thrown into the Blue Tower of Copenhagen Castle, where she remained for the next twenty-two years. While there she composed one of the most moving documents in Danish literature—*Jammersminde* (Memorial of Woe).[1] In this she described for her children, vividly and with noble resignation, the early years of her captivity. The first draft was completed in 1674, but the work was not published for nearly 200 years.

Frederik lacked his father's wide cultural interests, and his reign is not otherwise outstanding for artistic achievements. It is perhaps significant that Didrik Buxtehude, the greatest of Denmark's composers before the nineteenth century, left his post as organist in Elsinore in 1668 to spend the rest of his life in Lübeck, where he was visited by both Bach and Handel. And, while *Hexaëmeron*, the main work of Anders Arrebo, often referred to as the 'father of Danish poetry', was first published in 1661, it had been composed under Christian IV, its author having died in 1637. It was in any case a long and tedious reconstruction in verse of the Biblical story of the Creation whose

[1] The latest English translation was published in 1929 as *The Memoirs of Leonora Christina.*

main merit was that it was written in Danish. But the first of the absolute kings did, like his contemporary Charles II in England, take a considerable interest in the advances in scientific knowledge which marked the seventeenth century, and he took over Ole Worm's collection when that worthy man died in 1654 tending victims of plague in Copenhagen. The scientific scene in Denmark at this time was dominated by the remarkable Bartholin family, of whom Thomas, professor of medicine, published an outstanding treatise on the lymphatic system in 1652, and his brother Rasmus in 1669 discovered, though he could not explain, the phenomenon of double refraction of light through felspar.

The seal was set on the new order in Denmark by the Royal Law (*Kongelov*), drawn up in 1665. It constituted the only absolutist constitution in the world, and the second of its forty paragraphs granted the King of Denmark–Norway more authority than was claimed by any other European monarch at the time. He was 'hereafter (to) be regarded by all his subjects as here on earth superior to all human laws and knowing no other superior or judge over him in matters spiritual or temporal save God alone'. Only three restrictions were placed on him: he was to adhere to and cherish the Lutheran faith; to allow no diminution of his prerogatives; and to maintain the integrity of the territories which he had inherited. The document also laid down in considerable detail the order of succession to the throne, which was to follow both the male and female lines. Its existence was known to only a very limited circle (it was not published until the early eighteenth century), and the responsibility for its composition has been the subject of some dispute. Sehested can be discounted. He seems never to have favoured such boundless authority as was given in the Law and was out of favour in 1665; he died in Paris the following year while on a diplomatic mission. Two men, however, undoubtedly played a large part in the composition: Christoffer Gabel, Sehested's chief rival and his successor as effective head of the royal administration, and Peder Schumacher, who actually wrote the final copy of the Law. Like Gabel, Schumacher was a member of the bourgeoisie, the son in fact of a Copenhagen wine merchant of German origin. He had risen by his wits to the posts first of the royal librarian and then of treasury secretary, and it was he who was destined to carry on Sehested's work of reconstruction after a period of comparative stagnation under Gabel. He was admitted to the *statskollegium* in 1669 and recommended by Frederik to his son Christian, who succeeded his father in the following year.

# CHAPTER X

# The End of the Seventeenth Century and the Great Northern War (1670-1720)

CHRISTIAN V was a conscientious ruler who performed his duty as he saw it to the best of his abilities. His abilities were, however, rather limited. And his strong sense of the dignity pertaining to an absolute monarch led him to distrust more intelligent men who might make his deficiencies too glaring and to surround himself with ministers among whom he could maintain an illusion of befitting omniscience. Men of ability were certainly employed by him, but their periods of power were generally short and their hold on office tenuous.

The classic example of this characteristic of the reign is the career of Peder Schumacher. As has been seen, he had already come far under Frederik III. And very early in the new reign he was ennobled, adopting, as was the custom, a new name to go with the dignity—that of Griffenfeld (after his Norwegian estate). At first he was outshone in public by Frederik Ahlefeldt, member of a family which had acquired great influence under King Frederik thanks to the patronage of the Queen, and by Ulrik Gyldenløve, a bastard son of the previous monarch and an extremely popular Norwegian viceroy. It was the latter who was responsible for the first Danish building of importance in the fully developed Dutch Baroque style, the mansion on Kongens Nytorv in Copenhagen, known, since he sold it to Christian V's widow, as *Charlottenburg* and now housing the Royal Academy of Arts. While Ahlefeldt, the King's representative in Slesvig and Holstein, took over foreign affairs, Gyldenløve made himself responsible for commerce and the navy. But Griffenfeld gathered a number of key posts into his hands and came to exercise real power in the Danish Chancery. In 1673, when still under forty years of age, he was given the title of chancellor of the realm and was thereafter often referred to by foreign diplomats as 'chief minister'. The rather indolent Ahlefeldt and Gyldenløve were temporarily overshadowed. After his final elevation, Griffenfeld became more and more deeply immersed in foreign affairs, and it was his foreign policy that brought about his dramatic fall only three years later.

His principal desire was for Denmark to forge strong links with France, now rapidly becoming the most formidable power in Europe, and to replace Sweden as Louis XIV's Baltic ally. When war broke out between France and the Dutch in 1672, Griffenfeld advised strongly against Danish participation on the side of the latter, but during the two years following Denmark concluded alliances with Louis's enemies which forced her in 1675, when Sweden, by virtue of an agreement with France, attacked Brandenburg, finally to join in on the side of the anti-French coalition. The Chancellor's known opposition to the war was enough by itself to strain his relations with the jealous King, who had long been eager to take part in the hope of regaining from Sweden the Danish provinces which had been lost to her under his two predecessors. And when Denmark's allies discovered, through a letter intercepted in Hamburg, that Griffenfeld had been intriguing with the French Court after his country had become a belligerent, and communicated this news to one of his enemies in Copenhagen, his fate was sealed. His power and the arrogance with which he exercised it had left him with few friends at Court, and Christian was easily persuaded that he must act against the Chancellor in order to assure his allies of his own loyalty to their cause. Griffenfeld was consequently arrested, arraigned before a special tribunal and condemned to death for high treason and peculation. Of the former he was certainly innocent. There can be no doubt that he had lined his pockets with bribes from office-seekers and that his great fortune had not all been acquired by creditable means, but few statesmen of the age were wholly guiltless of such practices, and Griffenfeld hardly deserved on this count the punishment prescribed.

On 6th June 1676 he was led to the scaffold, but just as the headsman's axe was about to fall, a message from his master was read commuting the sentence to one of life imprisonment. For four years he was closely confined in Copenhagen Castle, but in 1680 he was transferred to the island of Munkholm in Trondheim Fjord in Norway, where he was allowed rather more freedom of movement. And just before his death in 1699 he was permitted to reside in Trondheim itself. For all his faults, there can be little doubt that his fall deprived Denmark of the services of a brilliant mind, the like of which she greatly needed, and, as will be seen, his successors soon adopted just that line in foreign policy which he had advocated.

The Griffenfeld period witnessed further developments in the system of administration introduced by Sehested in the early 1660's, including the appearance of a privy council (*gehej-mekonseil*), a small body of advisers who met frequently with the King to discuss particularly foreign policy. The new council was modelled on the French *conseil d'en haut* and had been fore-shadowed under Frederik III. Griffenfeld was himself its first secretary. The *statskollegium* faded more and more into the background and was finally abolished after the latter's fall. At the same time there was an increase in the importance of the chief secretaries of the various colleges until they took on something of the character of the French and English secretaries of state.

The creation of a new nobility more dependent on the Crown than the old one was given a new form in 1671 when the novel ranks of baron (*friherre*) and count (*greve*) were instituted. The recipients were given not only estates to enable them to sustain a suitable standard of living but also extensive taxation privi-leges, thus undermining that equality of financial burdens which the burghers appeared to have won in 1660–1. Griffenfeld was among the first to be honoured with the latter title, as he was one of the first to be made a member of the revived Order of the Elephant. This had originally been founded by Christian I in the fifteenth century, but had since fallen into desuetude. An entirely new knightly order, that of the Dannebrog, and an elaborate table of ranks were also established to provide addi-tional bribes with which it was hoped to ensure the loyalty of royal servants.

The early years of Christian V's reign was also a period when the reputation enjoyed by Danish science since the days of Tyge

Brahe was further enhanced by Ole Rømer and Niels Steensen and when a poet of considerable distinction emerged in Denmark in the person of Thomas Kingo. Rømer was a pupil of Rasmus Bartholin. In 1671 he was invited to pursue his researches in the newly founded French Academy of Sciences. And it was while he was in Paris in 1676 that he published his calculation of the speed of light. While it is this discovery on which his fame now largely rests, he did a great deal of useful if less spectacular work in inventing new and improving old scientific instruments, including a thermometer with a Fahrenheit scale, and after he returned to Denmark, in 1681, was extensively employed by the government; at the end of his life he was chief of police and first burgomaster in Copenhagen, where he had introduced the first regular system of street lighting. Steensen was a more complex character. Born a few doors away from the house of Griffenfeld's parents in Copenhagen, he revealed his genius for the first time while studying medicine in Leyden in the early 1660's and later demonstrated for the first time that the heart was a muscle. But his interests were extraordinarily wide. While staying with the Duke of Tuscany he managed, for example, to establish the character of fossils, and he has been called the founder of geology. In Florence, however, he was converted to Catholicism, which made life in Denmark, whither he returned in 1672, unbearable. He soon left again to spend the rest of his life in Germany, where he abandoned scientific research for religious devotion and died in 1686 as Bishop of Schwerin. Kingo was also deeply religious, but it was his faith which led him to make his special contribution to Danish culture. In 1674, while rector in his birthplace of Slangerup in Zealand, he brought out his first great collection of hymns. Three years later he was appointed Bishop of Fyn and in 1681 published a second volume. He was largely responsible for the new official hymn-book, which was issued in 1699 and contained some eighty of his own pieces. Many of his hymns have remained among the most popular with Danish congregations to the present day.

Fresh attempts were made at the end of the reign of Frederik III and the beginning of that of Christian V to foster the development of the Danish economy in accordance with 'mercantilist' principles under the direction of a new College of

Commerce set up in 1668. New monopoly trading companies were founded, including one for the West Indies, where the island of St. Thomas was acquired as a base, and another to secure slaves from the Guinea Coast of West Africa, where the forts of Frederiksborg and Christiansborg had been built in the early 1660's. And new industries, such as a tobacco factory, were established in Copenhagen. But none of these had much more success than the similar enterprises for which Christian IV had been responsible, and, while Copenhagen continued to grow as the result of immigration from the countryside until it reached a population of about 60,000 in the 1670's, many smaller towns appear to have been stagnating, if not actually in decline. This situation was inevitably reflected in the state of the Crown's finances, which was not improved by the new tax exemptions and the lavish Court which Christian V, unlike his father, insisted on maintaining. But the chief drain on the nation's resources was the war against Sweden, which raged on for a further four years after Griffenfeld's fall.

From the purely military point of view Denmark gave a good account of herself in this. An invasion of Sweden proper, it is true, ended unsuccessfully. The main Danish army under Christian's personal command landed in Skåne in the summer of 1676 and managed to occupy all of the province except Malmö together with most of Blekinge further east. But in a bloody battle outside Lund at the end of the year the Swedes were victorious, and after a further setback in 1677, the Danes retired to the fortresses of Hälsingborg and Landskrona. On the other hand, Sweden's German possessions and the territories of Sweden's ally the Duke of Holstein–Gottorp were occupied, Gotland was seized and successfully defended, and the Danish navy swept its opponents from the Baltic. Admiral Niels Juel, the greatest of the country's sea-heroes who had gained his battle experience under the Dutchmen Tromp and De Ruyter, won a decisive victory over a superior Swedish fleet in Køge Bay in the Sound in July 1677; twenty of the thirty-six Swedish ships were destroyed at no cost to Juel.

But while Denmark did much to redeem her tarnished military reputation, French diplomacy managed to isolate her from her allies and prevent her from making any gains in the peace which was finally concluded in Lund in 1679. And the war had cost her dear. Such slight economic gains as had been made before it were largely wiped out, and, in spite of a great increase in taxation, the Crown's debts had mounted alarmingly. The last ten years of Christian's reign were indeed dominated by the problem of finance, a problem complicated by a serious crisis in Danish agriculture which was just beginning and by the unsettled economic conditions which prevailed throughout most of western Europe in the later seventeenth century. In an effort to produce a more equitable distribution of the tax burden, work was begun on a new land survey to replace one which had been hastily drawn up in the early 1660's and then found to be seriously defective. The new one, completed in 1688, was a thorough piece of work; it recorded much more accurately than ever before the value of each estate and remained the basis of the land taxation system for a century and a half. At the same time the demesnes of some of the lesser nobles were again made liable to tax, and attempts, unfortunately not wholly successful, were made to prevent demesne land from being extended by the absorption into it of the holdings of peasant tenants.

The concern of the absolute monarchy for the rights and welfare of all classes below the Crown and the desire it had to preserve a social balance are perhaps demonstrated most forcibly in the Law Code promulgated in 1683. It was the outcome of work which had begun soon after the revolution of 1660–1 and was the first code for all Denmark; up to this time the country had been subject to the medieval provincial codes supplemented by royal decrees. It did remove all remaining vestiges of local self-government such as the election of pastors by their congregations, abolished juries, laid down harsh punishments for all offences which could be construed as being in any way directed against the State, and retained the death penalty for blasphemy, bigamy and infanticide. But on the whole it was a progressive measure. It recognized equality before the law for all the king's subjects, and the role of torture was considerably reduced. It was indeed looked upon in its day as a model and was translated into the leading European languages; and a copy of it was requested later by Peter the Great with the idea of making it the basis of a new Russian law code.

After the middle of the 1680's the work of reform tailed off.

This was partly because several schemes which had been begun immediately after and because of the introduction of absolution had now come to fruition and partly because the stimulus provided by the war was growing weak, but it was also because of Christian V's policy of divide and rule, which he had pursued since Griffenfeld's fall. He could assert himself only by surrounding himself with rather meagre talents and then playing off one adviser against another to prevent one of them from gaining the ascendancy which the Chancellor had once enjoyed. But the financial situation in the early 1690's was becoming so alarming again that he had to call on expert opinion to try to put things right. The man to whom he turned was Christian von Plessen, one of the large number of immigrants from the duchy of Mecklenburg who were to play a considerable role in Danish political life in the eighteenth century. Plessen first attracted the King's attention while he was acting as agent for Christian's brother George, who married the future English Queen Anne in 1683. He took over the Treasury in 1692, and his firm hand soon produced an improvement. He unified the taxation system, stopped many leaks and, by increasing confidence in Danish credit, was able to raise loans in Amsterdam, the great banking centre of seventeenth-century Europe, on much more favourable terms than hitherto had been possible.

The accession of Frederik IV, Christian V's son, in 1699 brought Plessen's work to an end, but he had done it so well that the Crown's finances remained in reasonably good shape, with income matching expenditure, until Denmark entered a period of eleven years of continuous warfare in 1709. The new King, though poorly educated for his duties, was considerably abler than his father and was able to take on his shoulders a much greater share of government. It was apparently he who was largely responsible for the re-establishment in 1701 of a national militia of 15,000 men for the purpose of making his realm less dependent on the professional army, made up mostly of foreign mercenaries, which had proved inadequate in the crisis of the previous year.[1] Each peasant selected by his landlord to serve was to do so for six years, but service meant only training on Sunday afternoons and attending company and

[1] See below, p. 139.

regimental manoeuvres for a few weeks each year; the rest of the time he was free to cultivate the soil. And in the year following, again it seems on Frederik's own initiative, the institution of *vornedskab* was abolished for peasants born since the King's accession. Though its effects would not be felt for some time, this measure did much to increase Frederik's popularity, a popularity which he retained throughout his reign with most of his subjects. A costly pleasure trip which he undertook to Italy in 1708 did, however, bring criticism, and some eyebrows were raised when he twice married bigamously, the second time to his chancellor's daughter. He must also bear most of the responsibility for the consequences of Denmark's participation in the Great Northern War of 1700–21.

After 1679 Denmark, having learnt to her cost the power and influence wielded by France and sorely tempted by the subsidies offered by King Louis to states who were willing to do his bidding, decided to conclude the French alliance for which Griffenfeld had always been pressing. In the expectation of support from Versailles, especially as Sweden was beginning to swing towards Louis's enemies, Christian V in 1684 reoccupied the Gottorp lands in Slesvig, which he had had to return to the Duke as part of the peace settlement of 1679. But he was forced to relinquish them again in 1689 under pressure from Sweden, Brunswick (which was particularly alarmed by the revival in 1686 of Danish claims to overlordship of Hamburg) and the 'Maritime Powers' of England and the Dutch Republic. The latter were now united under William III and, in alliance with the Emperor, had just become engaged in the Nine Years' War against France. Denmark took no active part in the conflict beyond hiring out to William some of the troops which she could ill afford to support for use in Ireland and Flanders, and when she attempted to exploit her neutrality to increase her trade, she found her merchant ships snapped up by the belligerents' warships and privateers and their cargoes confiscated on various pretexts. This led her in 1691 to join Sweden, whose trade was suffering from the same cause, in the first League of Armed Neutrality; joint convoys were organized and reprisals taken until England and the Dutch Republic, the main offenders, agreed to pay compensation to Scandinavian merchants for losses they had sustained. With the end of the war

and the accession to the throne of Sweden of the young and inexperienced Charles XII in 1697, Christian was tempted to
open negotiations with Russia and Saxony for the formation of
a coalition to destroy Swedish power in the Baltic. His son
completed the alliances in 1699, and in 1700 the Great Northern
War opened with a Saxon attack on Swedish Livonia and a
Danish attack on the Duke of Holstein–Gottorp.

But England and the United Provinces fulfilled their treaty
obligations to Sweden by sending a fleet to the Sound, where it
helped to cover a landing by Swedish forces north of Copenhagen. Frederik was unprepared for action so swift and in such
strength, and by the Treaty of Travendal he agreed to respect
the Duke's independence and to leave the anti-Swedish league.
While Charles XII advanced victoriously through Poland and
forced Augustus of Saxony to make peace, Denmark enjoyed
again the benefits of neutrality in a great European war; her
East India Company in particular prospered, and she once
more lent troops to the anti-French coalition in the War of the
Spanish Succession, which broke out in 1701. But the opportunity offered by the defeat of Charles by Peter of Russia in the
Ukraine in 1709 proved to be too much of a temptation to
Frederik and his advisers. The original alliances with Russia and
Saxony were re-formed, and at the end of the year a Danish
army landed in Skåne. In 1710 it was decisively defeated near
Hälsingborg by the Swedish marshal Magnus Stenbock and had
to withdraw to Zealand. But revenge of a sort came three years
later when the same Stenbock and the army with which he had
been defending the Swedish possessions in north Germany were
forced to capitulate at Tønning in Holstein. Then Charles XII
was slain in Norway in 1718. The war, however, dragged on for
a further two years before Denmark made peace at Frederiksborg.

Denmark did secure by this the abolition of the exemption
from payment of Sound Dues which Sweden had enjoyed and a
significant accession of territory in the shape of the Slesvig lands
of the Duke of Holstein–Gottorp. But against these gains must
be set the very damaging effects of the war on her economy, and
it may even be questioned whether all the trouble which the
possession of the whole of Slesvig brought those who guided her
foreign policy in the first half of the eighteenth century made

its acquisition worth while. Such problems had to be faced by Frederik IV himself, for he lived on for a further ten years after the war's end.

# CHAPTER XI

# *The Early Eighteenth Century (1720-66)*

---

AT the end of the Great Northern War the extent of the lands ruled directly or indirectly by the King of Denmark was impressive. On the European mainland they consisted, besides Denmark proper, of the ancestral duchies of Oldenburg and Delmenhorst in north-west Germany, Slesvig (the 'ducal portion' of which was claimed by the Duke of Holstein–Gottorp but had been guaranteed to Denmark by France and Britain in the peace settlement), the 'royal portion' of Holstein and, above all, Norway. Further afield, both Iceland and The Faeroes, part of the Norwegian Crown in the Middle Ages, recognized Danish suzerainty, and a claim to Greenland which had been revived under Christian IV had gone unchallenged. And, finally, Danish trading companies owned the islands of St. Thomas and St. Jan in the West Indies, in India the posts of Trankebar on the Malabar Coast and Danmarksnagore in Bengal, and a number of forts on the coast of what is now Ghana. But a glance at the map will indicate how scattered was this 'empire', while mention of Iceland, The Faeroes and Greenland suggests that much of it was barren and thinly peopled; large parts of Norway are even today unfit for agriculture.

The only important export from Jutland and the islands was cattle, and the kingdom's total population was only about 750,000 at a time when the new kingdom of Prussia, itself as yet a minor power, could boast over 2,000,000 inhabitants. About a tenth of all Danes lived in Copenhagen, the centre of the country's economic life, but about a quarter of this number was made up of troops and a large part of the remainder depended to a greater or lesser extent on the Court. Overseas trade had expanded encouragingly during the first peaceful decade of the eighteenth century, but the war had upset it once more, and recovery was slow. It was greatly hindered by a great fire which in 1728 destroyed nearly half of Copenhagen's buildings, including Christian IV's Town Hall and University. And a number of similar fires occurred in provincial towns, still largely half-timbered, in the same period.

The agricultural crisis which had begun soon after the introduction of absolutism reached its height after the Great Northern War, and the condition of the peasant tenantry which made up the bulk of the Danish population was generally wretched. Many on the islands were still tied to the soil by *vornedskab*, and particularly harsh treatment was meted out by the bailiffs of the large number of German nobles who had been attracted to the country by the low prices of land, and of absentee burghers who had acquired royal estates and were interested only in the profit they could make out of them. Labour services were often ill defined and punishment for failure to perform them adequately, against which there was no appeal, might be severe. Any gain the peasant might make was soon swallowed up in royal taxes, Church tithes and seigneurial dues. The 'Land Question' loomed large in Denmark for most of the eighteenth century.

Frederik IV is commonly regarded as the best of Denmark's absolute monarchs. As has been pointed out, he took an active and intelligent part in government and showed considerable concern for the welfare of his subjects. He also, though not of a scholarly disposition, took an interest in his realm's developing cultural life. It was during his reign that the Enlightenment from England and France began to affect northern Europe, and Dano–Norwegian literature (the written language of the two countries were hardly distinguishable in the eighteenth century) may be said to have come of age with the work of Ludvig Holberg. Born in Bergen of well-to-do parents, Holberg graduated from the University of Copenhagen, and in 1704 undertook the first of a series of long visits to other European countries; these included one to England between 1706 and 1708, during which he studied in Oxford. In 1717, when thirty-three years old, he was appointed to a chair in his old university. He first attracted public attention by his witty satire on contemporary Danish society in the long poem *Peder Paars*, but he is best known for the stream of comedies (thirty-two in all) which he wrote, mainly in the course of a few months in 1722–3, for the newly established permanent theatre in Copenhagen. In each of these he poked fun at the foibles of a social type—the armchair politician in *Den Politiske Kandestøber* (The Political Tinker), the peasant in *Jeppe på Bjerget* (Jeppe of the Hill), the half-educated pedant in *Erasmus Montanus*. While it would be as misleading to build up a picture of Danish society in the 1720's on the basis of these dramas as to see French society under Louis XIV wholly through Molière, with whom Holberg is inevitably compared, the young professor was a keen observer of his fellow men and can do much to enliven his era for the attentive reader.

But it was architecture which, as with most of his immediate predecessors, interested the King most. Soon after his accession work was begun on the palace of *Frederiksberg* on the western outskirts of Copenhagen. Classical in concept, it reveals Frederik's admiration of both Versailles and Italy. Subsequently considerably altered, it is now a military academy. The same influences are evident in the palace of *Fredensborg* in northwest Zealand which was constructed as a country retreat immediately after the end of the Great Northern War. The red Chancery Building of 1716–21, which adjoined the south side of the old Castle of Copenhagen, is more pompous and baroque. Frederik also caused extensive alterations to be made to the Castle itself in the later years of his reign.

These years were saddened by the deaths of all his children by his second wife, to whom he was 'legally' married after the death of his first in 1721, and he turned more and more to the solaces of religion. He was strongly attracted by Pietism, a puritanical brand of Lutheranism which had emerged in north Germany at the end of the seventeenth century as a reaction against the dry formalism of the established Lutheran Churches. It had much in common with the later Methodism, especially in its emphasis on good works and its emotional overtones. Under its inspiration the King gave his backing to missionary enterprises at home and abroad, including that organized by the Norwegian priest Hans Egede among the Eskimoes of Greenland; in 1721 Egede founded at Godthåb on the west coast of the island the first European settlement there since

Viking times. Frederik was also responsible for the promulgation just before his death in 1730 of a 'sabbath ordinance', which laid down heavy penalties for non-attendance at church and for indulging in worldly pleasures on Sunday.

The influence of Pietism in Denmark reached its height under his son Christian VI. Christian was physically unattractive, with a long nose, spindly legs and a shrill voice, and his sensitivity to these failings accentuated his naturally stiff manners and shyness; he speedily surrounded himself with an elaborate etiquette, and discouraged all contact with the general public. To make matters worse, both he and his German wife were ardent Pietists who frowned on such frivolities as card-playing, dancing and theatrical performances; the previously gay Court assumed a sombre air. The only form of relaxation which Christian indeed allowed himself was hunting, of which he was a great devotee. Under these circumstances Holberg devoted all his energies to serious scholarship, including the production of a history of Denmark, which became the standard work on the subject for the remainder of the eighteenth century; the theatre for which he had composed his comedies had been destroyed in the great fire of 1728 and was not rebuilt. More favoured was his younger contemporary, the sensitive Hans Brorson, Denmark's second great hymn-writer after Kingo. He issued his first collection in 1732 and at the end of the decade gathered together all his previous output in *Troens Rare Klenodie* (Faith's Rare Jewel), the poems of which reflect their author's passionate faith, which was intensified by personal tragedy.

The change of regime made no difference to Court expenditure, which absorbed most of the land tax. Luxury was often defended by contemporary economists as encouraging the circulation of coin, but the government was able to keep its books balanced only by further extensive sales of land. Much money also went on building projects, in particular the great palace of *Christiansborg*. This was begun in 1733 on the site of the completely demolished Castle of Copenhagen. Its main influence was South German baroque, but parts of it were made the responsibility of two great Danish architects—Laurids de Thurah and Niels Eigtved (see Plate 8b). Thurah was also commissioned by the King to design the charming hunting-lodge of

*Eremitagen* (The Hermitage) in the park of Dyrehavn to the north of the capital. This still stands, but a large part of Christian's palace was destroyed by fire in 1794.

Against Christian's faults as a ruler must be set a strong sense of duty and the interest in the lot of his lowlier subjects which he had inherited from his father and which were reinforced by his religious beliefs. Like Frederik, he ruled as well as reigned and preferred to work, particularly in the fields of military and foreign affairs, with individual advisers rather than with a committee of ministers. Between 1735 and 1737 indeed the Privy Council was reduced to two members. Elementary education, if for rather limited ends, figured prominently in the Pietists' social programme, and Christian, while continuing his father's policy of establishing primary schools on royal estates, went further. In 1736 compulsory confirmation, for which a certain reading knowledge was required, was introduced, and in 1739 an ordinance envisaged the setting-up of schools throughout the country at which peasant's children could acquire a degree of literacy and religious instruction. Owing to local opposition from both peasants and landlords and lack of funds, these spread slowly, and large areas of the country were ignorant of them, but it was a beginning.

On coming to the throne Christian also abolished the national militia set up in 1702. Although, as had been seen,[1] service in this took up a comparatively small part of the conscript's time, it was a burden which was deeply resented and even avoided by flight, partly because of the harsh discipline imposed during training sessions. Unfortunately the abolition came at a time when the decline in the number of *vornede* was beginning to have an appreciable effect on the mobility of agricultural labour in the eastern islands, and the disappearance of the militia threatened to make this worse. Still seriously crippled by the depression on the land, many landowners betrayed an almost pathological fear that their estates would be deserted. Military leaders also protested, and both groups warned the King of the unfortunate consequences which might flow from the act. To his credit, Christian resisted the urgings of some to restore *vornedskab*, but in 1733 he agreed to a decree which reconstituted the militia and on more onerous terms than before. One able-

[1] See above, pp. 137–8.

bodied man between the ages of eighteen and thirty-six was to be selected by each landlord from approximately every hundred of his acres and was to serve for eight years. And to ensure the maintenance of a large pool from which to draw, not only for the militia but also for the filling of vacant tenancies (tenants were not in practice enlisted), no male peasant was in future to leave the estate of his birth between his fourteenth and thirty-sixth year or until his service with the militia had expired. This was the *stavnsbånd* (ascription law), which remained in force for over half a century. It could perhaps be justified when first introduced by the agricultural depression. But it was continued long after conditions had changed for the better, and its terms indeed grew harsher. By 1746 the age-limits had been extended to nine and forty years, and those peasants who had served were compelled to take up a vacant tenancy if one were offered to them. It was in fact little distinguishable from the old *vornedskab* and unlike that applied to Jutland and Fyn as well as to the Zealand island group (Bornholm and Schleswig–Holstein were alone exempt, and in the latter serfdom proper was common). It must, however, be noted, that probably very few tenants wished to give up a plot once they had obtained one and that many landlords who had managed to lease all their land were willing to grant landless peasants permission to live away from the estate in exchange for a small payment.

For twenty years after the end of the Great Northern War the European powers managed to avoid a serious conflict among themselves, but the attack by Frederick II of Prussia on Austria in 1740 opened a new period of large-scale warfare which inevitably had repercussions in the Baltic region. The Scandinavian monarchies were particularly affected by the reactions of Russia, who had in 1721 replaced Sweden as the leading power there. Denmark's relations with Russia were very strained for some time after the Great Northern War because of the support given by the latter to the Duke of Holstein–Gottorp, who refused to accept the loss of his lands in Slesvig. The first crisis passed in 1727 with the death of his mother-in-law, the Tsarina Catherine I; Russian patronage was subsequently withdrawn from him. But the question complicated Danish foreign policy for nearly fifty years after this.

When in the 1730's Europe began to divide into two opposing

alliance systems with France and Spain on one side and Britain, Russia and Austria on the other, Denmark leaned at first towards the latter in the hope of gaining additional guarantees against the Duke's claims, but at the end of the decade she showed more interest in a French alliance, which offered her large subsidies; one was eventually concluded in 1743. In the same year came a crisis in Dano–Swedish relations. These had been generally friendly since 1720; old jealousies seemed so have been forgotten when neither country offered a serious threat to the other. But the childlessness of the Swedish King and Queen did rouse hopes in the hearts of some Danes of reviving the Kalmar Union by securing the election of a Danish prince as their heir. Then in 1743 the ruling Hat Party in Sweden raised the succession question in an attempt to keep themselves in power at the end of a disastrous war with Russia for which they were responsible. Christian VI's son, Crown Prince Frederik, gained the support of a large body of Swedish peasants, but the Hats managed to force through the acceptance of the Russian candidate, in return for which the Tsarina allowed them to retain most of Finland when peace was made. The Russian choice was, however, a member of the house of Holstein–Gottorp, and Denmark feared that he would use his power to upset the settlement in Slesvig. For a time war seemed inevitable, but calmer counsels fortunately prevailed, and the Scandinavians began once more to draw together in face of Russian attempts to dictate their policies.

Dano–Norwegian trade in particular benefited from the long period of peace which the monarchy enjoyed after the end of the Great Northern War as well as from the decline of Dutch commerce with the Baltic in the period, and its successes in the 1730's contrasted sharply with the difficulties being faced by the country's agriculture. The size of the merchant navy grew steadily, and a new Asiatic Company set up in 1732 extended its field of operations to China and enjoyed quite striking gains during the following years. The West India Company did less well. In 1733 the island of St. Croix, larger than the two other Danish possessions in the Caribbean, was purchased from France and in the following year the company took over trade with the Guinea Coast. But in 1754 it had to be dissolved, and its forts were taken over by the State. As in the seventeenth century, Denmark's overseas trade was run largely from Copenhagen, and it was the merchants of the capital who profited from the expansion; as a body they were able to exert considerable influence on the College of Commerce.

Pietism, never widely popular in Denmark, had by the 1740's lost much of its original drive, and the accession in 1746 of Frederik V, the former claimant to the Swedish throne, who had none of his father's puritanical outlook, was greeted with an almost audible sigh of relief. Under him the Court recovered its former gaiety, and cultural life revived. A new public theatre was opened in 1747, and, although Holberg had become more and more deeply involved in his historical and moral-philo-sophical writings, he agreed to become the theatre's adviser and wrote six new comedies for it. And the visual arts also bene-fited. The new monarch had himself painted no fewer than seventy times by the Swedish-born Carl Pilo, who was ap-pointed director of the new Royal Academy of Art, founded in 1754 (the year of Holberg's death). It is hardly surprising that Frederik continued the building traditions of his dynasty. Hardly indeed had *Christiansborg*[1] been completed than plans were drawn up for a whole new elegant northern suburb of Copenhagen intended to celebrate the three-hundredth anni-versary of the accession of the first Oldenburger to the throne of Denmark. 'Frederiksstaden' proved much too ambitious for the financial resources available. *Frederikskirke* (known popularly as 'the Marble Church' because it was intended that it should be built entirely of Norwegian marble) had, for example, to be abandoned half completed after twenty years and was finished only at the end of the nineteenth century to a more modest specification. But Eigtved, now the dominant architect in the country, did see the completion of his impressive *Amalienborg* complex of four noblemen's palaces in the new rococo style around an octagon; they were taken over by the royal family at the end of the century after *Christiansborg* had been ravaged by fire. The open space between them was embellished at the beginning of the following reign by a fine equestrian statue of Frederik V, commissioned by the Asiatic Company from the French sculptor Jacques Saly.

Frederik took little interest in any other serious business.

---

[1] See above, p. 144.

While much more approachable than his father had been and in several other ways a more attractive figure, he also lacked Christian VI's strong sense of duty and, in reaction to the puritanical atmosphere in which he had grown up, he soon abandoned himself to a life of pleasure, leaving affairs of State to his ministers; under him Denmark became in effect a bureaucracy. Fortunately these ministers included men of considerable competence. The one closest to the monarch was Adam Moltke til Bregentved, the grandfather of Denmark's first constitutional prime minister and a relative of the great Prussian marshal of the Napoleonic period. He was not a member of the Privy Council until 1763, but while enjoying only a Court office he wielded great power and influence, though with commendable modesty and restraint. His principal assistant was the intellectually more brilliant Johan Hartvig Ernst Bernstorff. Like Moltke, Bernstorff belonged to a family which had originated in Mecklenburg, but he had been born in Hanover, where his grandfather was chief minister to the Elector, later the English King George I. From 1751 to 1770 he directed both Denmark's foreign policy and her economic life.

The main problems which he faced in the former sphere were relations with Russia and the question of the Gottorp lands. Both were again linked, for the Duke of Holstein–Gottorp had been chosen heir to the Russian throne just before his cousin had won the votes of the Swedes. The latter had renounced all his claims to the disputed territories by the time he became king in 1751 and indeed agreed to the betrothal of his son and heir, Prince Gustav, to a Danish princess. But the Duke himself refused to make any concessions, and when he finally became Tsar as Peter III in 1762 he immediately concluded an alliance with Prussia, against whom Russia had previously been fighting in the Seven Year's War, and prepared to use the forces of both powers against Denmark. The Danish government called in the French general the Comte de Saint-Germain to reorganize the sadly neglected army and sent the Danish fleet to blockade the Russian base of Kronstadt outside St. Petersburg. Fortunately, however, Peter was deposed by his wife Catherine before any serious clash occurred, and she preferred to reach a peaceful settlement on behalf of the new duke, her son Paul. In an alliance which she concluded with Denmark in 1765 both sides looked forward to an agreement before Paul should come of age in 1773, and as a result of the subsequent negotiations it was arranged in 1767 that the Gottorp lands in both Slesvig and Holstein should be exchanged for Oldenburg and Delmenhorst.

Denmark remained neutral during the Seven Years' War, as she had done during the previous War of the Austrian Succession, and in spite of some interference with her merchant ships by the belligerents, after Sweden's entry into the war on the French side had brought a new league of armed neutrality to an end, her commerce again benefited greatly. In the Mediterranean, for example, Danish ships were often the only ones on which merchants were willing to load their goods.

Bernstorff was still attached to mercantilist economic doctrine, which was reflected in his (not very successful) attempts to enliven Danish industry. But at the same time both he and Moltke were fully abreast of current European thought, in particular of the ideas popularized by the French *philosophes* which were beginning to penetrate Denmark to a significant extent in the middle of the eighteenth century. These included the theories of the *physiocrates*, who emphasized strongly the importance of agriculture and the benefits to be obtained from rational farming methods and greater freedom for the peasantry. Experiment in agricultural techniques and organization was encouraged in Frederick V's reign by the improvement in market conditions which took place during it. The important trade in cattle was seriously hit by epidemics in the 1740's, but corn prices rose appreciably. This may have been helped to a certain extent by the ban on the import of foreign grain into Denmark and south-eastern Norway which was imposed in 1735, but the main reason seems to have been a marked rise in population in most parts of western Europe which was now taking place. Some Danish landlords sought to exploit the situation by simply demanding increased labour services from their tenants, who had no legal redress in the absence of written agreements and before courts which were largely under their masters' control. But others were more far-sighted and realized that they would themselves eventually benefit from prosperous and contented tenants. In the vanguard of the reform movement was Count Stolberg, steward of the estates owned by Christian VI's widow at Hørsholm north of Copenhagen; he gained his mistress's consent to commute labour services on them for money rents. A number of landowners like Moltke did likewise. But a few wished to go further. Among them was Bernstorff. In 1767, just after the death of Frederik V, he allowed his tenants to withdraw from the common fields and, on certain conditions, to leave the village altogether and settle on 'enclosed' plots on the outskirts of the estate. The most intelligent and adventurous peasant could for the first time experiment with new methods unrestrained by the conservatism of his neighbours, though he still lacked legal guarantees that he and not his landlord would benefit from any improvements he might make.

The government's approach to the Land Question remained extremely cautious; there was even a further tightening up of the *stavnsbånd*. But, inspired in particular by Erik Pontoppidan, the learned Bishop of Bergen, the remarkable step was taken on the occasion of the King's thirty-second birthday in 1755 of inviting suggestions from all classes of society for the improvement of Denmark's economic life, the best of which would, it was promised, be published in Pontoppidan's *Economic Magazine*. The result was a torrent of proposals. Most of them dealt with purely technical aspects of agriculture, but they included criticisms of a much more far-reaching nature, covering such topics as the three-field system and the *stavnsbånd*. It is significant that there were at the same time no strictures passed on the system of government; absolutism was generally looked upon as the best means of carrying through any reforms that were necessary.

# CHAPTER XII

## Enlightened Reform and Catastrophe
## (1766-1814)

THE half century covered by this chapter can lay claim to be
the most dramatic and significant in Danish history. It opened
with a fierce struggle for power by a group of younger men,
who wished to exploit the peculiar character of absolutism at
the time to change rapidly all aspects of Danish life in accord
with the ideals of the Enlightenment. Their defeat by more conservative forces was followed by a period of stagnation, succeeded in its turn by one of remarkable progress and peaceful
reform, during which many of the main characteristics of
modern Danish society emerged before the country's tragic
entanglement in Continental conflicts, so long averted, brought
economic depression and, with the loss of Norway, the end of
any claim she might have had before to the status of a major
European power.

Over forty of these years were occupied by the reign of
Christian VII. Seventeen years old when he came to the throne
on his father's death, he was obviously intelligent, but he proved
as attracted by a life of dissipation as had Frederik, and the frequent unconventionality of his behaviour gave rise to considerable concern; periods of indifference and lethargy alternating
with fierce outbursts of drunken rage indicated the onset of
schizophrenia. Soon after his accession he married Caroline
Matilda, the fifteen-year-old sister of King George III of
England. Though she was far from beautiful, her youth and
charm apparently won the heart of every Dane who met her
except her husband. She bore him a son in 1768, but for most of
the time Christian paid her little attention or treated her with

undisguised contempt. Soon after the birth of the Crown Prince, the couple undertook a visit to England and France, on which, to the great relief of his entourage, the King conducted himself reasonably well and made a good impression. But once he was home again his actions became more and more quixotic, although it was not until 1771 that he became incapable for most of the time of conducting even the minimal business which the ruler had to conduct in the bureaucratic State which had emerged under his father.

Moltke and Bernstorff were retained in office by the new King. But they lost ground rapidly to younger favourites, who came to form a distinct Court party and who urged Christian to assert his authority, by-pass the Council and replace the cautious advisers whom he had inherited with bolder men like themselves. They believed that they had discovered an excellent instrument with which to carry out their policies in an Altona doctor named Johann Friedrich Struensee. Struensee had secured appointment as Court physician, and in this capacity accompanied the King on his foreign tour, for the success of which he secured a certain amount of the credit. And as a result of the intimate contact he enjoyed with the royal couple, he gained complete mastery over them. The courtiers who had sponsored him found that they had introduced a cuckoo into the nest. By early in 1770 Struensee was in effective control of royal policy, and in September of that year Bernstorff was finally dismissed. The doctor immediately set about the task of bringing Denmark up-to-date. He never seems to have drawn up a logical programme of reform, and much of his work had about it a piecemeal character which suggests a response to circumstances and a desire to keep abreast of all the latest theories in various spheres. For Danish traditions he had nothing but contempt; he never even bothered to learn a word of the national language, although at a period when the medium used both at Court and in the administration in Denmark was German this is not as surprising as it might at first sight appear. And, while he betrayed all the weaknesses of the bureaucratic mind, he remained loyal to a small circle of friends and helpers and undoubtedly worked extremely hard.

During the sixteen months he remained in power a constant stream of orders issued from the royal cabinet over his signature affecting every aspect of Danish life. The Privy Council was swept away and the Colleges reduced to mere executive departments with no say in policy-making. The German Chancery was replaced by a more rationally organized Foreign Ministry, and the Treasury under Struensee's brother was transformed into the supreme administrative organ like the General Directory set up in Prussia earlier in the century. The salaries of officials were raised to compensate them for the abolition of perquisites. The moral code was deprived of many of its legal sanctions; the practice of permitting parents to incarcerate their refractory children in State prisons was brought to an end. And the death penalty was abolished. Little, however, was done to improve the State's finances; taxation was reduced, but Court expenditure was largely untouched, and a government lottery proved to be a sorry fiasco. Nor did much come of plans to improve the lot of the peasantry, in whom Struensee took comparatively little interest. And in the field of foreign affairs he was forced to rely on the advice of others; he was compelled to renew the alliance with Russia which had been the ostensible cause of Bernstorff's dismissal.

Not until he was appointed royal secretary in July 1771 did Struensee attract much attention outside the Court, and his earlier reforms were often attributed to others within his circle. But by the end of the year all Copenhagen was talking about him, in particular about his relations with the unhappy young queen. Rumours about the latter were in fact well founded; Caroline had responded to his sympathetic attentions so far as to become Struensee's mistress. There were, however, many other reasons for the widespread displeasure: industrialists had suffered from the withdrawal of State subsidies; privileged merchants were threatened by the freeing of trade; the burghers of Copenhagen found their city's autonomy destroyed. And a bad harvest increased unrest in the countryside. The bulk of the Danish nobility treated Struensee with suspicion from the beginning; it was this rather than any hostility to the aristocracy as such which forced him to rely so heavily on members of the middle class. One of the first actions which he had taken had been to free the Press from censorship, and he had been praised for this by no less a person than Voltaire. But as criticism mounted he felt obliged to reimpose restrictions. He made no attempt to court popularity or to explain what he was trying to do, with the result that the worst interpretation was often put on quite innocent measures. Nothing was known of the King's illness outside the Palace, and it became widely believed that he was being kept prisoner there and maltreated.

The first open opposition came from the Royal Guards; at Christmas-time of 1771 they mutinied against an order for their disbandment. When this happened plans for a counter-coup against Struensee were already well advanced. The plotters gained the ready participation of Juliane Marie of Brunswick, Frederik V's second wife, and her son Frederik, both of whom deeply resented the contempt with which they had been treated by the Secretary, and on 17th January 1772, after a masked ball at the Palace, he was arrested. At the same time the Queen was spirited away to *Kronborg*. The dazed King, after being easily persuaded to sign the necessary orders, was paraded through the streets amid the cheers of the populace. Struensee was speedily put on trial. Of the many charges laid against him, only that of having issued orders in the King's name without due authorization both had substance and was punishable under Danish law, but the outcome was a foregone conclusion. He was condemned to death and beheaded after undergoing the gruesome ritual reserved for those adjudged guilty of treason and *lèse-majesté*. Caroline Matilda was saved from further humiliation only by her brother's intervention; a British man-of-war bore her to Hanover, where she died four years later.

Power was now exercised by a triumvirate consisting of Queen Juliane, her son and the bourgeois minister Ove Høegh-Guldberg. Prince Frederik was a nonentity dominated by his mother. Juliane was not without ability, but she in her turn was guided by Guldberg, who had gained entry to the Court as tutor to Frederik V's children and for the next ten years controlled Denmark's domestic policy. This had two main distinguishing features: conservatism and 'Danishness'. All who had been associated with Struensee were dismissed, but the *status quo* was not completely restored. Perquisites, for example, were not reintroduced, and Guldberg showed himself in no hurry to revive the power of the Colleges. He came in fact to rule more and more as Struensee had ruled—from the royal cabinet through orders signed by the King and him alone. This caused growing discontent among senior officials. Nor were many of them enamoured of the second aspect of Guldberg's policy. Struensee's rule intensified a reaction which had been gathering momentum for some time against the German influence which had marked Danish Court and government since the late seventeenth century. Orders were now issued that Danish should be employed as the language of command in the army, and in 1776 it was laid down that no foreigner should in future be employed in royal service. Danish also returned as the language of the Court.

This 'national' movement was also reflected to a certain extent in the new vigour shown by Dano–Norwegian literature during the Guldberg period, though its debt to German writing, in particular to German 'pre-Romanticism', was considerable; the influential German poet Gottlieb Klopstock lived in Copenhagen throughout the 1750's and 1760's under Bernstorff's patronage. In the year after Struensee's fall, Johan Wessel, a young Norwegian who had settled in Copenhagen, caused a sensation with his play *Kierlighed uden Strømper* (Love Without Stockings), a witty parody, which can still be read with pleasure, on the kind of French tragedy which was so popular in Copenhagen in his day. And in 1780 the patriotic musical play *Fiskerne* (The Fishermen), containing a song which was later adopted as the Danish national anthem,[1] brought public honour to Johannes Ewald, the greatest of Denmark's eighteenth-century poets. But Ewald, already at thirty-seven the centre of the newly founded Danish Literary Society, had been writing Romantic works with themes from Norse mythology and Danish heroic legend for a decade and, weakened by a Bohemian existence, survived his triumph by only a year.

It was not only in the field of literature that Danish culture made considerable progress immediately after 1770; in 1776 Nikolaj Abildgaard, the country's greatest painter up to that time, began to teach at the Royal Academy, while his contemporary Jens Juel was succeeding Pilo as the most popular portrait painter among the nobility and wealthier middle class alike. And new arts, for which Denmark was to enjoy a world-wide reputation, were acquiring prominence. In the middle of

---

[1] See also above, p. 118.

the decade the Italian Vincenzo Galeotti took over direction of the new dance school attached to the Royal Theatre and laid the foundations of Danish ballet, while at the same time the Royal Porcelain Factory was established in the capital.

While Guldberg concerned himself with internal affairs, foreign policy under him was for seven years in the hands of J. H. E. Bernstorff's nephew Andreas Peter Bernstorff. He was an able and enlightened man whose relations with the triumvirate became more and more strained until an excuse was found to dismiss him. The outbreak of the War of American Independence in 1775 again provided Danish trade with the opportunities always open to neutrals when the great maritime powers of Europe clashed, and in 1780 Bernstorff took his country into the League of Armed Neutrality formed by Catherine II of Russia, on the basis of principles he had himself enunciated, to protect shipping from the belligerents' privateers. But at the same time he concluded a separate agreement on contraband with Britain, the most serious threat. This brought strong protests from Russia and the minister's fall.

The King's son Frederik was a young man of moderate intelligence whose main enthusiasms were military exercises and uniforms, but he had enough common sense to realize that when he should come of age Queen Juliane would probably do her best to keep him out of State affairs, where he would be a threat to the position of her own son. His fears were fed by Guldberg's critics at Court, who after 1780 included A. P. Bernstorff, and tension between himself and the governing trio grew towards an open breach. A plot was hatched to secure for him the powers of regent for his sick father, and in April 1784, at the first meeting of the Council he attended on reaching the age of sixteen, he carried through a single-handed *coup d'état* in persuading Christian to dismiss the Guldberg clique and grant him the reins of government. Guldberg and the others were caught completely unawares and put up no resistance; they retired into the shadows for ever more.

Frederik took his new duties very seriously and had as his helpers a brilliant circle of talent including A. P. Bernstorff, who resumed control of foreign affairs, Ernst Schimmelmann, who succeeded his father in charge of finances, the Anglophile Christian Reventlow, and the Norwegian jurist Christian

Colbjørnsen. It was a regime in which noble landowners were again dominant, but one which was at last willing to tackle the Land Question with the necessary boldness, and in 1786 the Great Land Commission was formed with Reventlow as chairman and Colbjørnsen as secretary.

The reaction against Struensee's reforms had brought a setback in State agricultural policy, but with the continuing improvement in market conditions on the land, intelligent landlords were more and more introducing reforms of one kind or another on their estates. There was, however, still considerable conservative opposition to change, with no common agreement among reformers as to what reforms were most desirable. Some wanted the government to go no further than to encourage landowners and their tenants to agree among themselves on mutually acceptable conditions of tenure and to draw up binding contracts without further outside interference. Others wanted legislation to give the peasantry the security which it lacked. Still others wanted to go so far as to break up the large estates and convert tenancies into freehold farms. The final settlement, reached after heated debates, granted the Danish peasant as much personal freedom as his English counterpart but much greater protection against economic exploitation. First, in 1786 and 1787 landlords were deprived of their right to impose degrading punishments on their tenants, and tenants were granted the right to compensation, adjudged by an independent tribunal, for improvements they had made, in the event of their being deprived of their plots; though at the same time they were adjured to act respectfully towards their social superiors. Then, in 1788 it was decreed that the *stavnsbånd* should be abolished in stages which would leave all peasants completely free by 1800. Labour services remained, but landlords were encouraged to define these in a contract with their tenants, if necessary with the help of State arbitrators. It is altogether remarkable that so much could be achieved in so short a time without any of the social upheaval which was about to burst on France, or any change in the form of government. It set a pattern for peaceful change which was to mark the development of Danish society henceforth.

The peasants seem generally to have been slow to take advantage of their newly acquired rights. And many labour-service contracts not only took a long time to work out but continued to impose a heavy burden when completed. But a growing number of landlords found it more profitable to commute such services for additional rent and to work their demesne with hired labour, and if this came to be in short supply, as it did in parts of Jutland, they might even sell off the whole estate to its tenants. Even when the demesnes remained intact, the tenancies were often disposed of to those who had worked them, and by 1820 over half Denmark's farmers owned their own land. At the same time there occurred a considerable speeding-up of the enclosure movement which had begun in the middle of the century. It took many years to complete the process; indeed the last enclosure in Denmark did not take place until 1861. But every year more and more individual farms were created and old village communities broken up with enormous consequences not only for the appearance of the countryside but also for the social life of its inhabitants and the structure of Danish agriculture.

The more immediate effects of all the changes in this period are difficult to assess with any precision, but the production of corn undoubtedly increased considerably, and by the beginning of the nineteenth century the majority of peasant-farmers appear to have been enjoying a much more comfortable existence than had the peasants of Holberg's day; they had, in addition, acquired a self-respect which they had hitherto lacked. On the other hand, many of the new small landowners found themselves in difficulties when the price of grain fell once more, and a rapid increase in population, which cannot have been unconnected with the reforms, led to a shortage of land. As a result a growing proportion of country-dwellers came to consist of cottagers who eked out a meagre existence on very small plots, and of day labourers who had no land at all. These classes were unprotected by the new laws and hard hit by any rise in the price of grain which would benefit their landowning brethren. A new social problem was emerging as an old one was solved.

It was not only on the land that reforms took place after 1784. Colbjørnsen speeded up legal processes and improved prison conditions. A regular system of poor relief was instituted, financed by compulsory contributions from the community's more fortunate members. A more liberal tariff, which abolished many import prohibitions, came in 1797. Schimmelmann was able in 1792 to introduce measures which would mean the end of the slave trade with the Danish West Indies by 1803, although he failed to secure the abolition of slavery itself. He headed a commission which in 1789 proposed the introduction of universal free elementary schooling, although this was not acted upon until the great School Law of 1814, which made education compulsory for all children between the ages of seven and confirmation at fourteen. Crown Prince Frederik did not play a particularly active role in all this work, but he did take a special interest in certain problems, including the position of Jews in Denmark; in 1798 they were granted the right to marry Christians and to enter secondary schools.

The death of A. P. Bernstorff in 1797 marks the end of the most vigorous period of reform. Henceforth, power came to be wielded more and more, by Prince Frederik, thanks both to divisions within the Council and to his frequent absences in the south of the country as a result of the increasingly threatening international situation, which enabled him to avoid discussion and adopt what amounted to 'cabinet government'. Military and foreign policy was almost monopolized by him, and the bureaucracy came to lose much of its autonomy. The Council ceased to meet altogether after Frederik's accession to the throne in 1808. Reventlow in particular put up a vigorous opposition to these developments, but he lacked support and had gradually to give ground. His task was made more difficult by the fact that Frederik was reasonably competent, practical, conscientious and sympathetic to the needs of his subjects. The only outside influence to which he appears to have been subject was that of the Landgrave of Hesse, whose daughter he married in 1790. He made few changes in the personnel of his government when he assumed full power on Christian's death; Bernstorff was succeeded by his son. But new men who owed their position to the loyalty they had shown the Prince as his officers rather than to their social status slowly undermined the influence of the landlords who had come to power in 1784. And Frederik's control of foreign affairs proved disastrous as he grew more and more out of touch with popular feeling.

A. P. Bernstorff continued Denmark's now long tradition of neutrality in European conflicts which had brought such prosperity to the country's carrying trade. He was forced by the Russian alliance to go to war with Sweden in 1788, but was easily persuaded to make peace again under pressure from Britain and Prussia, and he refused to join any monarchical crusade against Revolutionary France. But attacks by Britain's warships on Danish merchantmen trading with France after the two countries went to war in 1793 forced him to take action, and in the following year Denmark joined Sweden in a new league of armed neutrality. This and French victories on land persuaded Britain to adopt a more conciliatory attitude. It was then France who became the greater menace to Danish commerce; in 1798 the Directory threatened to confiscate all ships found to be carrying British goods. In reply Denmark adopted convoys and refused to allow her merchant ships to be searched. As Britain's strength grew once more, such convoys became involved more and more frequently in clashes with her warships. In 1800 a regular engagement took place between a Danish frigate escorting a convoy through the Channel and a British squadron, which ended in the capture of the frigate, and in August of that year a British embassy to Copenhagen, backed by a fleet of nineteen vessels, compelled convoys to be abandoned. But only four months later Denmark concluded a league of armed neutrality with Russia, Prussia and Sweden and arranged for the resumption of convoys. In the following January all Danish ships in British ports were seized.

At the end of March Admiral Hyde Parker arrived in the Sound with a fleet of fifty-three warships, and a few days later sent in his second-in-command Horatio Nelson to attack the Danish fleet in the harbour of Copenhagen. The Danes were taken by surprise, but put up a stout defence against a materially superior foe and badly mauled Nelson's squadron when it attempted to break through the line of block-ships protecting the harbour mouth. But his threat to burn all captured vessels enabled the peace party in the capital, led by Reventlow and Schimmelmann, to gain the upper hand, and an armistice was arranged. The subsequent negotiations resulted in Denmark's withdrawal from the League, which in any case broke up shortly afterwards with the murder of Tsar Paul, its principal architect. Danish commerce was more leniently treated for a few years by both sides. But in 1806 Napoleon introduced his

Continental System under which all trade between occupied Europe and Britain was forbidden, and Britain replied with Orders in Council banning all overseas trade with French-occupied lands. Denmark's relations with Britain thereupon began to deteriorate, while French pressure on her from the south increased. Neutrality was ceasing to be a viable alternative.

Denmark's entry into the war on the French side has been the subject of some dispute between British and Danish historians of the period. The Danes on the one hand admit that their government acted with lack of foresight and that it vacillated dangerously before taking action. But they claim that Canning, Britain's foreign secretary, gave it little opportunity to show its true colours and by his high-handed behaviour turned a potential ally into an enemy. There is no doubt that Canning was misled about Danish intentions. His policy was not, however, based on any single report but on his interpretation of a number of acts committed by the Danes, such as the withdrawal of troops from the Duchies after a clash with French troops, which threatened to close a valuable channel into the Continent for British exports and re-exports, and their strong protest against the blockade imposed by Britain on the mouth of the Elbe. He also feared that, even if Denmark should join Britain against France, she would not be able to prevent Napoleon from seizing her valuable fleet, adding it to his own and possibly avenging Trafalgar. Peace between France and Russia seemed to be almost certain, and the Emperor seemed bound to turn on Denmark next to stop up a serious leak in his System.

In 1807 Canning consequently sent a special embassy to Denmark, accused her of preparing her fleet for action against Britain, and demanded that she both hand it over for the duration of the war and conclude a defensive alliance. In July he followed this up with the despatch to the Sound of a fleet of forty-six warships under Admiral Gambier and an army of 31,000 under Viscount Wellesley (later Duke of Wellington). Danish reactions were delayed both by King Frederik's absence in Kiel keeping an eye on the southern border of his territories and by a widespread belief that Gambier's intention was to relieve British forces then stationed in Swedish Pomerania. And when the British envoy Jackson high-handedly renewed the

earlier demands under threat of the forcible seizure of the
Danish ships, he could offer no guarantee against French occupation of at least the Danish mainland. Frederik refused such
humiliating conditions and hurried north to lead the defence of
his capital. On 16th August war was declared and British
troops landed north of Copenhagen, which they proceeded
to invest. There were few Danish troops in Zealand, and
the city's defences were in bad shape. Wellesley hesitated
before opening a bombardment, but did so finally on 2nd
September. The firing lasted for five days, during which over a
thousand buildings, including the university, were destroyed
and numerous casualties suffered by the inhabitants. Only then
did Frederik decide to abandon the unequal struggle. By the
terms of the capitulation the Danish fleet of fifteen line-of-
battle ships, fifteen frigates and many smaller vessels was surrendered for good, four ships which were being built were
destroyed and a British garrison was installed in Copenhagen
for six weeks.

Canning, after being fiercely attacked in the House of Commons for his action, did promise to return the fleet three years
after the end of the war, but by then it was too late for such
concessions. In October Denmark concluded an alliance with
France, and at the beginning of November declared war on
Britain. In 1807 Napoleon, having crushed Austria and Prussia
and made a pact with Tsar Alexander, seemed likely to emerge
the victor in the struggle. And the outbreak of war between
Russia and Sweden in the following year raised King Frederik's
hopes of regaining control of both sides of the Sound; 14,000
Danish troops joined a French force under Marshal Bernadotte
which was gathered in Zealand in preparation for an invasion
of southern Sweden. But the enterprise had to be postponed
until 1809. By then British warships were able to block the
Sound, and when news arrived of the anti-French uprising in
Spain most of the large contingent of Spanish troops in Bernadotte's army deserted. When Russia and Sweden made peace
in September, Denmark had to follow suit.

The most serious consequence of Frederik VI's decision to
join France was that his country had to become part of the
Continental System and bring to an end her increasingly
valuable trade with Britain. The ban was for several years

applied very strictly, and British command of the seas prevented most other commerce outside the Baltic. Denmark's overseas possessions were occupied by British troops immediately after the outbreak of war, and the British fleet cut all links with Iceland and The Faeroes; even communications with Norway became extremely difficult. Over half the country's merchant fleet was seized. Danish privateers managed to win some rich prizes in the early months, but this source of wealth dried up when Britain began to organize convoys in northern waters. Within the country the economic situation deteriorated rapidly. In spite of attempts to fix prices, inflation gathered apace, and the burden of taxation became heavier and heavier. In January 1813 all existing banks were replaced by one note-issuing State Bank, whose resources were provided by a forced loan from landowners, the currency was reformed and a devaluation of 10 per cent was carried through. But the government found it impossible to balance the budget, and new loans increased an already large public debt. The new freehold peasants benefited from the inflation, which rapidly reduced the debts which they had incurred in purchasing their land. But the landless labourer was hard hit by the failure of wages to keep pace with prices. Industry benefited to a certain extent from its protection against British competition, but had to face stiff French competition on the European market.

It is hardly surprising that in these circumstances the war became more and more unpopular with the Danish public. In the Duchies, where there was a large German-speaking population, unrest was encouraged also by the growth of the German nationalist movement to the south, but economic conditions in this area were better than in Denmark proper, partly because of the wholesale smuggling of colonial goods, which were transported from the British-occupied island of Heligoland. In 1810 no fewer than 6,000 of the inhabitants were engaged in the traffic, in which profits of 70 per cent were not uncommon. Many Danish merchant houses also did well out of the illegal trade, and the government found that a valuable income could be obtained from the sale of licences exempting individual merchants from the Continental System, whose application became more and more relaxed until by the time peace returned it had ceased to operate altogether.

In spite of the general unpopularity of the war, the King refused to leave the sinking ship. He not only feared French reprisals, such as the occupation of the Duchies, if he should step out of line, but also hoped for Napoleon's support in a bid for the Swedish throne. In Sweden, Marshal Bernadotte had been elected heir to the childless Charles XIII and had engineered his future realm's entry into the anti-French coalition, which promised him Norway to compensate for the loss of Finland to Russia in 1809. Frederik was offered other territory for Norway should he follow Sweden's example, but in July 1813 he concluded a new treaty with France. After the decisive defeat of Napoleon at the battle of Leipzig, Bernadotte, in command now of the Allies' forces in northern Germany, invaded Jutland and compelled the Danes to conclude peace at Kiel in January 1814. By the final terms Britain gained Heligoland, and Denmark had to exchange Norway for Swedish Pomerania, which in 1815 was exchanged in its turn with Prussia for the Duchy of Lauenburg on the southern border of Holstein. But Iceland, The Faeroes and Greenland, although historically part of the Norwegian crown's dominions, remained under Danish rule, and the Danish possessions in the West Indies and India were returned.

# CHAPTER XIII

## *National Romanticism and National Liberalism (1814-50)*

THE end of the Napoleonic Wars brought some relief to the Danish economy, but its recovery was delayed both by the general post-war depression, which affected most of Europe, and by factors peculiar to Denmark herself. The overseas market for her agricultural produce was considerably restricted by the English Corn Laws and the loss of Norway; the price of grain plummeted, and much of it was in fact diverted into illegal peasant stills. The groups hardest hit by the new agricultural recession, which lasted until the late 1820's, were the growing army of cottagers, who could often find no work, and the owners of large estates, which occupied about 10 per cent of the cultivated land. The smaller landowners, who were less dependent on the market, withstood the storm rather more successfully, but their incomes dropped, and the movement from leasehold to freehold tenure, which had acquired a considerable momentum since the later 1780's, was slowed down appreciably; indeed many recently created freeholders tried to sell back their land to its previous owners. Shortage of money hampered internal trade, in which profit margins, especially in grain dealings, had to be cut back drastically. Copenhagen suffered from the growth of direct links between provincial towns and Hamburg, whose merchants were able and willing to grant long-term credit and where goods could often be purchased more cheaply than in the capital because not subjected to the Sound Dues; Copenhagen's population grew at less than half the rate of that of other urban centres.

The Danish merchant fleet had been halved during the war,

166

when many of the markets which had fed it in the late eighteenth century had been captured by Britain, especially in the Far East. One by one the great merchant houses collapsed; there were no fewer than 250 bankruptcies declared in Copenhagen between 1816 and 1820, and the King was driven to help favoured individuals out of the privy purse. British competition also hurt Danish industry, which made very slow progress in spite of State assistance. Both the currency and the credit system were weak. The notes issued by the State Bank declined rapidly in real value, and the Bank itself was closed and in 1818 replaced by a National Bank, which was administratively independent of the government. But the *riksdaler* continued to fall until 1827. Much of the blame for this state of affairs was thrown on the Jews of Copenhagen, many of whom suffered in a brief wave of petty persecution.

Little worthy of note occurred in Danish political life between the Peace of Kiel and 1830. At the end of the war Frederik VI, conscious of the criticism which had been directed against his policy, abandoned the 'cabinet rule' he had adopted on his accession and governed henceforth with the aid of a council made up largely of bureaucrats. Most of these men were as conservative in their outlook as the King had now become. Their energies were devoted largely to cutting government expenditure and consolidating the large State debt in the hope of improving the financial situation. Frederik himself was, however, popular with most of his subjects, for whom he became something of a father-figure who was considered to have their welfare at heart, and absolutism was so far questioned by only a handful of academics and students.

But at the same time new ideas, which were to have significant political repercussions, were transforming cultural life. Traits usually associated with the Romantic Movement can be found in the works of Ewald and other Danish writers of the later eighteenth century. But the breakthrough of Romanticism proper in the country is usually dated from the lectures on contemporary German philosophy delivered in Copenhagen in 1801 by a young Dano–German geologist named Henrik Steffens, who had just returned from an extended stay in Germany. These fired the imagination of the twenty-two-year-old poet and playwright Adam Oehlenschläger, who had already

167

preached passionately in favour of choosing literary themes
from Norse rather than from Classical mythology. After a long
meeting with Steffens, Oehlenschläger composed a series of
poems which appeared at the end of 1802, the most famous of
which was inspired by the theft of the Gallehus horns[1] earlier
that year. A long journey abroad which Oehlenschläger undertook a few years later brought a certain disillusionment with
German Romanticism, and the works which he produced after
his return lack the brilliance of his earlier efforts. He nevertheless remains Denmark's most important Romantic poet, and his
greatness within Scandinavian literature as a whole was acknowledged in 1829, when he was 'crowned' in Lund by Sweden's
leading Romantic poet, Esaias Tegnér.

Oehlenschläger's interest in the distant Scandinavian past
was shared by perhaps the most influential of all nineteenth-
century Danes—Nikolaj (N. F. S.) Grundtvig. Extraordinarily
widely read in a number of European literatures, he devoted
seven years after the end of the Napoleonic Wars to the study
of Anglo-Saxon and Norse manuscripts. But it was Grundtvig's
educational and religious ideas which made the greatest impact
on his countrymen. In 1810 he experienced a form of religious
awakening and alienated many of his former friends with his
subsequent attacks on rationalism. He sought to develop an
undogmatic, tolerant Christianity imbued with the virtues of
the heroes of Norse myth. He expressed his ideas in a series of
fine hymns intended to inspire a national revival in the dark
days which followed the war. In 1825 he broke with the leaders
of Copenhagen intellectual life and turned to the countryside,
seeking to guide the revivalist movement there which had made
great progress since the late eighteenth century. The popularity
of his latitudinarian views with many younger pastors helped
indeed to win back for the established Church much of the
ground which it had lost. Grundtvig's political attitudes were
somewhat idiosyncratic. After 1830, however, he abandoned
much of his earlier conservatism and came to profess great faith
in the wisdom of 'the people'; Danish liberalism was highly
coloured by his teachings.

The visual arts continued to be dominated throughout the
1820's by the Neo-Classical style popularized by Abildgaard.

[1] See above, pp. 27, 116.

In painting the dominating figure was Abildgaard's brilliant pupil Christoffer Eckersberg, who returned to Denmark in 1816 after several years abroad and soon established himself as the founder of Danish Naturalism. As professor at the Royal Academy of Art he trained a number of very able men, of whom Constantin Hansen decorated the hall of the university with large-scale scenes from Classical mythology. Neo-Classicism, however, reached its apogee with the sculptor Bertel Thorvaldsen (see Plate 9). Most of his life was spent in Rome, where he first gained international recognition with his statue of Jason executed in 1803. He returned to his native land finally in 1838 to a tumultuous reception, and on his death six years later was buried in the courtyard of the special museum built to house his works in the heart of the capital.

The revolutions which took place in Germany in 1830 following the overthrow of the Bourbon monarchy in France quickened political life in Denmark. Many rulers of states within the German Confederation were now forced at last to grant to their subjects the constitutions which had been promised to them when the Confederation was formed in 1815 but which had been forthcoming only in a few cases. Holstein and Lauenburg were part of the Confederation, and their duke, King Frederik, found himself faced with demands for the establishment in them of a representative body. The chief spokesman of the Holstein liberals was a young official named Uwe Jens Lornsen, who had learned his politics while studying in German universities. The Danish government's immediate reaction to his agitation was to dismiss him from his post, condemn him to a term of imprisonment and finally drive him into exile.

But the King and his ministers, much alarmed by the uprisings in other countries, decided to set up advisory bodies of leading citizens not only in Holstein but also in Slesvig and the kingdom itself. This decision, announced in 1831, was widely welcomed. In 1834 the first elections were held for four councils, one for Holstein to meet in Itzehoe, one for Slesvig to gather in the town of that name, one for Jutland to assemble in Viborg and one for the islands to convene in Roskilde, away from the excitable atmosphere of the capital. They were to be called every other year and to be chosen on a very restricted franchise, largely based on landed property. The poorer groups of society were thus excluded, and the conflicting interests of those who were to be represented—large and small landowners and burghers—could be expected to ensure that the councils (*stænderforsamlinger*) would be no danger to royal power. They were granted the right to petition the King, but their main task was the discussion of proposals made to them by his ministers, who were under no obligation to accept their recommendations. They did nevertheless give valuable political experience to a segment of the King's subjects, and encouraged the spread of liberal ideas, at least among the urban middle classes.

In the same year as this reform was implemented the first liberal newspaper appeared in Denmark—*Fædrelandet* (The Fatherland). It was edited by the passionate poet Carl Ploug as a weekly, but later became a daily publication. It campaigned for responsible representative government with popular control in particular over financial matters. Prosecution of its publishers by the Crown only strengthened the liberal cause, which could claim its first important gain in 1837, when the government agreed to the introduction of regularly elected town councils. These were followed in 1841 by elected bodies in counties and parishes also. The franchise for them was as restricted as for the provincial assemblies and they tended to be dominated by office-holders. But the door which had been opened in 1834 was hereby opened a little wider and would consequently be all the more difficult to close again. For the small farmers, the experience gained on parish councils proved particularly valuable and did much to increase their political consciousness.

In 1839 Frederik VI died, genuinely mourned by the great majority of his subjects. He was succeeded by his fifty-three-year-old cousin Christian, the son of the Prince Frederik who had been a member of the Guldberg regime. Christian had been chosen by the Norwegians to be their king during the country's short-lived period of independence in 1814 and had approved its liberal Eidsvoll Constitution. For this reason his accession raised the hopes of the Danish liberals, who made to him a number of appeals to grant a proper constitution also to Denmark. While he did not reject the idea outright, his statements on the subject were evasive, and the Press soon resumed its criticisms of the Crown. The new king was in fact a very intelligent, sympathetic and cultured man who favoured many of the practical reforms which had been pressed for in the provincial assemblies, but he believed that his subjects were as yet too inexperienced to be allowed to share government with himself and his ministers and realized above all the difficulty of evolving a constitution which would satisfy the inhabitants of Slesvig and Holstein.

These were becoming more and more sharply divided into two opposing camps. One, which came to be referred to as the Schleswig–Holstein party, was drawn largely from the liberal German-speakers in the towns and had strong links with the liberals of Germany itself. Its members wanted a separate constitution for a united Schleswig–Holstein and were supported by the great German landowners of the area. The latter, although politically very conservative, believed that such a union would serve their own interests and looked forward to the day when the greatest of them, the Duke of Augustenborg, a descendant of one of King Frederik II's brothers, should inherit the Duchies and rule them as an independent political unit. This would come, it was claimed, when the male line of the Oldenburgs should die out, for, while in the Danish kingdom the Royal Law of Frederik III ensured succession in the female line, this did not apply to the lands ruled by the king as duke. The other party was drawn from the Danish-speaking farmers of north and central Slesvig, who, alarmed by the spread of the use of German northward through Slesvig, wanted a closer union with the kingdom and a weakening of the ties which bound their duchy administratively to the overwhelmingly German-speaking Holstein. After 1838 the language question regularly disrupted meetings of the Slesvig assembly, where, because of the electoral arrangements, the Danish-speakers found themselves in a small minority. Christian VIII was opposed to the extreme claims made by both interests and worked hard to restore harmony between them, but, try as he might, he found the task of reconciliation becoming more and more difficult as time went by.

The Schleswig–Holstein Question, which was to bedevil both Denmark's political life and the country's foreign relations for the following quarter of a century, was to a large extent the outcome of the National Romantic movement with its accent on language as the primary distinguishing feature of a people, who,

Askov
Ribe · Rødding
Dybbøl · Als
Augustenborg
Flensborg
Isted
Slesvig
Dannevirke · Nør
Kiel
Ejder R.
Holstein
· Itzehoe
Hamburg
Lauenburg

······· Boundaries of Slesvig
         before 1864
—·—·· Northern boundary
         of Slesvig 1864–1920
———— Southern boundary
         of Denmark since 1920
⬚⬚⬚ Zone II in referendum
         of 1920
⚔ Site of battle

0                          40
       Miles

6. The Schleswig–Holstein Question 1814–1920

it was claimed, should be granted the right of political self-determination. In the Duchies, German and Danish nationalism met in a head-on clash which on both sides reinforced feelings of separatism. Danish nationalism came to full flower in the 1830's, when Grundtvig first put forward his demand for an educational system based on Christian and patriotic principles and on a study of history and poetry as well as practical subjects —'Education for Life' as he called it. These ideas strongly influenced the Folk High School movement after 1844, when the first of such schools was established, significantly enough, at Rødding in Slesvig. It was with Grundtvig's encouragement that Bernhard (B. S.) Ingemann, a teacher at Sorø Academy in the heart of Zealand, Denmark's foremost secondary school, began in 1824 the publication of a series of epic novels celebrating Denmark's medieval golden age—the Valdemar Period —while in the same year Steen Steensen Blicher issued the first of his realist short stories set in the isolated part of Jutland south of Viborg where he was a poor pastor. But Blicher played a more active part in the nationalist movement; in 1839 he organized the first of a series of national assemblies at Himmelbjerget in the beautiful lake district of Jutland east of Silkeborg.

Nationalism also affected the visual arts, in which Christian VIII was particularly interested, and music. N. L. Høyen, Denmark's first art historian, called in these years for the evolution of a truly national style of painting, a call which a number of young artists tried to answer, among them Johan Lundbye with his somewhat idealized impressions of the Danish countryside from the 1840's. And Friedrich Kuhlau, although remembered chiefly for his piano studies, wrote a considerable amount of music based on folk-ballad material. Even the internationally most famous of all Denmark's literary figures, Hans (H. C.) Andersen, who began writing his fairy-tales in 1835 after first attracting attention as a novelist, owed a certain debt to National Romanticism, which was, in northern Europe at least, closely associated with the collection of folk-tales. Andersen's stories were, however, largely original and composed for the first time with children as well as adults in mind. His second collection of 1843 firmly established his reputation in the genre.

Up to about 1840 political agitation was largely confined to the urban middle classes under the leadership of liberal academics. But the improvement in conditions on the land which took place during the 1830's led to the growth of activity among the small farmers. In provincial assemblies their representatives began to put forward further demands like the complete abolition of labour services, the transformation of leasehold into freehold tenure by law, the abolition of the distinction between 'privileged' and 'unprivileged' land (the former paid 20 per cent less in taxes) and the extension to all classes of society of the liability to perform military service. In 1842 this movement acquired a mouthpiece in the newspaper *Almuevennen* (The Peasants' Friend), edited by the ex-shoemaker I. A. Hansen. When the government attempted to restrict the activities of agitators who were touring Zealand, the farmers' leaders reacted by closing ranks with the urban liberals, who agreed to support their programme of reform on the land in exchange for the farmers' backing of the liberals' demands for a constitution. The link was institutionalized in 1846 with the formation of the *Bondevenners Selskab* (Society of Farmers' Friends) with Hansen as secretary. It is to this period that can be traced the origins of the political party later known as the Left (*Venstre*).

The return of economic prosperity had been helped both by the return of financial stability, largely thanks to the strict control exercised by the National Bank (the *riksdaler* reached par again in 1838, and notes were redeemed in 1845 for the first time in nearly a century) and particularly by developments in England. The rapid growth of population there led to a pressing demand for grain, and, after tariffs were reduced in the late 1820's, the Corn Laws were finally abolished altogether in 1846. This provided Denmark with a motive for both an increase in the area under cultivation and the introduction of new methods to improve the yield of the land already under the plough. Drainage was ameliorated, the use of clover and the potato spread and effective harrows came into use.

The growth of education after the act of 1814[1] enabled a larger section of the rural population to appreciate the benefits which could accrue from change and to apply new ideas. The schools which were built in the countryside in the early nineteenth century were often primitive and truancy was common, especially at harvest time when farmers needed their children

[1] See above, p. 160.

in the fields, but by the middle of the century nearly all men at least were literate, and the teacher had become an important figure in village life, often acting as the spokesman for the local population.

Other branches of the economy also made progress during the 1830's and 1840's. Although the towns retained a legal monopoly of internal trade, the liberals' call for greater economic freedom met with some response. And, while most industry remained in the hands of small craftsmen, a new era dawned in 1829 with the introduction of the first steam engine into the paper factory at Strandmøllen at the mouth of the Molleå north of Copenhagen, and in the same year came the formation by Hans (H. C.) Ørsted, the discoverer of electromagnetism, of the Copenhagen Polytechnic, the forerunner of the present Technological University. Ørsted also contributed to the spread of scientific knowledge by public lectures.

Such economic advances helped to increase pressure on the Crown for further political concessions, and Christian VIII does appear, during the 1840's, to have come round to the idea that absolutism could not be maintained for very much longer. But nothing had been done by the beginning of 1848, when a series of events brought about the first serious crisis in Danish politics in the nineteenth century. In January, Christian died and was succeeded by his son Frederik, a man of dignity and warmth who won the hearts of his subjects but who possessed a somewhat capricious temperament and only limited political sense. The fact that, in spite of two marriages, he still lacked a male heir, raised the question of the succession in the Duchies in an acute form. He had hardly had time to settle on his throne[1] when the revolution in Paris which led to the short-lived Second French Republic began a chain of liberal revolts in Germany. As in 1830, these strongly affected the Duchies, where tension was at breaking-point. The Schleswig–Holsteiners, who had in 1846 rejected a royal decree or 'Open Letter' declaring that the Danish law of succession applied also to Slesvig and Lauenburg, decided in the middle of March to send a deputation to Copenhagen to demand not only a constitution for a Schleswig–Holstein state but that state's entry into the united Germany

---

[1] Frederik dispensed with a coronation, and no subsequent Danish king has been crowned.

which seemed about to emerge. The Danish liberals, now led by the fiery young lawyer Orla Lehmann, who had made the cause of the Danish-speakers of Slesvig his own, immediately countered with a demand for a constitution which would be valid for the kingdom and Slesvig. This was the so-called Ejder Programme, named from the river Ejder which formed the border between the two duchies, a programme which had emerged in the early 1840's. It constituted the main platform of a National Liberal party.

On 20th March the liberals of Copenhagen called a mass meeting in the Casino Theatre which was attended by over 2,000 citizens. It was there resolved to petition the King for a constitution and for the appointment of a Council made up of men willing to put it into operation. The next day the petition, composed by Lehmann himself, was carried to *Christiansborg* at the head of a great procession. On receiving the document, Frederik announced that he had already accepted the resignation of his councillors and added characteristically: 'If you, gentlemen, will have the same trust in your king as he has in his people, he will lead you honestly along the path of honour and liberty.' After this the crowd dispersed peacefully, and the next day a new Council was appointed. It was headed by the old conservative adviser Count Adam Moltke, but it included Lehmann, the able theologian Ditlev (D. G.) Monrad and other National Liberals. The Colleges were at the same time replaced by ministries under the direction of single ministers, and the King declared that he regarded himself a constitutional monarch. Absolutism in Denmark was at an end.

The new government's most urgent task was to answer the demands of the members of the Schleswig–Holstein deputation, who had meanwhile arrived in Copenhagen by ship from Kiel. They were told that, in accordance with the Ejder Programme, a constitution would be drawn up for the monarchy and Slesvig but that Holstein would be granted a separate charter. The Schleswig–Holsteiners in the Duchies had, however, already decided to take the law into their own hands. On receiving news of the events which had taken place in the capital on 20th March, they had formed a provisional government of their own led by the Prince of Nør, brother of the Duke of Augustenborg, who claimed that the King was in the hands of the mob and

9. Self-portrait of Bertel Thorvaldsen (1810). Property of Danish Royal Academy of Fine Arts. *Thorvaldsens Museum, Copenhagen*

10. *Summer Evening at the Skaw* by Michael Ancher (1888). *Royal Museum of Fine Arts, Copenhagen*

was therefore no longer a free agent. He was supported by most of the local officials, and the fortress of Rendsborg, which contained a large quantity of stores and ammunition, was seized in a bold coup. Such action meant civil war, and the rebels called on the German states to aid their cause.

The inhabitants of the kingdom immediately rallied round the King and his ministers in a great upsurge of national feeling; youthful volunteers came forward in large numbers. And they were joined by others from Norway and Sweden; a Swedish regular army corps was sent to Fyn to aid in the defence of Denmark against what was seen as the threat of aggressive German nationalism. Lehmann and Ploug in particular had linked Danish liberalism with the so-called Scandinavianist Movement, which, fed by Romanticism and the resentment felt by many Swedes at the loss of Finland to Russia, sought closer cultural and political ties between Denmark, Norway and Sweden and even eventual political union. Nør's army was at first compelled to retreat before superior Danish forces, but it was soon reinforced by Prussian troops and volunteers from other German states, who enabled it to occupy Slesvig and even push northwards into Jutland. The civil war had become an international one, and in August Russian pressure secured an armistice; the Duchies were during it to be governed by a joint Prusso–Danish committee.

The pause in the fighting allowed elections to be held for a Danish constituent assembly. The vote in these was given to all male householders over the age of thirty, a reflection of the unity of the nation during a crisis in which all classes were called upon to make sacrifices. But about a quarter of the Assembly's 150 seats were reserved for royal nominees. The representatives met in *Christiansborg* in October. As soon as their deliberations began, three groups of roughly equal size emerged—a conservative Right of large landowners and government officials, who were strongly opposed to the introduction of a wide suffrage and many of them indeed to any genuine constitution at all; a Left, made up largely of small farmers but led by professional men, who, in spite of the fact that only about a third of those eligible to vote for the Assembly had done so, wanted universal manhood suffrage and economic and social reforms which would benefit in particular the rural population; and a Centre of moderate liberals drawn from the urban middle classes, like the lawyer Carl Christian Hall, who wished for the kind of personal freedoms preached by all European liberals at this time but who were divided on the desirability of giving all men the right to vote. The new ministry put forward a very liberal project, largely the work of Lehmann and Monrad, which envisaged a *Rigsdag* of two houses, both elected by universal male suffrage. It was therefore welcomed by the Left and by the left-wing Liberals, but was strongly criticized by the Right and also by some more conservative Liberals. A vigorous Press campaign in its favour organized by Monrad, however, helped to secure its approval by a comfortable majority in May 1849, and it received the royal assent the following month.

Under the June Constitution, as it came to be called, legislative power was to be shared between the Crown and a *Rigsdag* made up of a lower and upper house—*Folketing* and *Landsting*—both elected by all men over the age of thirty who were not in receipt of poor relief. The hundred members of the *Folketing*, who had to be over twenty-four years of age, were to be chosen every three years at constituency meetings of all those entitled to vote. But, as a concession to the Right, the *Landsting* was to be selected indirectly (half the house every four years) by electoral colleges, and those who sat in it were to be at least forty and possess a certain amount of property. The government could shorten the life of a *Rigsdag* and order fresh elections if it considered this expedient. And neither house was given any power over the choice of the king's ministers, although these were stated to be 'responsible' and liable to impeachment, and all laws were to be countersigned by them. Freedom of the Press, assembly and religion were guaranteed, and a form of *habeas corpus* was enshrined in the document.

The war in the Duchies had broken out again in the month before the passing of the Constitution, and the Danish army, after being defeated at Kolding, had to retire to Fredericia. But at the beginning of July it launched a successful counter-attack, and a few days later Prussia, under strong pressure from Russia and Britain, agreed to an armistice once more. A year later it made peace, and at the same time the deserted Schleswig-Holsteiners were severely beaten at Isted; the Danes were able after this to reoccupy the Dannevirke. In January 1851 the rebel army and government were dissolved. But while the Danes were reorganizing Slesvig as part of the kingdom, Austrian and Prussian troops, acting on behalf of the German Confederation, had at the end of 1850 reoccupied Holstein, and they threatened to remain there until Denmark bound herself to restore the *status quo*. In Copenhagen the National Liberals lost ground to the Right as the possibility of carrying through the Ejder Programme became more and more remote, and finally an agreement was reached in London by which the June Constitution would apply to the kingdom alone and Slesvig would be treated quite separately. With this the reactionary powers were satisfied, and their troops withdrew.

# CHAPTER XIV

# *The Struggle for the* Helstat *(1850-64)*

THE failure of the Ejder Programme led to the complete withdrawal of the National Liberals from the government at the beginning of 1852, and during the two years following cabinets were made up wholly of Conservatives. The Left, which was particularly well represented in the *Folketing*, continued to work with the Liberals on many reform projects, but, with the battle for the constitution in the kingdom won, the two groups began to draw apart; the Liberals tended to look down on the farmers, while the latter were somewhat mistrustful of their largely urban-based allies and on certain issues sided with the large landowners of the Right and the ministry.

The most pressing political problem immediately after the end of the war was the working-out of a constitution for the *Helstat* (i.e. the kingdom and the Duchies together) which would ensure that the interests of all its inhabitants were fairly represented without a breach of the undertaking given to the European powers in 1851–2 that neither would Slesvig and Holstein be united nor would Slesvig be bound more closely to the kingdom to the exclusion of its southern neighbour. In 1853 the ultra-conservative Anders (A. S.) Ørsted, the physicist's brother, became chief minister and tried to carry through such a constitution by royal decree. The Left and the Liberals were immediately up in arms and forced him to resign. A cabinet headed by a National Liberal and containing a number of other members of the party took office and in 1855 presented to the *Rigsdag* a project of a rather more liberal complexion. It provided for a National Council (*Rigsråd*) of eighty members, twenty of whom were to be appointed by the Crown, thirty elected by the *Rigsdag* in Copenhagen and by the provincial assemblies in the Duchies, which had been restored in their old form after the collapse of the rebellion, and the remaining thirty directly by the king's wealthier subjects. This National Council was empowered to discuss matters like defence, finance and foreign policy likely to affect all the territories, while more local matters were to be dealt with by the *Rigsdag* and the Assemblies.

The *Rigsdag* approved the plan, and the *Rigsråd* met in 1856, but its German-speaking members immediately voiced their discontent. The Schleswig–Holsteiners had been deeply antagonized by the restrictions on freedom of speech in Slesvig which had recently been imposed by its Danish governor and by the government's language policy, which was aimed at strengthening the position of Danish in central Slesvig. Their representatives in the *Rigsråd* now protested that the Assemblies had not been consulted before the new constitution was implemented and that they found themselves outnumbered by the *Rigsdag*'s nominees. They received strong support from the German Confederation, which threatened to reoccupy Holstein if the Danish government continued to foist the new constitution on the Duchies against the wishes of their inhabitants. Schleswig–Holsteinism was again becoming a serious menace to the unity of the *Helstat* and to international peace. Under strong pressure from the other Great Powers interested in the problem, especially Russia, which supported the Holstein nobility as a conservative element, the moderate liberal Hall, who took office in 1857 at the head of a largely National Liberal administration, finally agreed in 1858 to suspend the operation of the constitution while a solution was sought in consultation with the Assemblies of Slesvig and Holstein. Such negotiations were made no easier by the constant interference of foreign governments, most of whom called for Danish concessions, and discussions dragged on for the next five years without coming any nearer to a satisfactory conclusion.

The 'fifties, in spite of the preoccupation with the question of the Duchies, saw the continuation of the work of political, social and economic reform which had began even before the end of absolutism. The local government franchise was extended; all taxpayers, whatever their income, were granted the right to vote for half the councillors. On the land, labour services owed by cottagers had been abolished during the war, and it was now decreed that those still owed by other tenants should as soon as possible be commuted for money rents. The distinction between 'privileged' and 'unprivileged' land[1] was abolished, compensation being paid to owners of the former. The Liberals refused to support the Left's demand for the abolition of leasehold tenure by law, but the transition to universal freehold was considerably speeded up by a law of 1854, which allowed tenants to set up credit associations through which to borrow money to purchase their holdings, and by one of 1861 which allowed landlords to take into their demesnes one holding for every ten which were sold to their tenants. As a result the proportion of leasehold tenures fell from nearly 30 per cent in 1850 to only about 10 per cent in 1870 (by the time leasehold was finally abolished in 1919 there were very few such holdings left).

But the most important group of measures was that passed through the *Rigsdag* in 1856–7 which, as had been promised in the June Constitution, swept away the remaining vestiges of the urban monopoly of trade and industry and the monopolies enjoyed by the handicraft gilds in towns. The law dealing with the latter, which was not fully implemented until 1862, marked the conclusion of a struggle which had opened at the end of the 1830's. During it the larger gilds had fought hard to retain their privileged position, but they had been weakened after 1848 by the large number of Germans among their members; they were among the victims of the nationalist reaction which marked these years. The freeing of trade meant the appearance of shops in villages for the first time.

This legislation undoubtedly encouraged the quite impressive advances which took place in various sectors of the Danish economy in the years following, but other factors were also responsible for this. Grain prices were kept high by the continuing demand in England, now rapidly becoming industrialized, and in the third quarter of the century production of cereals rose by 60 per cent as a result of both higher yields and a greater area of land under cultivation. Agricultural societies to instruct farmers in new methods spread throughout the country, and the Folk High Schools[2] undoubtedly helped to break down rural conservatism. In 1856 the government amalgamated a number of

[1] See above, p. 174.
[2] See above, p. 173, and below, pp. 194–5.

institutions to form the Agricultural College in Copenhagen. The improved standard of living enjoyed by smaller proprietors and tenants was reflected in the construction in country districts of larger stone-built houses with tiled roofs, wooden floors and separate bedrooms.

The growing prosperity on the land created an increasing demand among the farmers for goods which were produced in and imported through the towns. Industry in the kingdom faced serious competition from that in Holstein after the customs barrier on the Ejder was removed in 1853, but it benefited from the activities of the Industrial Society, founded in 1838, and from an improved financial structure; private provincial banks began to appear in the 1840's, and in 1857 the powerful Society of Wholesale Merchants (*Grosserer Societet*) helped to found the *Privatbank* in Copenhagen. For many years the latter was guided with great success by Carl (C. F.) Tietgen, the most outstanding of Denmark's nineteenth-century industrial entrepreneurs, whose name was to be linked to a number of other important undertakings.

Even in the 1840's more and more trade from outside Europe was beginning to flow through Copenhagen instead of Hamburg, and in the 1850's the capital's share of Baltic commerce also rose rapidly. Hamburg became even less important to Danish merchants after a financial crisis which hit it in 1857 and prevented it from continuing to offer them the favourable credit facilities they had enjoyed there before. But the most influential factor in Copenhagen's subsequent rise to leadership of the country's economic life was the abolition of the Sound Dues in the same year. This was a move for which the Wholesalers' Society had been pressing for some time, but it came about finally as a result of the refusal of the United States to pay the exaction any longer. This encouraged other trading nations to put pressure on the Danish government, which finally agreed to surrender its rights in exchange for compensation of 67,000,000 *kroner*. The tariff walls around the country had been coming down since 1836 and were reduced to their lowest point by the Customs Law of 1863, which remained in force until 1908. The merchant fleet grew rapidly, especially after the repeal of the English Navigation Acts in 1846. Most of it was still under sail, but the Scottish-built steam-ship *Caledonia* had begun to ply between Copenhagen and Kiel as far back as 1819, and by 1862 there were forty-three Danish vessels using this source of power.

Steam was also beginning to play an important role in land communications in the shape of the railway. A line had been opened across Holstein from Kiel to Altona in 1843, and the following year the concession for the building of the first line in the kingdom—between Copenhagen and Roskilde—was won by the Industrial Society; the line was completed in 1847 and extended to Korsø on the western side of the island in 1857. After this, further progress was delayed by disagreement over development in Jutland. Jutish interests wanted a line running southwards to tap the German market, while Zealanders, more concerned with trade with England, pressed for one which would run across the peninsula and help link the capital with a port on the North Sea. Agreement to build both was finally reached in 1860–1, but less than 150 miles of track was in operation in 1864. Business was also encouraged by the construction of the first telegraph line in the country (between Hamburg and Elsinore) in 1854, three years after the issue of the first Danish postage stamp.

The decade of the 1850's did not witness any striking new developments in the cultural field; the end of the great age of literary Romanticism was symbolized by Oehlenschläger's death in its first year, and men of the movement's second generation, like Ingemann, had already made their mark. The intellectual scene in Copenhagen had long been dominated by Johan (J. L.) Heiberg, a writer of many elegant pieces for the theatre and critic with a biting wit, for whose journal Hans Andersen had composed some early poems. But Heiberg's most important role was to introduce Danes to the ideas of the great German philosopher Hegel. And it was partly by attacking these ideas that Denmark's own leading philosopher, Søren Kierkegaard, developed his own, which, while emerging out of Romanticism, also marked its death-throes. The physical weakness from which Kierkegaard suffered in childhood gave him a sense of isolation from his fellow men which remained with him throughout his life and which helps to account for the intense individualism of his message. He emphasized in this the sharp distinction to be drawn between reason and faith, of which the latter, he believed, was the only true basis for acceptance of Christian dogma. In his voluminous writings in the mid 1840's, beginning with *Enten-Eller* (Either-Or), he posited three possible 'life-styles', the aesthetic, the ethical and the religious—and claimed that only the last of these could provide man with a truly satisfactory answer to his problems. He did not become widely known until long after his death in 1855, but he is now regarded as the founding father of the Existentialist Movement.

Romanticism continued to influence the visual arts and music much later than literature. The new palace of *Christiansborg*, completed in 1828 to the designs of C. F. Hansen, was the last and the greatest monument to Neo-Classicism in Danish architecture, and the most important building of this period— J. D. Herholdt's University Library in Copenhagen—was in the revived Gothic style so popular with the Victorians. And much of the music of Niels Gade, the leading Danish composer of the century, was strongly influenced by the ultra-Romantic Mendelssohn, with whom Gade worked closely in Germany in his early years; he returned to Denmark in 1850 at the age of thirty-three and powerfully affected his even greater fellow countryman Carl Nielsen[1] and the Norwegian Edvard Grieg. He wrote nine symphonies, but his fame now rests largely on his smaller pieces for piano and chamber orchestra. Gade also wrote music for the ballet, and the enviable reputation enjoyed by Danish ballet today can be traced back to the middle of the nineteenth century, when it was raised to new heights by the remarkable Frenchman August Bournonville. His father had joined the Royal Theatre as a dancer in 1792 and took over from Galeotti as ballet master in 1816. August succeeded to the post in 1829 and held it until 1877, two years before his death. During this half century he produced over fifty ballets of very varied character, many of which are still in the company's repertoire, and trained some extremely talented dancers.

At the beginning of 1863 the Schleswig–Holstein Question appeared to be as far as ever from a solution, and the pressure on the cautious Hall from his National Liberal colleagues led by Lehmann to make a further attempt to implement the Ejder Programme was becoming well-nigh irresistible. The backing given by the German Confederation to the demands of the Schleswig–Holsteiners had given a great fillip to the Scandi-

[1] See below, p. 221.

navianist Movement. At the end of 1856 Ploug had proposed to King Oscar of Sweden the conclusion of a strong defensive alliance between their two countries as a counter to the menace from Germany, and Oscar had greeted the idea with some enthusiasm. The government in Copenhagen had rejected it on that occasion, but Scandinavianism continued to grow, and Oscar's son Charles XV, who succeeded his father in 1859, was its fervent supporter. Negotiations between the two powers were finally opened in the middle of 1863. The National Liberals were further emboldened by the outbreak of a nationalist revolt in Poland in this year. This not only reduced considerably the likelihood of Russia's interference on behalf of the Schleswig–Holsteiners, but, because of her savage repression of the insurgents, also strained her relations with the other Great Powers. Of these, Austria and Prussia were at loggerheads over the former's proposals for reform of the German Confederation; and the marriage between the beautiful Princess Alexandra, daughter of the heir to the Danish throne, and the Prince of Wales, later Edward VII, brought an upsurge of pro-Danish feeling in Britain. All in all, the international situation could, to all appearances, hardly have been more favourable for Denmark.

In March, Hall issued a 'patent' providing for a separate constitution for Holstein and Lauenburg. In July the Diet of the German Confederation threatened military action if the Patent, which it regarded as implementing the Ejder Programme, were not withdrawn. Hall refused. He entertained high hopes of support both from Sweden and from Britain, where Palmerston informed the House of Commons that if Germany threatened Denmark it would not be only Denmark with whom she would have to deal, a statement often misinterpreted as an offer of British aid. And in September the *Rigsråd* was presented with a new constitution for Denmark and Slesvig, similar to that of 1855 but providing for a bicameral *Rigsråd*. This was approved by the existing Council, from which most of the Schleswig–Holsteiners had withdrawn, but on 15th November, before it could be ratified, the King died.

Frederik VII had been a very popular monarch. His marriage shortly after his accession to an ex-ballet dancer named Louise Rasmussen, created Countess Danner, had been strongly criticized in high society, but it had helped to strengthen the image which he enjoyed as 'The People's King', and the influence which she had exercised on him had undoubtedly been beneficial; he once said it was wholly thanks to her 'that I have not already turned up my toes'. The new king, Christian of Glücksborg, a very distant cousin of his predecessor, was already forty-six years old, had been educated in Germany, and was suspected of harbouring pro-German and pro-Russian sympathies. He was indeed an opponent of the Ejder Programme and hesitated before approving the new constitution, especially as the international situation had become decidedly less favourable to Denmark since the beginning of the year. The German Confederation was preparing to send troops into Holstein to compel withdrawal of the March Patent, and Austria was seeking a *rapprochement* with Prussia in face of a threat from France, whose emperor Napoleon III was turning towards Prussia and Russia after Britain had reacted unfavourably to his proposal for a European congress to settle outstanding issues and consider a substantial redrawing of the political map of the Continent.

Christian IX, under strong pressure from the Danish public and his ministers, did finally sign, but with great reluctance and deep foreboding. His fears soon proved to have been justified. Prussia, France, Russia and Britain all called for the withdrawal of the constitution, which was claimed to be in breach of the undertakings given by Denmark after the war of 1848–50, while the new Duke of Augustenborg proclaimed himself Duke of Schleswig–Holstein in defiance of the Treaty of London, by which the Powers had in 1852 recognized Christian's right to succeed in the Duchies as well as Denmark. Hall and his colleagues believed that, in the event of an attack, Sweden at least would come to their aid, in spite of the fact that the alliance negotiations had run into difficulties, and had hopes that France might do the same. But they failed to persuade the King to give up his demand that the *Rigsråd* be consulted, and resigned. Monrad was called on to form a new ministry, which earned the nickname of 'The Million'—one figure and six nullities!

Monrad was confident that he could persuade the German powers to negotiate. But Bismarck, now chancellor of Prussia, did not intend to negotiate; he was bent on war to deprive Denmark of all three duchies and succeed in persuading Austria to act with him. In spite of the revocation of the March Patent two weeks previously, German troops had moved into Holstein before Monrad took office, and on 16th January 1864 the Prussian and Austrian governments presented an ultimatum: Denmark must either withdraw the November Constitution within forty-eight hours or suffer the invasion of Slesvig. Monrad offered to put the demand to the *Rigsråd*, but Austria and Prussia refused to allow him the time he needed. On 1st February their troops crossed the Ejder.

General de Meza, the Danish commander-in-chief, had to abandon the line of the Dannevirke to avoid being outflanked by superior enemy forces and withdrew his infantry to entrenchments on the Dybbøl Peninsula on the Baltic side of Slesvig; his cavalry retired into Jutland. News of the retreat, which had taken place in bitterly cold weather, caused a temporary panic in Copenhagen, and de Meza was dismissed. Appeals were made in vain to other powers. Sweden, the alliance negotiations with whom had broken down, feared that Russia might move against her if she should become involved; the Scandinavian Movement collapsed. Britain, while sympathetic, would not act without France; she also believed that Prussia and Austria would withdraw their troops as soon as the November Constitution had been repealed. And Napoleon III was waiting to see what advantage he might be able to take of the situation.

On 18th April the Dybbøl lines were stormed and overrun by the enemy after a devastating bombardment; the Danish troops who survived retreated on to the island of Als, and Jutland was evacuated. Two days after the defeat a conference of European powers opened in London. This managed to arrange a brief truce before considering a number of possible solutions of the question. Denmark's rejection of the idea that there should be a personal union between the kingdom and the Duchies opened the way for Prussia and Austria to demand that both Slesvig and Holstein should be separated completely from Denmark. Britain then revived a proposal for the division of Slesvig along linguistic lines; this also appealed to France. But no agreement could be reached on where the boundary should run; Monrad insisted on one skirting the river Sli and then following the

Dannevirke, but the Prussians and Austrians protested that this would leave many German-speakers under Danish rule. At the end of June the conference broke up having achieved nothing, and the fighting was resumed.

The Prussians succeeded in occupying Als almost immediately. Monrad continued to hope for foreign assistance and wished to carry on the struggle, but the Danish public now wanted peace, and he was forced to resign. The Conservative ministry which succeeded him negotiated an armistice, and peace talks were opened. It soon became obvious that Denmark could not hope to retain even a part of Slesvig, and by the Peace of Vienna in October she had to cede all three duchies to the victors, who shared their administration until after the Austro–Prussian War of 1866, when they became part of Prussia.

For this result, which meant the reduction of the lands of the Danish Crown in Europe by some 40 per cent, Danish policy must take a large part of the blame. The November Constitution had been imposed in the face of international agreements and without due regard to the likely reactions of the Powers. The fact that the rebellion of 1848–50 had been put down had led to over-confidence; the more sobering lessons which might have been learned from the previous crisis had been insufficiently absorbed. And an unwillingness to compromise at the conference table had meant the loss of what might otherwise have been saved. None of which makes the policy pursued by Bismarck any the more moral, but Danish mistakes did enable him to give it a certain moral colouring and to carry it through to a successful conclusion.

# CHAPTER XV

# The Foundation of Modern Denmark
# (1864-1914)

THE outcome of the second Schleswig–Holstein War was for all Danes a shattering experience. Some reacted by dreaming of revenge. Some wondered how long their small, militarily weak and not very rich country would be able to maintain its independence. Yet many determined that what had been lost should be balanced by exploiting to the full the resources which still remained. Typical of these men was Enrico Dalgas, an officer in the engineers, who in 1866 founded the Heath Society with the object of reclaiming the extensive wasteland of western Jutland and colonizing it with groups of the rural poor, who constituted such a serious social problem. In thirty years the total productive area of the realm was, by draining and afforestation, increased by over a sixth. And during the same period progress in many other fields laid the basis of the Denmark of today.

As in 1850, the politicians found themselves faced by a serious constitutional problem, for two constitutions—that of June 1849 and that of November 1863—were both valid for the territory to which Denmark had been reduced. Since the November Constitution had been evolved solely with the object of binding Slesvig to the kingdom, it seemed to many members of the Left logical that it should be repealed. But the Conservatives and many National Liberals wished to exploit the opportunity presented by the confusion to prevent the Left from securing a majority in both houses of the *Rigsdag* by introducing for elections to the *Landsting* the limited franchise which, under the November Constitution, was to apply to the upper house of the

*Rigsråd.* Once this had been done, they were quite content that the latter should be consigned to limbo.

The final collapse of the Ejder Programme had greatly weakened the National Liberals, who were widely blamed for the war and its consequences, and the Left had split into a number of factions, of which the largest was a right-wing group under I. A. Hansen. The Conservative government decided to rely largely on the latter to drive its constitutional measures through the *Rigsdag*, and Hansen agreed to co-operate on the understanding that certain reforms in which he and his colleagues were interested, like the abolition of leasehold tenure, should also be granted; the great landowners, who were in a strong economic position as a result of the agricultural boom in the middle of the century, had now largely taken over the leadership of the Right, and the idea was canvassed that farmers large and small should rule, in opposition to the urban middle classes who had provided the Liberals with their main support. The votes of Hansen's party enabled a new constitutional project to be passed. It received the royal assent in July 1866. Under it the *Folketing* was to continue to be elected on a basis of universal male suffrage. But of the sixty-six members of the *Landsting*, twelve were to be appointed by the government, one was to sit for The Faeroes, and the remainder were to be elected by colleges, half the members of which were to be chosen by all entitled to vote for the *Folketing* and half by the wealthier taxpayers. This meant in practice that a Conservative ministry could be sure of a majority in the upper house. No provision was, however, made for disagreement between the two houses.

Co-operation between Hansen's followers and the government came to an end as soon as it became apparent that the great landowners had no intention of abolishing leasehold tenure and were seeking again to conciliate the Liberals. When a new ministry under Count Holstein-Holsteinborg was formed in 1870 it indeed included a number of the latter; Hall was given the portfolio of education and religious affairs (traditionally combined in the Scandinavian kingdoms). Consequently all the groups of the Left came together to form the United Left Party, the first political party of a modern type which emerged in Denmark. Its programme included tax reform, the abolition of

# THE HOUSE OF GLÜCKSBORG

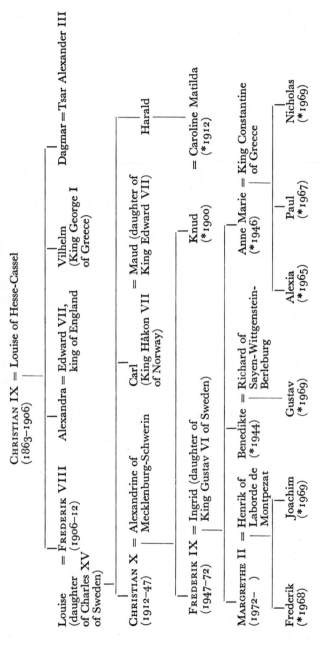

11. Thorvald Stauning. *Royal Library, Copenhagen*

12. Århus Town Hall (see p. 240). *Danish Tourist Board*

leasehold tenure, the re-introduction of the June Constitution, and parliamentary government (i.e. the appointment of ministers who could command a majority in the *Folketing*). The United Left won a majority of seats in the lower house in the elections of 1872, to which a majority of the Liberals, also becoming increasingly concerned by the rise of socialism, responded by joining the Conservatives in a national Conservative Party (*Højre*). Danish politics for the next thirty years were dominated by the struggle between the Left and the Conservatives, from whom the King regularly chose his chief ministers, over the principle of parliamentary government.

The struggle was fought against the background of a rapidly changing society; during the last three decades of the nineteenth century a new agricultural crisis completed the transformation of the old rural community which had begun at the end of the eighteenth century, and industry emerged for the first time as a key factor in Denmark's economy. The large-scale imports of North American and Russian grain into Europe, which were made possible by improved transport facilities, caused a sharp fall in grain prices in the mid 1870's. This stimulated a movement which had already begun in Denmark away from cereal-growing, on which, as many had warned, she had become excessively dependent, towards a more diversified agriculture with the accent on dairying and cattle-breeding. Barley and oats for fodder and new crops like sugar beet (a speciality of Lolland) also began to replace wheat and rye in importance, and after 1880 bread cereals even had to be imported. The growth in the number of cattle increased the amount of manure available, and this, together with imported artificial fertilizers, greatly improved productivity of cultivated land. And much work was done at the Agricultural College and by individual landowners on improving breeds of cows for milk and meat.

Many of the larger estates had earlier in the century begun to set up dairies on the model of those already existing in the richer and more progressive Holstein, and Danish butter began to be exported to Britain about 1860. In 1878 came the invention by the Swede de Laval of the centrifugal cream separator, a key advance in this field. Such appliances were at first confined to the dairies of the great landowners, but in the early 1880's smaller farmers, each of whom individually possessed too few cows to produce high-quality butter, began to band together and form small co-operative dairies in which these separators could be used. The first of these was established at Hjedding, north of Esbjerg in western Jutland, in 1882, and by the end of the decade there were nearly 700 throughout Denmark. To each of them the members contributed the basic capital needed for the raising of the initial loan, and at the end of the year any profit which had been made was divided among them according to the amount of milk each had delivered. But at meetings to decide policy each participant enjoyed only one vote. The quality of the butter produced was carefully controlled, and it could be kept fresh in an ice-cellar until collected. Export was also mainly in the hands of co-operative associations. The growing demand for bacon and eggs in England encouraged these branches of agriculture also to adopt the co-operative principle; the first co-operative pig slaughter-house was set up at Horsens in eastern Jutland in 1887. Co-operative retail societies soon sprang up in the villages; these purchased goods wholesale and in 1896 acquired a national organization—the *Fællesforening for Danmarks Brugsforeninger* or *FDB* for short—which imported in bulk and ran its own factories. Three years after this a Co-operative Committee appeared to co-ordinate all these activities. The whole movement, one aspect of a general effort being made at this time by the smaller farmers to free themselves from dependence on the larger landowners, is a vivid illustration of the sophistication and self-reliance which they had acquired and which distinguishes them so strikingly from the downtrodden peasants of only a hundred years before.

One of the chief factors contributing to this change in outlook was undoubtedly the Folk High School Movement, Denmark's most important gift to European education. After the loss of Slesvig, which placed Rødding on the other side of the national boundary, a school was founded at Askov in mid Jutland. This has remained ever since the most important of these colleges, but it was its younger sister at Ryslinge on Fyn, founded in 1851 by Christen Kold, which set the pace in new teaching methods. Under Kold, whose ideas also influenced the State elementary schools, less emphasis was placed on formal instruction and more on example and inspiration, with, as Grundtvig had wished, a strong nationalist and Christian bias. In the ten years from 1866 to 1876 the number of pupils attending folk high schools increased from about 1,000 to 4,000, and by 1914 this latter figure had been doubled. From 1892 the schools received financial support from the State, but they remained entirely autonomous. They ran two main types of course, one for young men in the wintertime lasting five months and one for young women in the summer before they became involved with the harvest. Many later leaders in agrarian political and social life first acquired a knowledge of Denmark outside their often rather isolated communities as well as an interest in national problems during such courses. And before the end of the century the idea had spread to the other Scandinavian countries.

Reforms such as those which have been described enabled Danish agriculture to weather the storm, but the process was nevertheless a painful one for many country-dwellers, and a growing number of them sought their salvation during these years in the towns. In 1870 some 25 per cent of all the 1,780,000 Danes were townsfolk. By 1910 the proportion had grown to 40 per cent. In Copenhagen many continued to live in rapidly deteriorating conditions within the lines of the old fortifications,[1] but new workers' quarters, no less overcrowded and insanitary than elsewhere in Europe, spread beyond them into the districts known as Vesterbro, Nørrebro and Østerbro, and similar areas grew up on the outskirts of other towns. Urban development was very uneven. The towns of eastern Jutland in particular grew rapidly; Århus overtook Odense as the second largest city, while new towns like Silkeborg in mid Jutland appeared. But other ancient centres like Ribe stagnated.

A considerable number of Danes chose to leave their country altogether. Even before 1870 the steady increase in population, combined with faster and cheaper methods of transport, had led to an acceleration of emigration. But it was a mere trickle compared with what followed. Between 1870 and 1914 some 300,000 left, mostly to settle in North America, and half of these went before the end of the century. It is true that Denmark was less affected by the movement than was either Norway or Sweden in the same period, but the social effects on her were nevertheless quite considerable, especially as a high percentage of those involved were able-bodied young men. The peak was

[1] See below, p. 198.

reached in 1882, when over 10,000 set sail, but this annual figure was approached again in 1890–2.

Industrial growth in Denmark was encouraged by the ending of the competition with Holstein in 1864, when a customs barrier was erected along the Kongeå, and by the low interest rates which prevailed in the early 1870's. The country's geographical position and possession of a large number of good harbours enabled her to import reasonably cheaply both raw materials and fuel which she lacked. Industry tended to concentrate in and around the ports, but the growth of the railway network also led to the creation of undertakings at new centres inland as well. Copenhagen was linked to the new port of Esbjerg, founded in 1868 particularly for the trade with England, and by 1895 nearly 1,400 miles of track had been built and most parts of the country were served. The ships of the United Steamship Company (*DFDS*), which was created by Tietgen in 1866, also helped to bind the islands and the mainland more closely together by regular sailings.

The growth of industry and with it of an industrial proletariat brought the spread of socialist doctrines. In 1871 the young post-office worker Louis Pio founded a Danish branch of Marx's International and began to publish in Copenhagen a weekly paper called *Socialisten*, which called for working-class solidarity in the fight against capitalism. The violent language in which Pio's demands were couched alarmed the authorities, and when, in 1872, he called for a mass demonstration in the capital in support of striking building workers, the demonstration was banned; when Pio threatened to ignore the order, he was arrested and condemned to a term of imprisonment. The demonstration was held nevertheless and had to be dispersed by hussars with drawn sabres. The International was outlawed, and a number of Pio's colleagues joined him in prison. But the setback was only temporary. In 1876 a Social Democratic Party was founded, and in the elections of 1884 two socialist deputies were returned to the *Folketing*.

The transformation of Danish society in the four decades following the loss of the Duchies was accompanied by a radical questioning of old assumptions in cultural as well as political life. The 1860's were a rather barren period in Danish literature, but it was just then that Georg Brandes, the young son of a

Jewish merchant in Copenhagen, was preparing what became known as the Modern Breakthrough, and at the end of 1871 he began delivering a series of lectures in the capital entitled 'Main Currents in Nineteenth-Century Literature', in which he launched a full-scale attack on the prevailing late-Romantic tradition. His free-thinking, positivist ideas, inspired by contemporary French thought in particular, shocked the Establishment. But they were taken up with enthusiasm by many of his contemporaries, of whom the most important was Jens (J. P.) Jacobsen, best known for his naturalistic novels *Marie Grubbe* (1876; English translation, 1914) and *Niels Lyhne* (1880; English translation, 1919), and the restless poet and novelist Holger Drachmann. The younger, in some ways yet more important, Henrik Pontoppidan was also associated with the Brandes circle; his main work, the novel series *Lykke-Per* (Lucky Peter), in which he studies the contrast between ideal and reality through the life of his main character, appeared around the turn of the century. Born in the same year as Pontoppidan (1857) but contrasting sharply with him, both in his view of life and his impressionistic style, was the pessimistic Herman Bang.

Danish painting was also affected by the Realist Movement, led in this field by L. A. Ring, who attempted faithfully to portray the landscape and simple people of his native Zealand. But the most important single influence on the painting of the period was French Impressionism, whose earliest and most faithful follower in Denmark was Theodor Philipsen. It also strongly affected the talented group of artists who in the 1870's began to foregather on the Skaw (Danish, *Skagen*), attracted thither by the brilliant play of light on the flat land and the sea of this northernmost tip of Jutland. The so-called 'Skagen School', many of whose works can be seen today in the Skagen Museum at Hjørring, include P. S. Krøyer and the husband-and-wife team Michael and Anna Ancher (see Plate 10).

The struggle over parliamentary government became intense after the appointment as prime minister in 1876 of Jacob (J. B. S.) Estrup, a strong-willed landowner who had been one of the chief architects of the Constitution of 1866. He was faced by an equally uncompromising Left, effectively led by Christen Berg, a schoolteacher from Jutland, who did much to organize local party groups and to build up a Press which would support his party's programme. He had in 1873 founded *Morgenbladet*, its most important journal, one of whose leading contributors was the lawyer Viggo Hørup, a prominent critic of the government in the *Folketing* and a coiner of catchy slogans like 'Nothing above and nothing beside the *Folketing*'. While Berg was a moderate, strongly influenced, as were many in his party, by the romantic nationalism of Grundtvig, Hørup represented the realist radicalism popularized by Georg Brandes, whose brother Edvard worked with Hørup on *Morgenbladet*. He formed an important link with the towns, and from this time the Left ceased to be a purely agrarian party interested only in the views of the smaller farmers.

After the elections of 1876, which brought great gains for the Left in the *Folketing*, the party's leaders, in an effort to force Estrup to surrender to their demands, adopted a policy of blocking his budget proposals until it was too late to have them approved in time for the new financial year. But he replied by proroguing the *Rigsdag* and issuing a provincial Finance Bill, embodying the taxes which had been approved, by decree. He defended his action by quoting a clause in the Constitution which gave the government the power to issue such decrees in an emergency when the *Rigsdag* was not in session, and claimed that such an emergency arose when the *Folketing* and the *Landsting* failed to agree. Divisions within the Left enabled him to get his budgets passed for a few years after this. But by 1880 the party was again united and could once more adopt an effective policy of obstruction; government bills, after a first reading in the *Folketing*, were referred to a committee which never met, and the expenditure proposed in budgets was drastically reduced.

The item of expenditure in which Estrup was most interested was defence, in particular a new ring of fortifications around Copenhagen to replace those which had been torn down in the late 1850's to allow for the capital's expansion. The Left were united in their opposition to the plan, which implied the abandonment of the rest of the country in the event of hostilities and withdrawal to Zealand until help should arrive from any ally. But they could not agree about an alternative. Hørup and the radical wing attacked 'militarism' in general and claimed that any amount spent on defence would be wasted since Denmark would never be capable of withstanding an attack by a great European power. 'What good will it do?' Hørup asked. The majority of the party only demanded a cheaper system which would at the same time protect the capital's communications with the rest of the country.

In spite of Estrup's patriotic appeals and the division within the Left, the elections of 1884 reduced the Conservative membership of the *Folketing* to only 19 out of 102; the party was obviously losing support even in the urban areas. The Premier's resolve was, however, unshaken. Confident in the support of the King and the *Landsting*, he continued to defy the majority of the lower house. And when it again rejected his budget, he repeated the tactics he had adopted in 1877 with the difference that the provisional Finance Bills now contained expenditure which had not been approved. The same thing happened for several years running. Unrest in the country grew, and an attempt was made on Estrup's life. He countered by forming a special corps of mounted gendarmes (the hated 'Light Blues'). And short of revolution, for which it was not prepared, there was little the Left could do as long as the Conservatives remained united. Work on the new fortifications went ahead, paid for out of the surplus in the Treasury created by economies in previous years. Constitutional government in Denmark was to all intents and purposes suspended for nearly a decade.

As time went on, a group emerged in the Left led by Frede Bojsen, a schoolteacher from Møn, which professed itself willing to bargain with Estrup in order that political life might be resumed. It offered to support the Conservatives' defence plan in exchange for social legislation benefiting the poorer workers. Moderate Conservatives (indeed Estrup himself) were impressed by the measures, such as old age pensions, which had been introduced by Bismarck during the 1880's and felt that similar enactments in Denmark might help to take some of the wind out of the sails of the socialists, who appeared to be gaining strength during the near-dictatorship. With Bojsen's support, two acts were passed in 1891 and 1892 which, though very modest, can be said to mark the beginnings of the Danish welfare state. One enabled local authorities to grant help to the needy aged in their areas and the other released government funds to help private health insurance companies to reduce their premiums and increase their benefits. The death of Berg in 1891 and Hørup's failure to win a seat in the elections of 1892 strengthened Bojsen's position within the Left and enabled him to conclude in March 1894 a pact with moderate Conservatives who were unhappy with Estrup's methods. By this a small amount of money was to be granted for the maintenance of the fortifications already erected, a guarantee was obtained that no more provisional laws would be employed, and agreement was reached on electoral and army reforms.

Estrup was forced to resign. But he was replaced by another Conservative prime minister, not, as many of the Left had hoped, by a ministry from among themselves. Bojsen's critics in his own party gained a majority in the *Folketing* as a result of the elections of 1895 and thereupon formed a new party of Left Reformers (*Venstrereformparti*) under Berg's successor, Jens ('I. C.') Christensen; Bojsen's Moderates were reduced to an ineffectual handful. Christensen was an effective parliamentary tactician who was able to exploit a weakening of purpose among Conservatives which resulted from Estrup's resignation. A group of so-called Free Conservatives had reconciled themselves to the fact that the demand for parliamentary government could not be resisted much longer.

The breakthrough came in 1901. In the elections of that year the Conservatives could get only 8 out of the now 114 seats in the *Folketing*, while the Reformers won 76 and the Social Democrats 14. King Christian finally agreed to invite the majority party to form a government. The man he approached was Professor J. H. Deuntzer, who was not even a member of the *Rigsdag*, but Christensen became minister of education and was generally recognized as the strong man of the new cabinet. Of the other members, only one was a farmer. This so-called *systemskiftet* (change of system) was celebrated with joyful demonstrations throughout the country and was with justification regarded as opening a new (though, as it turned out, not a calmer) chapter in Danish political history.

Although the Conservatives still controlled the *Landsting*, the Free Conservatives helped Deuntzer's ministry to pass most of its legislation during the next few years. In 1903 an Education Act established 'middle schools', which made it easier for pupils in State elementary schools to enter the 'Latin schools' (now renamed *gymnasier*) which prepared for matriculation. Tithes were abolished and popularly elected church councils instituted. The ancient, unevenly distributed land taxes, for the abolition of which the Agrarian Society had been struggling since its foundation in 1893, were at last replaced by a general property tax. And since the return from this was reckoned to be too modest for the government's needs, it was supplemented by progressive income and wealth taxes. The majority party appeared to be justifying its name.

But it contained both a moderate wing of farmers and a more radical wing of townsmen and poorer countrymen. After the winning of power the relations between these became increasingly strained, and in 1905 the radical minority broke away to form the Radical Left (*Det Radikale Venstre*). The Radicals differed from the majority of the Left largely over defence and social reform; they wished the army and navy to be reduced until they were fit only for police operations and urged the breaking-up of large estates so that landless labourers could become smallholders.

Smallholders had had too little to sell on the market to benefit much from the agricultural boom in the 1850's and 1860's, and they were hard hit by the depression which set in in the 1870's. Their numbers, however, grew. After 1880 credit associations enabled an increasing number of workers to buy plots and also to participate in the Co-operative Movement, especially in egg-production. And the flight from the land during the depression led many of the larger farmers to favour the idea of granting some land to labourers, though not so much as to make them self-supporting; in this way it was hoped to stem the flood while ensuring an easily accessible work force. An act of 1899 entitled anyone who had saved 10 per cent of the value of a piece of land to borrow a certain amount annually from the State towards mortgage repayments on it. Many, however, saw this as only a first step, and the smallholders' associations which began to appear campaigned for plots large enough to ensure their owners' independence. Their cause was strongly supported by both Radicals and Social Democrats.

The formers' defection forced Deuntzer to resign, but a new Left ministry was then formed by Christensen. International tension, especially the Russo–Japanese War, was at this time making defence a live political issue again, a fact symbolized by Christensen's assumption of the portfolios of war and the navy. He and many members of his party had come round to the idea that considerable expense on defence might be necessary to help Denmark to maintain her neutrality in the European war which was being widely forecast, and this attitude drew them towards both the Moderates (Bojsen's old group), now led by the historian Niels Neergaard and the teacher Klaus Berntsen, and the Conservatives, while it drove the Radicals and the Social Democrats closer together in opposition. The latter supported, however, a law of 1907 which granted State subsidies to the unemployment funds run by trade unions and to the poor relief funds administered by local authorities, as well as another law of 1908 which gave an equal vote to all taxpayers (including women) in local government elections.

Christensen appeared to be in a well-nigh invulnerable position, especially in view of his excellent relations with the new King Frederik VIII, with whom in 1908 he undertook a tour of Jutland. But in the same year he was struck down by a scandal. Peter Adler Alberti, whom Christensen had chosen to be his minister of justice, was forced to resign in July in face of strong attacks in the *Folketing* on his conduct of affairs, and in September he confessed to the embezzlement of large sums entrusted to him as head of the Zealand Farmers' Savings Bank. The Premier, although he had authorized a substantial loan to the Bank at Alberti's request, was in no way implicated in Alberti's crime, but he had had great trust in the latter and was undoubtedly shaken by the development. He chose to step down. His successor, the Moderate Neergaard, soon fell foul of the defence issue, on which none of the parties could reach agreement, and Christensen finally consented to enter a new Reform cabinet as minister of defence. He managed to work out a compromise acceptable to the *Rigsdag* by which fortifications were to be maintained until 1922, the seaward defences of the capital strengthened and the navy provided with new equipment, but the size of the army reduced.

This cabinet was in its turn forced to resign after a vote of no confidence, and Carl (C. Th.) Zahle formed the first Radical administration. Even with the support of the Social Democrats, Zahle did not command a majority in the *Folketing*, and in 1910 he went to the country in the hope of improving his position. The main issue on which he chose to fight was constitutional reform; he proposed the equalization of the franchise in elections to both houses and granting the parliamentary vote to women. But the Reformers and the Moderates emerged with a majority, and Zahle admitted defeat.

The two latter parties now reunited in a new Left Party. Christensen declined to form a cabinet because he was involved in judicial proceedings arising out of the Alberti scandal, and the task was undertaken by Berntsen. He himself put forward proposals for constitutional changes, but these were blocked by the Conservative majority in the *Landsting*. The Left suffered a serious setback in the elections of 1913 which gave a Radical–Social Democrat alliance a large majority in the *Folketing*; this alliance marks the beginning of that close co-operation between Radicals and Social Democrats which was to be one of the main features of Danish politics for the next fifty years. The Social Democrats in fact won more votes and one more seat than the Radicals, but their leader, the cigar-maker Thorvald Stauning, was not ready to take office, and Zahle therefore formed his second ministry. Firmly supported by the Social Democrats, it survived for seven years, the longest-lived cabinet since the resignation of Estrup. The final barrier to the acceptance of the Radicals' constitutional proposals fell in 1914, when the Conservatives at last lost their majority in the *Landsting*, but further progress was delayed by the outbreak of the First World War.

The Danish economy made considerable progress after the 1890's. The adjustments on the land to changed market conditions were completed; in 1914 there were five times as many pigs as in 1870, and the average milk yield per cow had doubled. Co-operative dairies handled 70 per cent of total production, and there were over 500 local co-operative retail societies. Most industrial undertakings were small. But the average size had been growing for some time; since 1870 many family firms, headed by the great engineering complex of Burmeister and Wain (which traces its origins back to 1843), had been turned into limited companies. And a number of really large combines, for example in iron and steel production, had appeared. The bulk of what was turned out was absorbed at home, and about half of it was associated with food-processing, but there was a growing export of high-quality articles; the ceramics produced in the Royal Porcelain Factory and the workshop of Bing and Grøndahl and Georg Jensen's silver were acquiring an international reputation.

Transit trade was helped by the creation in 1894 of a free harbour in Copenhagen in an attempt to meet the competition of the recently opened Kiel Canal. Imports, in which industrial goods from Germany played a large part, exceeded exports, but the gap was partly filled by the income from foreign investments and the earnings of the merchant marine. The latter's tonnage trebled between 1870 and 1914, and after 1900 was made up largely of steamships; the world's first ocean-going motor vessel was built in Burmeister and Wain's yards in 1912.

An inchoate Danish trade union movement had made some progress in the early 1870's, but it suffered a setback in the economic recession of the latter part of that decade and did not become a significant factor until after 1880. By 1900, however, many unions were organized nationally. The most outstanding labour leader of the period was the painter Jens Jensen from Fyn, a 'reformist' socialist who chaired the committee of Copenhagen unions for twenty-seven years and was elected mayor of the city in 1903; the fears which the latter event aroused in the hearts of many burghers were soon shown to have been completely unjustified. Jensen played a leading role in the formation in 1898 of the Danish TUC (*Det Samvirkende Fagforbund* or *DSF*). In reply the employers immediately set up their own national organization, and in the following year came the first great trial of strength between Capital and Labour in the country. The employers tried to impose their will on the workers by means of a general lock-out, but the latter managed to hold out for four months and achieved a compromise agreement—the so-called 'September Treaty'. The general rules of procedure laid down in this remained in force until 1960; and by the agreement the workers' right to organize was recognized but the conditions for calling strikes were strictly defined, and arrangements were made for arbitration. Thanks largely to the unions, the real wages of Danish industrial workers were in 1914 nearly double what they had been forty years before.

The last decade of the nineteenth century and the first of the twentieth form a rather confused period in Danish cultural life in which several trends manifested themselves. In literature, Brandes was strongly attracted by the ideas of Nietzsche in the late 1880's, and a reaction against the Realism which he had championed took the form about the same time of a revival of lyric poetry. The two most important writers in this genre were Johannes Jørgensen, who was converted to Catholicism in 1896, and his close friend Sophus Claussen, who was strongly influenced by the French Symbolists. A further reaction came after 1900 with the materialists Martin Andersen Nexø and Johannes V. Jensen. Nexø was Denmark's first important 'proletarian writer'. His monumental novel *Pelle Erobreren* (Pelle the Conqueror) appeared between 1906 and 1910 (English translation, 1913–16) and was followed in 1917–21 by its equally lengthy companion *Ditte Menneskebarn* (Ditte Child of Man; English translation, 1920–3); Nexø passed from socialism to communism and died in 1954 in East Germany. Jensen was, like the older Realists, attracted by Darwinism, as is apparent in his series of historical novels under the collective title *Den Lange Rejse* (The Long Journey; English translation, 1945).

A reaction against Realism also occurred in painting in the late 1880's. Of Denmark's two leading Symbolist painters, Vilhelm Hammershøi, who was strongly influenced by Impressionism, achieved international fame early, but it was J. F. Willumsen who was to dominate Danish painting during the first half of the twentieth century; he has been honoured with his own museum in Frederikssund north of Roskilde. A revival of interest in religious themes was led by Joakim Skovgaard; great murals by him can be seen in Viborg Cathedral. His pupil Niels Larsen Stevns also painted scenes from the New Testament, but is best known for the frescoes with which, between the wars, he decorated the walls of the Hans Andersen Museum in Odense. To an earlier tradition belong the so-called 'Fynboer' group (Poul Christiansen, Fritz Syberg, Peter Hansen and Johannes Larsen) who pictured the landscape and people of the island in highly individual ways. Architecture, which had suffered something of an eclipse since the middle of the nineteenth century, came to life again with the evolution of the National Romantic style at the end of the 1880's. Its finest fruit was Martin Nyrop's Copenhagen Town Hall, built between 1892 and 1905.

# CHAPTER XVI

# *The First World War and its Aftermath (1914-20)*

As soon as news came of German mobilization on 1st August 1914, the Radical cabinet in Copenhagen, with the full support of the other political parties, issued a declaration that Denmark intended to remain neutral in the coming struggle, but at the same time some army reservists were called up. And the entry of Britain into the war three days later caused a crisis which made it only too apparent how precarious the country's position was. Dano–German relations in the previous decades had been correct, though far from cordial; the loss of the Duchies still rankled with many Danes, and the attempted Germanization of the Danish-speaking population of Slesvig had caused considerable resentment. Germany now feared that Denmark would allow Britain to send a fleet through her waters to attack German ports on the south coast of the Baltic and decided to adopt measures to counter the threat; German ships immediately began to lay mines in the channel south of Langeland, and the government in Berlin demanded that the Danes should do likewise in the Great Belt between Zealand and Fyn. It made it clear that if such action were not taken by Danish mine-layers German vessels would perform the task, and even that German troops might occupy points on the Danish coast as additional security. Denmark feared that if she gave way Britain might regard it as an unfriendly act and make difficulties for Danish trade, which was so dependent on the British market. But after a flurry of talks involving political leaders, military chiefs and the King, it was decided that the risks involved in defiance were too great, and orders were issued to mine not only the Great Belt but also the southern part of the Little Belt and the Sound. At the same time, the army was increased to 58,000 men; even the parties which had previously opposed expenditure on defence agreed to vote the necessary sums. In fact the British government was very conscious of the difficult position in which Denmark was placed and had in any case no plans for sending warships into the Baltic; a telegram from King Christian X to his cousin George V was answered in the most amicable terms, and Anglo-Danish relations were unaffected.

While fear of Denmark's immediate military involvement in the war soon passed, concern for the effects of the crisis on her economy remained. Britain and Germany were her most important customers, and both her industry and her agriculture had become dependent on the raw materials, such as coal and artificial fertilizers, which they supplied. The government immediately asked for and obtained from the *Rigsdag* powers to impose price and export controls in order to protect essential stocks and opened negotiations with London and Berlin. After a brief run on the banks, Denmark also went off the gold standard; the Scandinavian currency agreement of 1873, which had established a common value for the *krone* throughout the area, lapsed. Both Britain and Germany needed Danish agricultural produce and proved quite willing to conclude trading agreements; Britain consented to continue to supply Denmark with raw materials and manufactured articles on condition that specified items were not re-exported to Germany. For the following two years some major sectors of Denmark's economy did even better than they had done before the war; an increase in foreign demand drove up farm prices, and, although not a few merchant ships were sunk by mines in the North Sea, many shipowners were able to make considerable profits.

Towards the end of 1914 the political parties were able to return to the question of constitutional reform. The Conservatives and the Left finally agreed to support a modified version of Berntsen's original project, which was approved in the *Rigsdag* by an overwhelming majority and received the royal assent on 5th June 1915. By it the *Folketing* was to be elected by all men and women over the age of twenty-five. Twenty-three 'national' seats and those for Copenhagen were to be filled by proportional representation, which favoured the Conservatives, but the remaining ninety-three members were to sit for single-member constituencies. Three-quarters of the *Landsting*, half of which was to be chosen every four years, was to be elected indirectly by all citizens over thirty-five, and the remainder by the outgoing house in accordance with the composition of the parties in it; these provisions in particular, which ensured the continuance of the house's conservative character, represented concessions by the Radicals to the Opposition. The new constitution did not come into force until 1918; it was generally thought undesirable that national harmony should be disrupted by an election campaign while the war was on. And the implementation of important reforms in the legal system which were approved in 1916 was also postponed, in this case until 1919. The most fundamental of these reforms were the clear separation of executive and judiciary, which had been promised in the Constitution of 1849, the introduction of juries to determine guilt in serious criminal actions, and of the oral conduct of trials.

The first serious political battle of the war years was fought over a rather unlikely issue. During the nineteenth century Denmark had rid herself of most of her colonial possessions; her Indian settlements were sold to the English East India Company in 1845 and her forts on the Guinea Coast five years later. But her West Indian islands she had retained. The opening of the Panama Canal in 1914 gave them considerable strategic importance, and in 1916 the United States revived an offer to buy them. The cabinet in Copenhagen decided to ask the *Rigsdag* to approve the sale; the population of the islands had been declining, they had long been a financial drain, and there had been considerable unrest among the largely Negro inhabitants. The proposal was supported by the Social Democrats, but the Conservatives set their faces against what they claimed would be an abrogation of the country's responsibilities, and the Left wished the matter to be postponed until after the war. Finally the government was strengthened by the addition of three new ministers without portfolio—Christensen, Stauning and the Free Conservative Christian Rottbøll—and it was decided to hold a referendum on the question. This—the first in Danish history—was held at the end of the year and produced a large majority in favour of the sale. At the end of March 1917 the islands were handed over in exchange for

$25,000,000 and reverted to their original name of the Virgin Islands.

By this time the economic situation in Denmark was beginning to worsen rapidly. At the beginning of 1917 Germany had proclaimed unrestricted submarine warfare; any ship, belligerent or neutral, sailing anywhere near Britain was liable to be sunk without warning. In spite of the arrangement of convoys from Bergen under the protection of British warships, the toll of Danish merchantmen and sailors lost in the North Sea rose alarmingly. And the entry of the United States into the war in April worsened the position still further. The Allies as a result felt themselves better able to impose a strict blockade on the Central Powers and severely restricted all exports to neutral countries through which they might reach the enemy. Danish farmers began to suffer considerable shortages of feed and fertilizers, and they found it more and more difficult to export; agricultural production sank. Industry meanwhile ran short of raw materials; many factories had to close down or at least to restrict output, and the number of unemployed rose until at the beginning of 1918 25 per cent of the organized labour force was out of work. Sugar, bread, butter, meat and coffee had to be rationed, maximum prices had to be imposed on fuel, which was very scarce, and on other commodities, and farmers were ordered to deliver minimum quantities of grain at fixed rates. The cost of other items, like clothing, rose rapidly, and wages, in spite of special supplements, failed to keep pace with inflation.

The fact that, in spite of these difficulties, many farmers continued to live well, that some industrialists still made healthy profits and that a number of speculators, such as those dealing in shipping shares and in the export of tinned meat to Germany (the 'goulash barons'), gathered together considerable fortunes encouraged the growth of extremism in the Danish labour movement. The number of lightning strikes and street demonstrations organized by syndicalists, who took heart from the success of the Bolsheviks in Russia and aimed at the total overthrow of the existing social and economic system, grew towards the end of the war. Although Stauning attended a radical socialist peace conference in Stockholm in 1917, he and the other leaders of the Social Democrat party and of the trade union movement firmly disassociated themselves from such methods and aims, an attitude which antagonized a section of the workers but enabled co-operation with the Radicals to continue.

Elections for the *Folketing* had to be held in the spring of 1918. In them Zahle won a fresh mandate, just in time to deal with another question concerning Denmark's overseas territories. The Icelanders had refused to recognize the constitutions of 1849 and 1866, and in 1874 they had finally been granted one of their own, which ensured the island a fair degree of autonomy. Many of them wished for complete independence, and the Radicals now agreed to go so far as to recognize Iceland as a sovereign state united with Denmark only by a common sovereign, though her foreign relations were to continue to be looked after in Copenhagen. The bill which the government presented to the *Rigsdag* embodying these proposals also laid down that if the Icelanders should, at the end of twenty-five years, vote unequivocally to break all political ties with Denmark, they should be allowed to do so. The debate on the measure was not so heated as that over the sale of the West Indian islands had been, and the Act of Union was passed by a large majority, but the Conservatives abstained when the final vote was taken.

When Germany collapsed at the end of 1918, many men throughout Europe looked forward to a permanent peace settlement based on President Wilson's Fourteen Points. These contained a promise that national frontiers should be redrawn in accordance with the wishes of the peoples who were living within them, and it was natural that Danes should think first of the fate of Slesvig. When the duchy had been absorbed into Prussia in 1866, a clause in the Austro–Prussian peace treaty had stated that the northern part should be allowed to return to Denmark if a majority of the inhabitants should express a wish for this by means of a referendum. But no referendum was held, and in 1878 Austria and Germany agreed to the abrogation of the clause. Now, in 1918, the leaders of the Danish-speaking population of Slesvig, who had resisted with considerable success the German attempts to destroy the Danish character of the region south of the Kongeå, appealed to the Danish government to request the Allies to allow them to benefit from the principle of self-determination. Some Danes thought that, since the duchy had been seized by force, it should be returned *in toto*, but all the political parties finally backed the cabinet's decision to ask the victors to arrange a referendum in northern and mid Slesvig to determine their future. A thorough survey conducted by the historian H. V. Clausen had shown that there was no hope of obtaining a majority for reunification in the southern part; it was too thoroughly Germanized.

The application was discussed by a special commission which met in Paris in February and March 1919, and in the Versailles Peace Treaty with Germany in June it was laid down that the Dano–German border should be fixed in accordance with the results of referendums in two zones of Slesvig. In the northern-most of these (zone I) a majority of its inhabitants was to determine whether it should go *en bloc* to Denmark or Germany, while in the southernmost, which embraced central Slesvig, including the important town of Flensborg, voting was to be by communes, a majority in each one deciding its individual fate. Voting in zone I took place in February 1920 under the eyes of international observers and resulted in a pro-Danish vote of 75 per cent. That in zone II came a month later, and its outcome was a sad blow for the Danes: not one commune produced a Danish majority. Flensborg, which had been a largely Danish-speaking town in 1864, was now 75 per cent German-speaking. A so-called Flensborg Movement had emerged in Denmark when the plans for the referendums were first mooted. Its main aim then was to get the town included in zone I. Having failed to do this, its followers went on to campaign for giving it a special status, and they received considerable support throughout the country. The movement indeed played a not inconsiderable part in the serious political crisis at Easter 1920.[1] The new Left cabinet which emerged from this, however, decided to abide by Denmark's original agreement with the Allies, and in June zone I was accordingly returned formally to the Danish Crown. On 10th July King Christian rode over the old frontier on a white horse to a tumultuous reception from his new subjects, and on the next day he attended a great reunion festival in the Dybbøl redoubts of hallowed memory.

[1] See below, p. 213.

# CHAPTER XVII

# Between the Wars (1920-39)

THE inter-war period in Denmark, as in many other European countries, was one of considerable political and economic instability. No single party was able to secure a safe majority in the *Rigsdag*, and minority or coalition ministries, involving a great deal of 'horse-trading' and unsatisfactory compromise, were the rule. Cabinets of the Left had to rely on the support of the Conservatives, with whom, in spite of certain views in common, they found it difficult to co-operate for very long. Social Democrats and Radicals worked together more successfully, especially as the former had become under Stauning a 're-formist' party, mainly interested, like the Radicals themselves, in social reform, but even here there was friction. In the forefront of political life and colouring it throughout were the country's economic problems. Denmark's heavy dependence on her overseas trade exposed her to all the fluctuations in world market trends, and successive governments grappled desperately with forces only half understood even by experts. Economic instability encouraged the emergence of both left- and right-wing extremism, which did nothing to lighten the burden on the leaders of the main political parties. Yet the continuing crisis did at the same time stimulate the evolution towards a juster social order, to which all the governments of the period contributed. And it seems to have done little, if anything, to stunt Danish cultural life, some aspects of which acquired during it an international reputation for the first time.

The First World War had brought with it a considerable extension of governmental control of economic life. This had evoked some criticism at the time from the Conservatives and the Left, both of whom adopted a *laissez-faire* attitude to industrial development, but they had generally accepted the necessity for some measure of State regulation as long as the emergency lasted. With the end of the conflict, however, they began to press more and more urgently for the removal of restrictions, which the Radicals and Social Democrats considered to be still necessary. They claimed that they enjoyed the support of a majority in the country and demanded the holding of fresh elections to prove it. And when in March 1920 Zahle failed to obtain clear support in the *Folketing* for his Slesvig policy, the demand was taken up by King Christian. Zahle refused to act until a new law extending proportional representation to rural districts had been passed, but the King countered by informing him that he had been dismissed and asking the lawyer Otto Liebe to head a caretaker government of officials to supervise immediate elections. The Socialists and the unions, already incensed by a threat from employers of a national lock-out in answer to strikes by workers for higher wages, were furious at Christian's action. They began organizing for a general strike to begin after the end of the Easter holidays, and there were violent republican demonstrations outside *Amalienborg*. Finally, after hurried negotiations on Easter Saturday, the King agreed to accept a new caretaker ministry agreeable to all parties and to wait until the law had been passed before elections were held. Never again has the monarch interfered in such a way in Danish political life. The general strike was called off, and the employers consented to certain wage increases; syndicalist agitation continued, but the labour front became much more peaceful.

The elections were held at the end of April and resulted in a serious setback for the Radicals, who lost nearly half their seats in the *Folketing*. Neergaard formed a Left ministry, which included Christensen as minister of education and Berntsen as minister of defence, as well as a number of younger men, like Thomas Madsen-Mygdal, chairman of the Danish National Farmers' Union (*DSDL*), who were to become prominent in the politics of the inter-war years. Some important pieces of social legislation had already been passed under the Zahle administration in 1919. Agreement had been reached on an eight-hour day for industrial workers, leasehold tenure had been finally brought to an end, and a large amount of land had been released for

smallholdings by the replacement of most of the clergy's glebe
land by fixed salaries and by the purchase by the State of the
third part of a number of large estates after the abolition of the
entail on them. During its four years in power the Neergaard
cabinet continued a social reform policy. In 1921 disablement
insurance was added to existing sickness benefits. In 1922 fixed
old age pensions were introduced for those who had been earn-
ing less than a certain level of income; no longer would local
authorities be able to decide who the recipients should be and
how much they should receive. And the State's contribution to
health insurance schemes and to union unemployment funds
were increased, with special provision made for those out of
work for a long period. This latter was a reflection of the serious
economic crisis which had hit Denmark, in common with the
rest of western Europe, in 1920 and which was the government's
main concern.

In spite of the difficulties which she had had to face in the last
years of the war, Denmark's economy had emerged from it in an
apparently strong position; the very large pre-war foreign debt
had been converted into an equally substantial credit. But the
need to import large quantities of raw materials at high prices
soon reversed the position once more, and in 1920 the revival of
competition led to a fall in prices which hit both industry and
agriculture. Industry was particularly affected by Germany's
recovery; unemployment figures rose sharply until in 1922 a
third of the labour force was out of work. Attempts by employers to save their profits by reducing wages, which were in
theory pegged to the cost of living, led to renewed industrial
unrest. This spread to the countryside, where savings on the
price of imported feed and fertilizers were offset by the lower
prices obtained for exports. The collapse of *Landmandsbanken*,
one of the biggest banks, due to its association with one of the
great speculative trading companies—which had appeared
immediately after the war and now disappeared one after the
other causing widespread distress in the lower middle classes—
brought a near-catastrophe, only averted by swift State intervention.

On top of everything else, Neergaard and his colleagues
found themselves faced at the end of 1923 with a sharp fall in
the exchange rate of the *krone*. Inflation did, it is true, cause a

revival in industry and a consequent reduction in unemployment, but there was a widespread fear that Denmark might be going the way of Germany, where the *Mark* had become practically valueless. One cause of the trouble was the excessive issue of notes by the National Bank after the war in an attempt to stimulate enterprise. Another was the growth of the country's trading deficit, which further undermined confidence abroad in the viability of her economy.

Unfortunately the Conservatives, on whose votes the government had to rely in the *Rigsdag*, could not agree with the Left on the best means of restoring stability. They wanted rigorous protection, which would reduce both imports and foreign competition. The Left, traditional free-traders who had rapidly dismantled wartime controls when they came to power, feared the effect which protection might have on the prices of basic consumer goods and on agricultural exports so vital to Denmark. They believed that all that was needed was a reduction in the number of notes in circulation by restricting credit through the National Bank. Meanwhile the value of the *krone* continued to fall, and in the spring of 1924 Neergaard was forced to go to the country. The election made the Social Democrats the largest party in the *Folketing*. Though its official programme still paid lip-service to Marxist theory, the moderation of its practice had won for it the support of a considerable section of the Danish middle class.

Stauning thereupon formed Denmark's first Social Democratic ministry; it was also the first Danish ministry to contain a woman—the historian Nina Bang, who received the education portfolio. But, like Britain's first Labour government, which came to office the same year, its position was weak. In the *Folketing* it could command a majority only with the support of the Radicals, and it was faced with a Left-Conservative majority in the *Landsting*. Its programme of extensive social reform, State control of the economy and disarmament had in the circumstances to be in large part abandoned, and it was forced to adopt a policy with regard to the crisis very similar to that advocated by Neergaard; the discount rate was raised and the note circulation reduced. Such measures did help to raise the value of the *krone*. In fact its value rose far more swiftly than had been anticipated, largely due to increasing confidence in it abroad which encouraged speculation. By 1926 it was back at par, and in 1927 Denmark returned to the gold standard. But over-rapid deflation caused a new crisis in both industry and agriculture. Danish goods became less competitive in foreign countries, and production had to be cut back; unemployment again increased, and profits shrank. In 1925 the employers tried, as in 1922, to solve their difficulties by means of a reduction of wages, backed by a lock-out. After two months, however, the unions forced them to abandon the attempt.

The Social Democrats proposed to tackle the new crisis with large-scale public works and a wealth tax to provide funds with which the State could subsidize industry and agriculture. The Radicals, however, found it impossible to support such a programme, and at the end of 1926 Stauning called an election in an attempt to secure a clear mandate. He failed. His party lost two seats, while both the Left and the Conservatives gained two. Two also went to the Single Tax Party (*Danmarks Retsforbund*), formed in 1919 to support the ideals of the American economist Henry George, who had advocated that land alone should be the source of all taxes, just like the French *physiocrates* of the eighteenth century. The Left obtained a promise of Conservative support, and its new leader Madsen-Mygdal formed a minority government. Its answer to the economic problem was a reduction in direct taxes and State expenditure. Cuts in old age pensions, which were fiercely attacked by the Social Democrats, were defended on the grounds that deflation had reduced the cost of living. Madsen-Mygdal was lucky. For a time the economic situation improved. The prices of agricultural produce rose, and the rationalization which had been forced on industry by the crisis began to pay off; unemployment declined, though its level remained disturbingly high.

The Left, however, found it very difficult to co-operate with the Conservatives. It refused to impose the high protective tariffs for which the Conservatives pressed, and the gulf between the two parties widened rapidly as the government extended its economy drive to the armed forces. In 1928 the Conservatives gained a vigorous new leader in the *Folketing*. Christmas Møller, still only in his mid 30's, dreamed of turning the party into one which would appeal to a far wider social spectrum than hitherto and which could play an independent role in political life. He realized that in order to do this it would have to make a clean break with the Left, and in the spring of 1929 he persuaded his followers to vote against the budget. This they were the more willing to do as it considerably reduced the service estimates. The election which followed Madsen-Mygdal's defeat was undoubtedly a sad blow for Møller. The Conservatives, far from benefiting from the breach with the Left, actually lost seats. The chief beneficiaries were the Social Democrats, who gained eight. Stauning formed his second ministry. But this time he made it a coalition with the Radicals, on whose votes he still relied. Peter Munch, who had taken over the leadership of the Radicals from Ove Rode, became foreign minister. He was on the left of his party and was in favour of much closer co-operation with the Social Democrats than his predecessor had been, a fact which made Stauning's position much stronger than it had been in 1924 and which enabled him to continue in office for the next eleven years.

Although Denmark was not directly involved in the First World War, the savagery with which it was fought was regarded with as much horror by sensitive men and women there as in other countries, and the optimistic materialism which had been so prevalent (though far from universal) before 1914 suffered a blow from which it never recovered. Some writers were, it is true, less affected than others: Pontoppidan, who shared the Nobel Prize for literature in 1917, and Johannes V. Jensen, who was to be awarded the same honour in 1944, retained a belief in human progress. But disillusionment with the past and fear for the future were common themes in the works of many of the younger men who emerged in the 1920's. Tom Kristensen, the leading Danish Expressionist poet, sought a radical reconstruction of society on new bases, while the more conservative Jacob Paludan in his first great novel *Markerne Modnes* (The Ripening Fields) of 1927 strongly criticized a number of features of the modern world.

The visual arts were less obviously affected. Painters continued after the war to look to France for their inspiration, and the various schools which succeeded Impressionism were well represented. Harald Giersing, a leading member of the influential 'Grønningen group', formed in 1915 and named after a thoroughfare in eastern Copenhagen, adopted an Expressionist technique in his landscapes and interiors, while Olaf Rude, who chose the scenery of Bornholm for many of his pictures, William Scharff and Vilhelm Lundstrøm were strongly drawn to Cubism and greatly admired by the abstract painters of succeeding generations. Kai Nielsen and Gerhard Henning had led a revival of Danish sculpture in the second decade of the century; the former unfortunately died at the early age of forty-two in 1924, but the Swedish-born Henning went on to produce a brilliant series of monumental female figures and to dominate the art of the inter-war period. Two buildings of the 1920's represent the latest development of dominant trends in Danish architecture before the breakthrough of functionalism in the following decade. The Copenhagen Police Headquarters near the city's main railway station, designed by Hack Kampmann and Aage Rafn and built between 1919 and 1924, is the culmination of a brief revival of Neo-Classicism which had begun with Carl Petersen at the beginning of the century, and Jensen Klint's Grundtvig Church in the Bispebjerg suburb of Copenhagen, which was begun in 1921 and completed in 1940, was an attempt to reproduce on a large scale a cross between Gothic town and country churches.

Just before the war and in its early years Denmark enjoyed an enviable international reputation for her motion pictures, the first of which dates back to 1898. In the peak year of 1912 no fewer than 161 films were produced in the country and constituted a valuable item of export. From about 1916 foreign competition, especially from the United States, became more and more serious, and output sank steadily until in 1930 it was down to two. Yet some excellent films continued to emerge during this last 'silent period', headed by Carl Dreyer's *Jeanne d'Arc* of 1928; Dreyer, who had started work as a director in 1920, was to become Denmark's most widely admired man of the cinema.

By the end of 1930 Denmark was beginning to feel the effects of the world economic depression. Prices fell, and markets were restricted more and more by tariff barriers. The country's agriculture and industry both found themselves faced with collapse. Many farmers were forced to sell their land to pay off their debts, and in the winter of 1932–3 there were again 200,000 unemployed, over 40 per cent of organized labour. Stauning managed to persuade the Left to agree to the institution of a government board to impose import quotas on key items and generally to control overseas trade. But the way in which regulations were enforced met with strong criticism from the Opposition, and Stauning decided to hold new elections in the autumn of the year. As a result, the Left lost five seats, thus strengthening the government's hand. But it still felt the need to conciliate the Left, and the party's new leader Oluf Krag was willing to negotiate. In January 1933 the Social Democrats, Radicals and Left reached an agreement, known as the Kanslergade Treaty after Stauning's residence in which the talks had taken place. By it the Left promised to support a law banning strikes and lock-outs for a year in order to dampen the industrial unrest caused by employers' attempts to cut wages, and also a code of social welfare worked out by Karl (K. K.) Steincke, the minister for social affairs. In exchange, the government would devalue the *krone* to assist the export of agricultural produce. Steincke's code consisted of four acts which replaced the multitude of piecemeal legislation passed since the end of the nineteenth century, and guaranteed to every Dane the right to enjoy a reasonable standard of living; no one would in future have to rely on the charity of local authorities.

In the same year came an agreement with Britain by which Denmark was to be allowed to supply up to 62 per cent of the former's bacon imports in exchange for an undertaking to accept certain British exports. Britain's policy of Imperial Preference, adopted in 1932, hit Danish dairy farmers particularly hard; their butter had now to compete with that from New Zealand on unequal terms. And British bacon imports fell in the late 1930's. Many farmers felt that they were being unfairly treated, and in the summer of 1935 a great deputation of some 40,000 of them, organized by the extreme right-wing Agriculturalists' Association (*Landbrugernes Sammenslutning* or LS), demonstrated outside *Amalienborg* and petitioned the King. This was followed by an unsuccessful attempt to embarrass the National Bank and the government by the agricultural wholesale organizations, who refused for a time to accept foreign currency. Stauning decided to try to improve his position still further by going to the country.

The Social Democrats fought the election in October with the slogan 'Stauning or Chaos' and won a resounding victory.

They gained six seats, while the Left, which had been the target of bitter criticism by the farmers over the Kanslergade Treaty, lost ten. Elections to the *Landsting* in the following year gave the government a majority in that house also for the first time. The economic situation remained unsatisfactory, but bacon prices were maintained by reducing the number of pigs and halving exports, and agriculture generally managed to adjust itself reasonably well to unfavourable market conditions; there was a record harvest in 1938. Industry also made progress. The prices which it had to pay for its imported raw materials remained high, and the State had to continue to exercise close control over foreign trade, but large-scale public works helped to keep down unemployment; a bridge linking Jutland and Fyn over the Little Belt, inaugurated in May 1935, was followed by one joining Zealand and Falster (*Storstrømsbro*), which was opened in September 1937 and is still the longest in Europe.

These bridges were not simply a lavish form of outdoor relief. They and the considerable extension and improvement of the country's road system which took place in the 1930's were made necessary by a rapid increase in motorized transport; special parking places had had to be instituted in Copenhagen in 1921. The railway network, partly privately owned and partly State-run, was already generally adequate by 1914, but services were considerably speeded up between the wars by the introduction of diesel trains and electrification. Denmark had also played a prominent part in the development of air transport. As far back as 1906 Jacob Christian Ellehammer had undertaken the first European flight in a heavier-than-air machine from Lolland, and in 1920 a regular connection between Copenhagen and London was opened by *Det Danske Luftfartsselskab*, Europe's first airline company.

Although, as has been seen,[1] certain individual Danes had won an international reputation for themselves in the field of applied art before the war, it was in the 1930's that 'Scandinavian Design' as a whole became universally recognized and admired as a pacesetter. In Denmark the tradition of fine silversmithing established by Georg Jensen was continued by his apprentice Kay Boyesen in a more functional style, while the high reputation of Danish furniture can be traced back in

---

[1] See above, p. 204.

particular to the work of Kaare Klint, son of the designer of the Grundtvig Church. Functionalism rapidly became the dominating influence not only in such spheres but also in architecture, and it was appropriate that the first important Functionalist building in Denmark, *Vesterport* in Copenhagen, should in 1931 become the home of the Permanent Exhibition of Danish Arts and Crafts (*Den Permanente*). In the same year and on a site not far away on the other side of the main railway station began to arise what is widely regarded as the purest example of the style in the country—the Meat Market (*Kødbyen*) by Poul Holsøe. But Copenhagen did not have a monopoly of striking new buildings. In 1928, on the initiative of a committee made up of representatives of the Århus Town Council and other local interests, a second Danish university was founded in the Jutish city, and work on permanent buildings in unfaced brick, for its various faculties, planned by Kay Fisker, Povl Stegmann and C. F. Møller, was begun in 1932; they were not, however, completed until after the Second World War.

From the early years of the century until his death in 1931 Danish music was dominated by Carl Nielsen, and his influence on younger composers has indeed remained strong until the present day. Nielsen, the son of a poor housepainter from Fyn, led a reaction against the late Romanticism of Gade and created a style at the same time individual, Danish and of the twentieth century. Of his six symphonies, for which he is best known, the first was written in 1891–2 and the fifth, in many ways the most important, in 1922. But he was a prolific composer, who tried his hand at nearly every musical form. The year after his death, the Royal Danish Ballet, which had tended to rest on its laurels since the golden age of Bournonville, began to be revivified by its new young ballet master Harald Lander, who not only revised much of the inherited repertoire but added many new works. And Lander worked particularly closely with Knudåge Riisager, one of the most important of Nielsen's successors.

Literature in the 1930's continued to mirror the moral confusion and discontent which had followed the First World War and was now reinforced by economic difficulties and the emergence of fascism. Certain aspects of the latter movement proved attractive to Kaj Munk, the Jutish clergyman who led a revival of Danish drama with plays like *En Idealist* (1929) and *Cant* (1931), on the theme of the individual's helplessness in the hands of Fate, and *Ordet* (The Word; written in 1924, but not published until 1932) about the validity of miracles. His fellow dramatist Kjeld Abell was at his best in satires on the emptiness of conventional bourgeois life such as *Melodien der blev væk* (The Melody that Got Lost, 1935; English translation, 1939). Also characteristic of the 1930's was the psychological novel. The bohemian Nis Petersen, although now chiefly admired for his poetry, first made his name with *Sandalmagernes Gade* (The Street of the Sandalmakers, 1931; English translation, 1932), a work in this genre set in the time of Christ. And H. C. Branner began to make his mark with short stories, in which he dealt particularly with personal relationships. The most popular Danish writer abroad in this period, Karen Blixen (also known under her pseudonym of Isak Dinesen), defies classification. Her earliest success, *Seven Gothic Tales*, was originally written by her in English and published in New York in 1934. Her masterpiece *Out of Africa*, which appeared in both an English and a Danish edition in 1937, was inspired by the seventeen years she spent on a coffee farm in Kenya.

Hitler's invasion of Austria in the spring of 1938 caused great concern in Denmark. The Social Democrats had by now abandoned the plans for drastic disarmament which they and the Radicals had tried to push through, against strong opposition from the Left and the Conservatives, after they came to power, but the Radicals in particular were still strongly averse to any extensive rearmament. Munch's attitude was the same as that which had been adopted by the Radicals in the late nineteenth-century debates on the question: that any attempt to resist an invasion would only cause unnecessary suffering. Yet further sums for the armed forces were now authorized, and in April a meeting was held in Copenhagen between representatives of Denmark, Norway, Sweden and the Benelux countries to discuss ways and means by which such smaller European powers might defend their neutrality in view of the apparent powerlessness of the League of Nations; at the end of the First World War, the *Rigsdag* had voted unanimously for Denmark to join the League, and in 1931 a six-year-old dispute with Norway over claims to eastern Greenland had been settled by the International Court in The Hague in Denmark's favour. And the conference agreed that international tension should as far as possible be relieved through the League. But Sweden and Norway were less vulnerable to German attack than Denmark, and when in April 1939 Hitler offered non-aggression pacts to all three kingdoms, she decided to sign one as a gesture of goodwill, while her two neighbours declined to do so.

The Danes were particularly sensitive to the fate of the Danish-speaking population of southern Slesvig and to the activities of National Socialists within the northern part of the duchy, which might, it was feared, be used as an excuse for German intervention as in Austria and Czechoslovakia. A Danish National Socialist Workers' Party had been formed in 1932, and in the elections which were held in April 1939 it managed to secure three seats in the *Folketing*; a further 8,500 votes were cast for the Danish Rally (*Nationalt Samvirke*), an extreme right-wing group sympathetic to fascism which had broken away from the Conservatives under Victor Pürschel. These elections as a whole constituted a setback for the government; the Social Democrats lost three seats. But it retained its majority and was able to get passed for the second time a constitutional project which involved the election of a second chamber, renamed the *Rigsting*, in the same way and by the same voters as elected the *Folketing*. In the event of disagreement between the two houses, they were to meet together and the issue to be decided by a majority of the whole *Rigsdag*. In a national referendum, however, the plan failed to secure a sufficient majority and had to be dropped.

# CHAPTER XVIII

# *The German Occupation (1939-45)*

WHEN the Second World War broke out in September 1939, the Danish government, as in 1914, affirmed the country's intention to remain neutral, but certain precautionary measures were adopted; a black-out was enforced, and a number of reservists were called to the colours. Fuel and some foodstuffs were rationed. The swift collapse of Poland was followed by the so-called 'phoney-war', during which Hitler and his generals prepared their plans for a massive attack westwards. They determined, however, that this should be preceded by the occupation of Norway, whose coast offered excellent bases from which German submarines and warships could harry Britain's sealanes. And to ensure communications with Norway, control of Denmark was necessary; little resistance was expected there, especially if surprise could be complete. In fact secrecy could not be maintained. The plan was leaked by discontented German officers to the Dutch military attaché in Berlin, and on 4th April 1940 the Danish envoy there was able to pass on the information to his government. In Copenhagen, however, the ministers persuaded themselves that the report was either a mere rumour or an attempt by the Germans to test Danish reactions. It had already been decided that any resistance to an attack would be pointless, and it was feared that overt countermeasures might provide an excuse for invasion.

On 8th April a large number of German ships were seen sailing northwards through Danish waters, and troop movements were observed across the southern border of Slesvig. The border was crossed about 4 a.m. on the following morning by detachments of German motorized troops, who soon crushed all resistance and swept forwards into Jutland. Almost simultaneously other units were landed at points on the islands and on the waterfront of Copenhagen. While bombers flew threateningly overhead, the German envoy informed the government that Denmark would be 'protected' for the duration of the war, but promised that there would be no interference by German military authorities in the country's internal affairs; any further resistance would, however, be answered with an aerial bombardment of the capital. Stauning and his colleagues were in no position to make more than a verbal protest and ordered an immediate cessation of hostilities to prevent unnecessary bloodshed.

As had been promised, the occupying forces behaved, at first at least, with 'correctness', and the initial public alarm caused by their arrival subsided; the lives of most Danes were little changed. Shortages of certain items made themselves felt, some more foodstuffs had in time to be rationed, and some others, such as tea and coffee, disappeared altogether, but no real hardship was suffered. Prices rose as the National Bank increased its note issue to compensate suppliers for the growing debt incurred by the Germans for goods which they in effect requisitioned. But the government imposed price controls, and inflation was kept in check. Inflation and German orders indeed helped to speed the wheels of industry, and unemployment, which had been high at the beginning of 1940, was somewhat reduced. Hitler decided to try to make of Denmark a 'model protectorate' to demonstrate that peoples who did not oppose the formation of the 'New Order' in Europe had nothing to fear. He also needed Danish agricultural produce, supplies of which might be interrupted if the Danes were given serious cause for complaint.

Immediately after the beginning of the occupation, a coalition government was formed by admitting three Conservatives and members of the Left into the cabinet. After demonstrations by Danish fascists and their sympathizers, aimed at destroying the democratic regime and replacing it with a Nazi-style dictatorship, it was considered necessary in July to strengthen the ministry still further. The most significant of the changes then made was the replacement of Munch as foreign minister by the sixty-three-year-old diplomat Erik Scavenius, who had occupied the same post during the First World War. He was no Nazi, but he believed that Danes must learn to accept the 'New Order', which, after Dunkirk, seemed as if it had come to stay, and that they should adopt a co-operative attitude to the representatives of German power in their country. Many of his statements were distasteful to his colleagues, and he became very unpopular with the ordinary man-in-the-street, but it was feared that any move to muzzle him or to contradict him officially might bring unfavourable German reactions. As it was, a number of ministers incurred the Germans' displeasure and were forced to resign; Christmas Møller, who had spoken out boldly against the occupying forces, was replaced as minister for trade as early as October, although efforts made two months later to force Stauning himself out of office were successfully resisted.

And German pressure increased as time went on. Severe restrictions on the freedom of the Press had been imposed in the early days of the occupation, and at the beginning of 1941 the *Rigsdag* had to approve harsher penalties for sabotage and spying. When in June of the new year Hitler turned against the Soviet Union, the government was compelled to ban the Communist party and arrest its leading members, and in addition to allow the formation of a 'Free Corps' of volunteers, including some regular army officers, to fight on the eastern front. In November, Scavenius, against the strong opposition of several members of the cabinet, took Denmark into the Anti-Comintern Pact. Although he managed to avoid committing the country to any real obligations as a result, news of the move led to the holding of a large anti-German demonstration in Copenhagen.

This was the first serious sign of the trouble which lay ahead for the occupying forces. Previously, while comparatively few Danes had shown much love for the Germans, and the latter had soon given up hope of using the Danish Nazi party as an instrument to secure absolute power in Denmark, opposition had been expressed largely by means of cold-shouldering German troops and officials. At the end of 1941, however, a regular resistance movement, in which outlawed Communists played a prominent part, began to take shape; an underground Press distributed tracts, and isolated acts of sabotage occurred. Allied agents were dropped into the country, but there was understandably some doubt abroad as to where Denmark's sympathies lay, and in April 1942 Christmas Møller escaped to London to explain the situation and, through the BBC, to call on his countrymen at home to do all in their power to hinder the German war effort. The government in Copenhagen, headed by the former finance minister Vilhelm Buhl after Stauning's death in May, condemned such an appeal, which ran counter to the official policy of conciliation still being followed. But Møller's popularity being what it was, his words undoubtedly had a far-reaching effect.

The Germans became more and more irritated by the attitude adopted towards them by the Danish public, and even some acts of the Danish government made them doubtful of its reliability. Hitler himself was particularly annoyed by the simple 'thank you' he received from King Christian in reply to a greeting he sent the monarch on his birthday in September, though no affront had in fact been intended. It was decided in Berlin that, while a policy of appeasement might be continued for a little time, Buhl must go. At the beginning of November, Scavenius was summoned for talks with Ribbentrop and ordered to arrange the formation of a new cabinet headed by a non-political figure and containing Nazis or their sympathizers. He persuaded the parties at home to accept a ministry headed by himself, and the Germans to drop their latter demand; and for a time tension was relaxed. The accommodating attitude of the new German plenipotentiary Werner Best eased Scavenius's task, and in March 1943 it was felt that circumstances warranted the holding of elections. In spite of strong German support, the Danish Nazis failed to increase their representation in the *Folketing*; the occupation had done nothing to shake the Danish electorate's allegiance to the old parties.

The Germans and their allies were now in retreat on all fronts, and not only did acts of sabotage by the underground movement, which was receiving a growing amount of aid from abroad, become more widespread, but manifestations of anti-German feeling by the general public became bolder; large-scale demonstrations were held in the cities, and strikes seriously disrupted production of war material. By the summer of 1943 Hitler had come to the conclusion that a policy of conciliation in Denmark would no longer work; the country threatened to become a weak link in the chain of defences

against invasion of 'Fortress Europe'. Best was therefore in-
structed at the end of August to present the cabinet with a list
of demands including a ban on strikes and demonstrations, the
surrender of all weapons and the imposition of the death
penalty for sabotage. When Scavenius and his colleagues refused to comply, the German military commander, von Henne-
ken, who had long been pressing for a tougher attitude,
assumed supreme power. A number of prominent public figures
were thrown into prison; the Danish army was disarmed and
its officers interned; and such naval vessels as their crews did
not have time to scuttle were seized. Civil administration continued as best it could under the direction of the permanent
heads of the civil service bureaux.

Resistance was consequently stepped up under the direction
of the Freedom Council, which was formed in September to
co-ordinate the activities of the various underground groups;
railway lines were blown up and considerable damage done to
factories manufacturing goods for the occupying power. But
perhaps the most remarkable single operation for which the
Resistance was responsible was the evacuation to Sweden at the
beginning of October 1943 of most of Denmark's 7,000 Jews
before they could be seized and carried off to gas chambers in
Germany and Poland. Such activity naturally brought reprisals.
Not only were houses raided and suspects dragged off to torture,
imprisonment and often death, but senseless acts of destruction,
like the burning of the Tivoli Pleasure Gardens in Copenhagen,
were perpetrated, and criminal elements were organized to
secure information on underground formations and plans and
to terrorize the civilian population. In January 1944 Kaj
Munk, who had abandoned all his earlier sympathy for
fascism and had preached fearlessly against Nazi tyranny, was
murdered. And the execution of informers by the Resistance
was answered by so-called 'clearing murders', the indiscriminate
shooting down of individual Danish men and women. In
September 1944 the police, after putting up an heroic defence,
were disarmed and taken off to German prisons. The population
thereupon organized a corps of unarmed volunteers to take over
police duties as best they could. This occurred soon after the
'Siege of Copenhagen'. At the end of June, the whole capital
had gone on strike in protest against the terror in its streets, the

execution of members of the Resistance and a recently imposed curfew. In an attempt to cow the city into submission, the Germans had immediately cut all its communications with the outside world and its supplies of gas, electricity and water. But after only a few days they had to admit defeat. Not only was the blockade lifted, but they agreed to a number of concessions laid down by the Freedom Council, including an end to acts of terror.

The Allies maintained close contact with the Freedom Council and helped it considerably, not only with supplies of arms but also, towards the end of the war, with bombing raids on various Gestapo headquarters to destroy the records kept in them. Shell House, the headquarters in Copenhagen, was made a target in March 1945. The building was burnt to the ground and a number of prisoners managed to make their escape, but others were killed, and by a tragic error part of the Frederiksberg district was also hit, and over one hundred of its inhabitants lost their lives. By May an underground army of some 43,000 was ready to assist allied troops when they reached Denmark from the south. German troops in Denmark, however, laid down their arms at the same time as those in north Germany and before American or British detachments had penetrated as far as Slesvig.

# CHAPTER XIX

## Denmark Since 1945

---

Just before the end of the war the political parties and the Freedom Council agreed on the formation of a coalition ministry under Buhl which included representatives of the Resistance movement, and less than a week after the German capitulation the *Rigsdag* reassembled. Almost immediately its members became involved in controversy over the punishment of those of their countrymen who had collaborated with the enemy and who could be considered guilty of other 'war crimes'. Many such offences were not covered by existing law, and the government proposed retroactive legislation to fill the gap. But a considerable number of deputies were doubtful of its morality, while, on the other hand, ex-underground fighters pressed for harsh penalties, extending to ministers who had held office during the Occupation. The legislation was finally passed, and the courts sentenced an appreciable body of men and women to fines and varying terms of imprisonment, but only forty-six persons were executed; and a commission recommended against bringing charges against wartime ministers.

The coalition could be kept in being for only a brief transitional period, and in October 1945 elections were held in preparation for a return to normal parliamentary government. They resulted in a serious setback for the Social Democrats and a considerable success for the Left; the Communists, whose negotiations with the Social Democrats to form a single party had broken down, emerged as the fourth largest group in the *Folketing* with eighteen members. The King called on Knud Kristensen, who had been minister of the interior in the coalition, to form a Left cabinet, which, with the support of the

Radicals and Conservatives, could count on a majority of one in the lower house.

The pattern of post-war Danish politics proved to be basically similar to the pre-war one, though with interesting variations. The scene has been dominated once more by the four 'traditional' parties. The Left and Conservatives have co-operated rather more happily than before against the Social Democrats; the Radicals, who have often held the balance in the *Folketing*, have, however, been able to exploit this position to bargain with both the latter and the 'bourgeois bloc'. The only serious challenge to the older parties has come from the Left, but it has constituted a threat to them for comparatively brief periods. Again no single party has been able to secure a large enough majority in the *Rigsdag* to rule without having to rely on the votes of others; all governments have been minority ones or coalitions of various kinds. Again the most serious problems facing politicians have been economic: inflation, unemployment and the country's balance of payments in particular. But again this has not prevented the carrying-through of significant social reforms and the further development of a Welfare State more advanced than that found in most other European countries.

The economic situation was certainly Kristensen's greatest worry when he took office. Both raw materials and food were in short supply. Overseas demand for Denmark's produce was weak; of her principal pre-war customers, Germany was still in chaos, and Britain lacked purchasing power. Prices were high and rising fast, and unemployment was widespread. The combination of adversities brought considerable unrest and frequent strikes, a number of which were, however, also called in protest against what were considered too lenient sentences passed on collaborators. The government introduced a drastic austerity programme: rationing was continued, strict controls were imposed on external trade, indirect taxes were increased to control consumption, an excess profits tax was levied and the currency converted to check inflation.

But the question which caused some of the bitterest political debates was that of south Slesvig. Immediately after the end of the war there had grown up among the German and Danish-speaking populations of the area a powerful movement in favour of reunion with Denmark. This gained considerable sympathy within the Left and the Conservative party. But the majority of *Rigsdag* members feared the complications which might result from any changes in the southern frontier at this stage, especially in view of the presence in the duchy of large numbers of refugees who had fled thither from eastern Germany before the advancing Russians and who would take some time to resettle. Consequently when, in October 1946, Britain, within whose sphere German Slesvig lay, proposed a frontier adjustment or an exchange of populations, both solutions were rejected as premature. Kristensen, however, expressed himself frequently in favour of a referendum, and this lost him the Radical support on which he relied. Finally, in October 1947 he suffered a vote of no confidence and was forced to go to the country.

The Left made gains in the election, but mainly at the expense of the Conservatives and not enough to secure Kristensen a majority. He therefore resigned, and, after some difficult negotiations, the new king Frederik IX, who had succeeded his father in April, called on Hans Hedtoft, the leader of the Social Democrats, who had won back some of the ground they had lost in 1945, to form another minority ministry. Christmas Møller, who had opposed the majority of his party over the south Slesvig question, had stood in the elections as an independent and failed to gain a seat. He died the following year.

During 1948 matters of foreign policy loomed large. Danish relations with the Soviet Union had been strained immediately after the war by the continued presence of Russian troops on Bornholm, which they had had to take by assault after its German garrison had refused to surrender. They were not withdrawn until May 1946. Now came the 'cold war'. None of the Scandinavian kingdoms wished to become involved in a 'hot war' between the Great Powers and they opened discussions between themselves about the conclusion of a defensive alliance to protect their neutrality. But, largely because Norway wished for closer links with the Western Powers than Sweden considered desirable, these discussions finally broke down in February 1949. Hedtoft reluctantly recommended Denmark's adhesion to the Atlantic Pact. In the *Rigsdag* only the Radicals, some members of the Single-Tax party and the Communists (now reduced to nine) voted against the proposal, and in April both Denmark and Norway became members of NATO.

As such, Denmark incurred the obligation of spending more on her defences, which increased the government's financial difficulties. With the help of Marshall Aid, both Danish agriculture and industry developed appreciably as the immediate post-war crisis was overcome. But the prices of the country's imports rose more rapidly than those of her exports, which still consisted largely of agricultural produce, and as a member of OEEC she was not able to impose the restrictions on foreign trade which had helped her in the inter-war years. Inflation, exacerbated by the devaluation of the *krone* in September 1949, also gave cause for concern. In October 1950 Hedtoft had to resign after being defeated on a motion introduced by a Single-Taxer to end butter rationing. He was succeeded by the Left leader Erik Eriksen at the head of a coalition of the Left and the Conservatives, which had to rely on Radical votes to overcome the opposition of the Social Democrats.

It was under Eriksen's aegis that agreement was reached between the main parties on a new constitution, which had been under discussion for some time. The main features of the project, which had to be passed by two successive *Rigsdags* and approved in a referendum, were an increase in the size of the *Folketing* from 151 to 179 seats and the abolition of the *Landsting*. In addition, parliamentary government was to be officially recognized for the first time, most types of law were to be able to be made the subject of a referendum if one were requested by at least a third of the *Folketing*, and an *ombudsmand*, such as Sweden had had since 1809, was to be appointed to investigate complaints against government departments and individual officials, both civil and military. While it was agreed that the voting age should be reduced from 25, agreement could not be reached on whether it should be to 21 or 23, and it was decided that this too should be put to a popular vote. The proposals were approved by a new *Rigsdag*, whose composition differed little from the old, and the referendum was held in May 1953. The poll was a low one, but the majority in favour was overwhelming, while by a smaller majority the voting age was fixed at 23. The royal assent was given in June, and the first elections for the single chamber took place in September. The Social

Democrats improved their position, and a promise of support from the Radicals enabled Hedtoft to form his second ministry.

The new *Folketing* for the first time contained two representatives from Greenland, to which the constitution granted the status of a Danish county. American bases had been established there during the war as the result of a pact concluded in Washington by Henrik Kauffmann, the Danish ambassador, who refused to recognize the government in Copenhagen after the beginning of the German occupation, and this arrangement had helped to break down the isolation from which the island had previously suffered. Hedtoft took a great interest in the welfare of the Greenlanders and in 1948 set up a commission, whose recommendations, including the establishment of an elected provincial council in Godthåb, were accepted in 1950. Considerable sums have subsequently been invested in Greenland by the Danish government, and, in spite of difficulties such as are always encountered when attempts are made to transform a primitive society into a twentieth-century one, the standard of living enjoyed by its inhabitants has, as a result, risen considerably. Greenland and The Faeroes were Denmark's only overseas possessions after Iceland, completely cut off from Copenhagen throughout the war, opted for complete independence in 1944. And a referendum held in The Faeroes in 1946 produced a small majority in favour of their independence also. But subsequent elections to the *Lagthing* (Provincial Assembly) in Torshavn returned a majority of members who wished to retain an association with Denmark. In March 1948 the *Lagthing* was granted complete control over internal affairs.

Though differences over foreign policy and defence prevented the Radicals from joining in a coalition government with the Social Democrats in 1953, they were in general sympathy with the new cabinet's economic and social programmes. Inflation and an unfavourable balance of trade were still the main economic problems, and the measures adopted by Hedtoft to combat them, which included higher taxes and a higher discount rate, proved to be inadequate. Early in 1955, Hans (H. C.) Hansen, who succeeded to the premiership on Hedtoft's death, secured Radical support for a more drastic 'package', the main feature of which was a new sales tax. Danish exports became more competitive on the world market, but unemployment rose, and strong pressure from the unions for higher wages, backed by strikes, seriously embarrassed the government. It lost four seats in the elections of 1957. But Eriksen was unable to form a new government, and, quite unexpectedly, the Single-Tax party, in the hope of gaining greater influence over policy and in spite of very different views on economic matters, offered to join the Radicals and Social Democrats in a coalition. The result was the first majority government in Denmark since the end of the war.

It adopted new anti-inflationary measures, and by the end of the year there were signs of a distinct improvement in the economic situation, though more to the benefit of industry than agriculture. The prices of imported raw materials began to fall, and the rapid growth of the West German market in particular provided business with incentive for expansion; during the next three years the problem of unemployment gave way to that of a shortage of labour, and the standard of living of the average Dane rose appreciably. The government still, however, had to keep a wary eye on inflationary tendencies, and it was largely for this reason that Hansen and his colleagues resisted demands from the Left and the Conservatives to reduce the high level of taxation. Additional funds were in any case required to meet Denmark's military obligations as a member of NATO and to pay for the social reforms which were approved in this period. In 1956 a new State pension, based on the income earned during the recipient's working life, was introduced, and much money was also spent on the building and renewing of schools and hospitals. In 1958 plans for comprehensive primary education passed the *Folketing*. The old 'middle schools' were to be abolished, and all children were to go to the same type of school throughout their compulsory seven years of education. At the end of the seven years, they would be enabled to begin a three-year practical course, at the end of the second year of which selection would be made for entry into a three-year grammar school.

The Common Market, formed in the spring of 1957, seemed to many Danes to constitute a threat to their newly won prosperity. Negotiations for the formation of a Scandinavian economic union were opened at the end of the same year and had reached an advanced stage by 1959, but they were overtaken by

British proposals for the formation of EFTA. A large section of the Opposition feared that membership of this body might affect Denmark's trading prospects even more seriously, but the *Folketing* approved her joining at the beginning of 1960. The boom did, in fact, appear to be losing some of its momentum soon afterwards, and industrial unrest grew.

It was against this background that elections were fought in November. The Single-Taxers appear to have lost support because of their participation in the coalition; none of their candidates were returned, and their ministers consequently left the government. The Radicals also suffered heavily, but decided to remain. And the Social Democrats, led, after Hansen's death at the beginning of the year, by the former finance minister Viggo Kampmann, gained six seats, though this was not enough to give the government a safe majority. The most striking feature of the election was the great success enjoyed by the Socialist People's Party (*Socialistisk Folkeparti*), a new group to the left of the Social Democrats which had been formed by Aksel Larsen after his expulsion from the Communist party for 'revisionism'. It won no fewer than eleven seats, doubtless largely as a result of a transfer of votes from the Communists, whose support had dwindled after the Soviet invasion of Hungary and who, like the Single-Taxers, disappeared from the *Folketing*.

Industrial unrest continued into 1961. And it was not only urban workers who were discontented. Farmers even stopped supplying foodstuffs to the towns for a time. Since the war Danish agriculture had been changing rapidly. An ever-growing drift of population from the countryside had created a shortage of labour there, and this had led to extensive mechanization and rationalization: the horse almost disappeared before the advance of the tractor; many smaller plots were amalgamated into larger units; and mixed farms gave way to specialized. In spite of this, however, many farmers still found it difficult to obtain adequate prices for their produce; industrial exports indeed gradually overtook agricultural exports in value. The government had agreed in 1958 to buy surplus cereals at higher than market prices, and now finally agreed to grant growers direct subsidies. The farming community and the Left, still very much the farmers' party, were the strongest supporters of Denmark's application in 1961 to join the Common Market;

membership would provide them with a large free-trade area for agricultural produce, which was not covered by the EFTA agreement. Even after negotiations between Britain and The Six broke down in 1963 they wished the government to continue its attempts. But most within the other parties agreed that Denmark could not afford the risks involved in entering without Britain, and not until the latter renewed her approach in 1967 did Denmark do likewise.

The farming subsidies, improved social services and inflation caused by the wage settlements which had ended a wave of strikes drove the government to increase the tax burden. But it was soon obvious that inflation called for more drastic remedies, and in March 1963 Jens Otto Krag, who had succeeded a sick Kampmann as prime minister in 1962, managed to force through the *Folketing*, though only by a bare majority, a temporary wages, prices and profits freeze. And in spite of the strong criticism which the measure received from the Opposition at the time, it undoubtedly helped to stabilize the economic situation so that it was already possible to relax controls in 1964.

The elections of 1964, when 21-year-olds voted for the first time, brought about little change in the party composition of the *Folketing*. But the Radicals lost one seat, and in accordance with a pledge made before the poll that they would withdraw from the government if they failed to make gains, their ministers resigned. Krag, though now without a majority, decided to carry on alone. His dependence on votes from outside his own party discouraged bold legislation, however, and only in the field of housing was much progress made during the following two years. Shortage of accommodation was one of the most serious social problems which Denmark had had to face since the end of the Occupation, and the one which it took her longest to solve. The freeing of the private building trade from government regulation in the late 1950's had helped somewhat to ease the situation, but the rents charged for the new flats which arose on the edge of urban areas, and in parts of the countryside to which industry was moving in search of cheaper land, were often extremely high, much higher than most rents for older urban properties. In 1966 the parties agreed on a plan to even out the differences in stages.

Krag called a new election in November 1966 after he had failed to get sufficient support in the *Folketing* for a programme of tax reform which included a value-added tax of 10 per cent. He lost a number of seats, but the Socialist Peoples' Party increased their representation to twenty, which meant that the two socialist parties commanded between them an absolute majority in the legislature. But disagreement over foreign and defence policy prevented their joining together in a majority coalition, and within twelve months economic policy caused a rift between them from which they both suffered. With the help of the People's Party, Krag managed to pass his value-added tax in July, but inflation, intensified by a devaluation of the *krone* following that of the pound, continued and the already large balance of payments deficit increased, while a slowing-down of industrial growth brought rising unemployment. At the end of the year the government was defeated as a result of the refusal of the majority of the People's Party representatives to agree to a new wage freeze. And in the subsequent elections both the latter and the Social Democrats lost heavily. The Radicals were the chief beneficiaries, and their leader Hilmar Baunsgaard formed a 'bourgeois coalition' with the Left and the Conservatives, which commanded an impressive majority.

The transfer of power did not, in fact, bring about any signicant changes in policy. The continuing unfavourable economic situation was met with a price freeze and an increase in the value-added tax. Unemployment declined sharply in 1969, and the freeze ended, but the trade deficit rose alarmingly, and the European financial crisis which began in the spring of that year caused a rapid dwindling of the country's gold reserves; the government had to impose a temporary ban on all foreign exchange dealings and raise the bank rate to the record high level of 9 per cent. And in October 1970 yet another price freeze was introduced, which lasted until March 1971.

In other spheres also the new government continued along lines which had been laid down by its predecessors. Pension benefits were improved and extended, and in 1969 agreement was reached on the raising of the school-leaving age to sixteen in 1972. And the abolition of all censorship of the printed word by the Krag government in 1967 was followed up in July 1969 with the removal of all restrictions on the publication of pic-

tures, an event celebrated the following October with a Porno-
graphic Fair in Copenhagen.

Such permissiveness was certainly not approved of by all
Danes, and a Christian People's Party, formed specifically to
oppose it, fought in the elections held in metropolitan Denmark
in September 1971. But it was the economic situation which
proved to be the main issue in the campaign and which was
mainly responsible for Baunsgaard's defeat. His own party
managed to retain its position in the *Folketing*, but his Conservative and Left allies lost ten seats between them, while the Social
Democrats gained eight and the Socialist People's Party, which
set its face firmly against Denmark's entry into the Common
Market, won six. The Christian People's Party failed to secure a
single place. In spite of its losses, however, the bourgeois coalition
still had a majority of one, and everything became dependent
on the results of the elections in the Faeroe Islands, which were
not held until the beginning of October. These gave the socialist
parties a majority of one, and Krag, having secured a promise
of support from the Socialist People's Party, formed an administration.

In spite of the obvious differences in the size and international
responsibilities of the two countries, the similarities between the
economic difficulties faced by Denmark and Britain since the
end of the Second World War are quite striking. The prosperity
of both rests to a very large extent on their ability to sell a high
proportion of their output in foreign markets, and both have
had to struggle hard to secure an export surplus; Denmark has
indeed not so far succeeded, and this remains the most serious
problem for her governments. And they have others, such as a
continuing housing shortage, or more strictly a shortage of accommodation at a rent which can be afforded by lower-paid
workers. Inflation and unemployment, though, as has been
seen, they have loomed large in the past, are, for the moment at
least, much less acute than in Britain. And the Danish standard
of living has been high since the late 1950's; the country has the
tenth highest per capita income in the world, and, while taxation is heavy, a substantial proportion of the income derived
from it is devoted to social services which have gone far towards
eliminating poverty. But, while the average Dane undoubtedly

enjoys his creature comforts (excessively so, some critics would claim), this has not prevented his governments from contributing handsomely to relieving the needs of less fortunate lands; by 1968 the aim of devoting 1 per cent of the GNP to aid to developing countries had been attained.

And material prosperity has apparently done nothing to diminish artistic achievement. The international reputation already won by Danish industrial design before the Second World War has grown still further after it. Fine but practical furniture, now made of man-made as well as natural materials, has in particular become an important export item as has a large range of delightful toys. Many designers have followed in Klint's tradition, and some figures more familiar in other fields have made important contributions. This is true, for example, of the silversmith Boyesen before his death in 1958 and of the architect Arne Jacobsen. Jacobsen's buildings, like the controversial Århus Town Hall (1938–42), on the design of which he collaborated with Erik Møller (see Plate 12), and his recent SAS Building in Copenhagen, belong to the international Functionalist style which became established between the wars. But many younger architects attempted after 1945 to unite this with national elements and, using a variety of materials, to blend their creations into the surrounding landscape. Among the most successful of these are Jørn Utzon's 'Kingo houses', built on the atrium principle, near Elsinore and *Louisiana* by Jørgen Bo and Vilhelm Wohlert, a perfect setting for modern works of art on the shores of the Sound at Humlebæk north of Copenhagen.

The Royal Danish Ballet, in spite of the departure of Lander for Paris in 1951, has maintained its world-wide renown during its frequent appearances in Europe and America, and its performances form the core of the Copenhagen Festival, held annually in May since 1950. The Danish cinema has won many prizes in international competitions. Bjarne Henning-Jensen's adaptation of Nexø's *Ditte, Menneskebarn*[1] was acclaimed in Venice in 1947 as was Dreyer's version of Munk's *Ordet*[2] in 1954. Henning Carlsen followed up his *Dilemma* (World of Strangers), a sensitive study of *apartheid* in South Africa, which appeared in 1962, with *Sult* (Hunger), a highly successful adaptation of a novel by the Norwegian Knut Hamsun and a joint Scandi-

---

[1] See above, p. 205.    [2] See above, p. 222.

navian production. An output of some twenty films each year shows the great vigour of the country's film industry.

Denmark's contributions to the remaining visual arts and to music are less well known outside her borders, though a number of her artists have lived for long periods abroad, notably the painters Asger Jorn and Richard Mortensen and the sculptor Robert Jacobsen in Paris. Abstract subjects have been the most popular with the younger painters who have emerged since the late 1930's (Jorn, Mortensen, Egill Jacobsen and Mogens Andersen above all), but the older Oluf Høst and Jens Søndergaard continued to produce their impressions of the landscapes respectively of Bornholm and Jutland which established their reputations before the war. And the highly individualistic Henry Heerup adopted the same primitivist approach in a number of figurative paintings as in his animal sculptures. In the same way the older sculptors Johannes Bjerg, Einar Utzon-Franck, Gottfried Eickhoff and Mogens Bøggild continued in the naturalistic tradition of Kai Nielsen, while the younger Robert Jacobsen and Erik Thommesen not only branched out into non-naturalistic and abstract forms but adopted new materials, iron by the former and wood by the latter. In music the influence of Nielsen has remained significant. But post-war Danish composers have looked far afield for their inspiration. Of the three most influential, the rather austere Vagn Holmboe has been attracted in particular by Bartok and Balkan folk-music, the more emotional and very prolific Niels Bentzon by Brahms, Berg and jazz and Herman Koppel by Hebrew melody.

A wider knowledge of Danish post-war literature has been hampered by the barrier of language, especially as some of the most significant work has been in poetry. This enjoyed a revival during the Occupation; the young Morten Nielsen was able to write very little before he was killed in tragic circumstances while training with the Resistance, but it is enough for us to estimate the loss. Between 1948 and 1955 a leading group of poets, of whom the most important was Erik Knudsen, was associated with the magazine *Heretica*. Yet the two most outstanding literary figures of recent years—Martin A. Hansen, the chief inspiration behind *Heretica*, and H. C. Branner[1]—have in fact been prose writers. The short story remained the medium

[1] See above, p. 222.

to which Branner made the greatest contribution, but he turned his hand happily to novels, radio plays and film scripts. The slightly younger Hansen also began publishing before the war, but it was during the Occupation, his experiences during which caused a deep personal crisis of conscience, that his stature was fully recognized. In much of his work, like *Orm og Tyr* (The Snake and the Bull), which deals with paganism and the early days of Christianity in Denmark, he looked back to periods when society was better integrated than in the twentieth century.

# Danish Governments Since 1848

| Dates of Office | First Minister<br>(1848–55 *premierminister*<br>1855–1918 *Konsejlspræsident*<br>1918– *statsminister*) | Party Composition and<br>(after 1870) position<br>in Folketing |
| --- | --- | --- |
| 22 Mar. 1848–16 Nov. 1848 | A. W. Moltke (Conservative) | Conservative and<br>National Liberal |
| 16 Nov. 1848–13 July 1851 | A. W. Molkte (Conservative) | Conservative and<br>National Liberal |
| 13 July 1851–27 Jan. 1852 | A. W. Molkte (Conservative) | Conservative and<br>National Liberal |
| 27 Jan. 1852—21 Apr. 1853 | C. A. Bluhme (Conservative) | Conservative |
| 21 April 1853–12 Dec. 1854 | A. S. Ørsted (Conservative) | Conservative |
| 12 Dec. 1854–18 Oct. 1856 | P. G. Bang (National Liberal) | Conservative and<br>National Liberal |
| 18 Oct. 1856–13 May 1857 | C. G. Andræ (National Liberal) | National Liberal |
| 13 May 1857–2 Dec. 1859 | C. C. Hall (National Liberal) | National Liberal |
| 2 Dec. 1859–8 Feb. 1860 | C. E. Rotwitt (No party) | |
| 8 Feb. 1860–31 Dec. 1863 | C. C. Hall (National Liberal) | National Liberal |
| 31 Dec. 1863–11 July 1864 | D. G. Monrad (National<br>Liberal) | National Liberal |
| 11 July 1864–6 Nov. 1865 | C. A. Bluhme (Conservative) | Conservative |
| 6 Nov. 1865–28 May 1870 | C. E. Krag-Juel-Vind-Frijs<br>(Conservative) | Conservative |
| 28 May 1870–14 July 1874 | L. H. C. H. Holstein-<br>Holsteinborg<br>(Conservative) | Conservative and<br>National Liberal<br>(minority) |
| 14 July 1874–11 June 1875 | C. E. A. Fonnesbech<br>(Conservative) | Conservative and<br>National Liberal<br>(minority) |
| 11 June 1875–7 Aug. 1894 | J. B. S. Estrup (Conservative) | Conservative (minority) |
| 7 Aug. 1894–23 May 1897 | T. Reedtz-Thott (Conservative) | Conservative (minority) |
| 23 May 1897–27 Apr. 1900 | H. Hørring (Conservative) | Conservative (minority) |
| 27 Apr. 1900–24 July 1901 | H. Sehested (Conservative) | Conservative (minority) |
| 24 July 1901–14 Jan. 1905 | J. H. Deuntzer (Left) | Left (majority) |
| 14 Jan. 1905–12 Oct. 1908 | J. C. Christensen (Left) | Left (majority) |
| 12 Oct. 1908–16 Aug. 1909 | N. Neergaard (Left) | Left (majority) |
| 16 Aug. 1909–28 Oct. 1909 | L. Holstein-Ledreborg (Left) | Left (minority) |
| 28 Oct. 1909–5 July 1910 | C. Th. Zahle (Radical) | Radical (minority) |

# Danish Governments Since 1945

| Dates of Office | First Minister (1848–55 premierminster 1855–1918 Konsejlspræsident 1918– statsminister) | Party Composition and (after 1870) position in Folketing |
|---|---|---|
| 5 July 1910–21 June 1913 | K. Berntsen (Left) | Left (majority) |
| 21 June 1913–29 Mar. 1920 | C. Th. Zahle (Radical) | Radical (minority) |
| 30 Mar. 1920–5 Apr. 1920 | O. Liebe (No party) | Non-political caretaker |
| 5 Apr. 1920–5 May 1920 | M. P. Friis (No party) | Non-political caretaker |
| 5 May 1920–9 Oct. 1922 | N. Neergaard (Left) | Left (minority) |
| 9 Oct. 1922–23 Apr. 1924 | N. Neergaard (Left) | Left (minority) |
| 23 Apr. 1924–14 Dec. 1926 | Th. Stauning (Soc. Dem.) | Soc. Dem. (minority) |
| 14 Dec. 1926–30 Apr. 1929 | Th. Madsen-Mygdal (Left) | Left (minority) |
| 30 Apr. 1929–4 Nov. 1935 | Th. Stauning (Soc. Dem.) | Soc. Dem. and Radical (majority) |
| 4 Nov. 1935–10 Apr. 1940 | Th. Stauning (Soc. Dem.) | Soc. Dem. and Radical (majority) |
| 10 Apr. 1940–8 July 1940 | Th. Stauning (Soc. Dem.) | All-party coalition |
| 8 July 1940–3 May 1942 | Th. Stauning (Soc. Dem.) | All-party coalition |
| 3 May 1942–9 Nov. 1942 | V. Buhl (Soc. Dem.) | All-party coalition |
| 9 Nov. 1942–30 Aug. 1943 | E. Scavenius (Radical) | All-party coalition |
| (Resignation accepted by King, 5 May 1945) | | |
| (30 Aug. 1943–5 May 1945 | Departmental Government) | |
| 5 May 1945–7 Nov. 1945 | V. Buhl (Soc. Dem.) | All-party coalition |
| 7 Nov. 1945–13 Nov. 1947 | K. Kristensen (Left) | Left (minority) |
| 13 Nov. 1947–30 Oct. 1950 | H. Hedtoft (Soc. Dem.) | Soc. Dem. (minority) |
| 30 Oct. 1950–30 Sept. 1953 | E. Eriksen (Left) | Left and Conservative (minority) |
| 30 Sept. 1953–29 Jan. 1955 | H. Hedtoft (Soc. Dem.) | Soc. Dem. (minority) |
| 29 Jan. 1955–28 May 1957 | H. C. Hansen (Soc. Dem.) | Soc. Dem. (minority) |
| 28 May 1957–19 Feb. 1960 | H. C. Hansen (Soc. Dem.) | Soc. Dem., Radicals and Single-Tax (majority) |
| 19 Feb. 1960–18 Nov. 1960 | V. Kampmann (Soc. Dem). | Soc. Dem., Radicals and Single-Tax (majority) |
| 18 Nov. 1960–3 Sept. 1962 | V. Kampmann (Soc. Dem). | Soc. Dem. and Radicals (majority) |
| 3 Sept. 1962–25 Sept. 1964 | J. O. Krag (Soc. Dem). | Soc. Dem. and Radicals (majority) |
| 25 Sept. 1964–Feb. 1968 | J. O. Krag (Soc. Dem). | Soc. Dem. (minority) |
| Feb. 1968–6 Oct. 1971 | H. Baunsgaard (Radical) | Radical, Left and Conservative (majority) |
| 11 Oct. 1971– | J. O. Krag (Soc. Dem.) | Soc. Dem. (minority) |

# Suggestions for Further Reading

THE following brief survey of books and articles on Danish history has been drawn up on the same principles as the bibliography at the end of my history of Sweden, viz. the comparatively few recent studies in English have been given fairly full coverage, while the choice of works in Danish, both for reasons of space and because even many of the items listed are not readily available outside Scandinavia, is highly selective. For more detailed guidance on the latter, reference should be made to: B. Ericksen and A. Krarup (eds.), *Dansk historisk Bibliografi* (3 vols., Copenhagen, 1917–27); and its continuations by H. Bruun, *Dansk historisk Bibliografi 1913–42* (4 vols., Copenhagen, 1966–70) and *Dansk historisk Bibliografi 1943–7* (Copenhagen, 1956). One or two important contributions in French and German have also been included. An asterisk marks books and articles through which the ordinary reader may most easily approach the subject in more detail. All books in Danish were published in Copenhagen unless otherwise indicated.

The leading Danish historical journals are: *Historisk Tidskrift* (1839–  ), one of the oldest in Europe still being published and not to be confused with the Swedish and Norwegian periodicals with the same title; *Fortid og Nutid* (1914–  ), which is mainly concerned with cultural and local history; and *Historie* (the new name adopted in 1968 by *Jyske Samlinger*). Articles on Danish history have also figured in the Swedish *Scandia* (1928–  ), and (in English) on Danish economic history in the *Scandinavian Economic History Review* (1953–  ). For a brief survey of Danish historiography, see W. Westergaard, 'Danish History and Danish Historians' (*Journal of Modern History*, vol. 24).

245

# Suggestions for Further Reading

(a) *General Histories and other works covering all Periods*

There are many chapters on Denmark in the lavishly produced *Scandinavia Past and Present*, edited by J. Bukdahl *et al.* (3 vols., Odense, 1959),* and authoritative articles on all aspects of Danish life in the very attractive official handbook *Denmark*, published by the Danish Foreign Office (latest edition, 1971).* J. P. Trap's great topographical survey, *Danmark* (14 vols., 5th edn., 1953–70), is a mine of information for the historian. J. H. S. Birch, *Denmark in History* (London, 1938),* is the most detailed history of the country in English, though the briefer *A History of Denmark* by John Danstrup (2nd edn., Copenhagen, 1949)* and Palle Lauring's popularly written *A History of the Kingdom of Denmark* (2nd edn., Copenhagen, 1963, transl. D. Hohen)* are easier reading. The best survey in a language other than a Scandinavian one is L. Krabbe's *Histoire de Danemark* (Copenhagen and Paris, 1950). The latest single-volume history in Danish is Kjeld Winding, *Danmarks Histoire* (3rd edn., 1958), where the emphasis is on political development. Of multi-volume works, A. Friis *et al.* (eds.), *Schultz Danmarks Histoire* (6 vols., 2nd edn., 1941–3), has not been wholly superseded by the attractively illustrated *Danmarks Histoirie*, edited by John Danstrup and Hal Koch (14 vols., 2nd edn., 1969–70). J. Hvidtfeldt *et al.* (eds.), *Historikergruppens Danmarks Historie* (2 vols., 1950–3), is particularly useful for social change. Erik Arup's *Danmarks Histoirie* (3 vols., 1925–55), which reached the seventeenth century before the author's death, is important not only for its scholarship but also because of the criticisms made in it of many accepted views.

Particularly aspects of Danish history are covered by: A. Nielsen, *Dänische Wirtschaftsgeschichte* (Jena, 1933), and K. Hansen (ed.), *Det danske Landbrugs Historie* (5 vols., 1924–43); Ib Koch-Olsen, *Danmarks Kulturhistorie* (2 vols., 1968), B. L. Grandjean, *Dansk Kunst* (with English transl., 1952), V. Poulsen, *Danish Painting and Sculpture* (transl. S. Mammen, 1955),* T. Paulsson, *Scandinavian Architecture* (London, 1958),* G. Albeck *et al.* (eds.), *Dansk Litteraturhistorie* (4 vols., 1964–6), P. M. Mitchell, *A History of Danish Literature* (Copenhagen, 1957),* and J. Horton, *Scandinavian Music: a Short History*

# Suggestions for Further Reading

(London, 1963);* H. Koch and B. Kornerup (eds.), *Den danske Kirkes Historie* (8 vols., 1950–66), and L. S. Hunter (ed.), *Scandinavian Churches* (London, 1965).* The lives of individual Danes are recorded in often quite lengthy articles in P. Engelstoft (ed.), *Dansk Biografisk Leksikon* (27 vols., 1933–44).

## (b) *Prehistory*

The standard work is J. Brøndsted, *Danmarks Oldtid* (3 vols., 2nd edn., 1957–60). In English the best study is O. Klindt-Jensen, *Denmark Before the Vikings* (London, 1957),* but the older *Scandinavian Archæology* by H. Shetelig and H. Falk (transl. E. V. Gordon, Oxford, 1937) contains much useful material and embraces the Viking period. Two books by P. V. Glob, the present director of the National Museum in Copenhagen, have recently been translated: *The Bog People* (transl. R. L. S. Bruce-Mitford, London, 1969)* with some rather gruesome pictures but a good description also of the life of the times; and *Danish Prehistoric Monuments* (transl. J. Bulman, London, 1971).

## (c) *The Viking Age*

Of the large number of general works on the Vikings which have appeared in English of recent years: J. Brøndsted, *The Vikings* (Harmondsworth, 2nd edn., 1965),* is a good survey; H. Arbman, *The Vikings* (London, 1961), is a well-illustrated volume in the 'Peoples and Places' series; G. Turville-Petre's *The Heroic Age of Scandinavia* (London, 1951)* is concerned largely with the literary evidence; P. H. Sawyer, *The Age of the Vikings* (London, 1962), gives a controversial interpretation of Scandinavian expansion based on a wide reading of the sources; and both Gwyn Jones, *The Vikings* (Oxford, 1968),* and P. G. Foote and David M. Wilson, *The Viking Achievement* (London, 1970),* are very full and take account of the latest research. Art is dealt with in D. M. Wilson and O. Klindt-Jensen, *Viking Art* (London, 1966). The religion of pagan Scandinavia both before and during the Viking period is well covered in H. R. E. Davidson's *Pagan Scandinavia* (London, 1967)* and E. O. G. Turville-Petre's *Myth and Religion of the North* (London, 1964).

Articles on the Danish settlements in England include: F. M.

## Suggestions for Further Reading

Stenton, 'The Danes in England' (*Proceedings of the British Academy*, vol. 13)* and 'The Scandinavian colonies in England and Normandy' (*Trans. of the Royal Hist. Soc.*, 1945); and P. H. Sawyer, 'The Density of the Danish Settlement in England' (*Univ. of Birmingham Hist. Journ.*, vol. 6). The same subject is dealt with in chapters of F. M. Stenton, *Anglo-Saxon England* (Oxford, 2nd ed., 1946),* and in H. Shetelig, *Viking Antiquities in Great Britain and Ireland* (Oslo, 1940), particularly the introduction. In Danish, there is a recent short study by Niels Lund, *De danske Vikinger i England* (1967). A. V. Storm has written on 'Early English influence on the Danish Church' in volume 13 of the *Saga Book of the Viking Society*.

### (d) *The Middle Ages*

The chapters by H. Koht in the *Cambridge Medieval History*, vols. VI and VIII (Cambridge, 1929, 1959),* provide a very useful introduction, and 'Denmark Between the Viking Age and the time of the Valdemars' is the title of an article by A. E. Christensen in the first volume of the new publication *Medieval Scandinavia* (1968– ).* But the best coverage in a language other than Danish is still to be found in Lucien Musset's *Les peuples scandinaves au moyen age* (Paris, 1951). Constitutional development up to the end of the fourteenth century is the subject of Aksel E. Christensen's *Kongemagt og Aristokrati* (1945), while Niels Skyum-Nielsen's *Kirkekampen i Danmark 1241–90* (1963) has Jakob Erlendsen as its central figure. S. Tägel's study in Swedish of *Valdemar Atterdag och Europa* (1962) has recently been followed by a Swedish study of the king's daughter: Michael Linton's *Drottning Margarethe* (Gothenburg, 1971). All sides of Scandinavian medieval culture are looked at in *Nordisk Kultur* (30 vols., 1930–56) and in the yet incomplete *Kulturhistorisk Leksikon for nordisk Middelalder* (15 vols. so far, 1956– ). A. Olrik has edited a *Book of Danish Ballads* (transl. S. Dampier, New York, 1939). There is much on early medieval architecture in Denmark in A. Andersson, *The Art of Scandinavia*, vol. 2 (transl. V. Menkes, London, 1970). And historiography is examined in A. Campbell, 'Saxo Grammaticus and the Scandinavian Historical Tradition' (*Saga Book of the Viking Society*, vol. 13). The early chapters, helpful for foreign policy,

248

# Suggestions for Further Reading

in C. E. Hill, *The Danish Sound Dues and the Command of the Baltic* (Durham, 1926), fall within this period.

### (e) *The Sixteenth Century*

There is a brief survey of the Danish Reformation in the fifth chapter (by N. K. Andersen) of *The New Cambridge Modern History*, vol. II (Cambridge, 1965),* and in G. Johannesson, 'Die Kirchenreformation in den nordischen Ländern' (*XIe. Congrès International des Sciences Historiques: Rapports, IV*; Gothenburg, Stockholm and Uppsala, 1960). Various aspects of it are looked at in Kai Hørby's *Reformationens Indførelse i Danmark* (1968), while one of the leading figures of the struggle, Poul Helgesen, is examined in unfamiliar guise in W. Glyn Jones's 'Paulus Helie and the Danish Reformation' (*The Month*, vol. 210). Foreign policy can be approached through the relevant part of Hill's book (see above, section d); a very full account of negotiations is given by the commentaries in the early volumes of L. Laursen and C. S. Christianson (eds.), *Danmark-Norges Traktater 1523–1750* (1905– ). There are two articles in English by W. Kirchner on particular aspects of the diplomacy of the period: 'A milestone in European history: the Dano–Russian treaty of 1562' (*Slavic and East European Review*, vol. 22) and 'England and Denmark 1558–1588' (*Journal of Modern History*, vol. 17). For social life, T. Troels-Lund's *Dagligt Liv i Norden i det sekstende århundrede* (7 vols., 6th edn., 1968–9) is a great classic which has not, in spite of its age, been superseded.

### (f) *The Seventeenth Century*

There is a biography of Christian IV in English by J. A. Gade (London and Cambridge, 1928).* The introduction of absolute monarchy is fully examined in C. O. Bøggild-Andersen, *Statsomvæltning i 1660* (1936), and the same author is in the process of publishing a life of *Hannibal Sehested* (2 vols., 1946, 1971). Much light is thrown on the background to the event by E. L. Petersen in 'La crise de la noblesse danoise entre 1580 et 1660' (*Annales*, vol. 23), and the *Kongelov* has been analysed by E. Ekman in 'The Danish Royal Law of 1665' (*Journal of Modern*

# Suggestions for Further Reading

History, vol. 29). Any study of the later seventeenth century in Denmark must begin with E. Holm's *Danmark-Norges indre Historie under Enevælden 1660–1720* (2 vols., 1885–6). A rather jaundiced view of Denmark under Christian V was given by the British envoy Robert Molesworth in his *Account of Denmark as it was in the Year 1692* (London, 1694). *Danmark-Norges Traktater* (see above, section e) have reached 1700. British relations with Denmark in this century are dealt with in: the introduction by J. F. Chance to *British Diplomatic Instructions 1689–1789, III: Denmark* (London, 1926); H. L. Schoolcraft, 'England and Denmark 1660–1667' (*English Hist. Rev.*, vol. 25); Michael Roberts, 'Cromwell and the Baltic' (in *Essays in Swedish History*, London, 1967); M. Lane, 'The Relations between England and the Northern Powers 1689–1697: I, Denmark' (*Trans. of the Royal Hist. Soc.*, 3rd ser., vol. 5); P. Torntoft, 'William III and Denmark–Norway 1697–1702' (*Eng. Hist. Rev.*, vol. 81); and in the early part of B. N. Thomsen and Brinsley Thomas, *Dansk-Engelsk Samhandel 1660–1963* (Århus, 1966). Basic material for economic development in general is contained in the first volume of A. Friis and K. Glamann, *A History of Prices and Wages in Denmark 1660–1800* (London, 1958). Demographic developments since 1645 are well treated in Axel Lassen's *Fald og Fremgang* (1965). Anders Vedel is the subject of an essay by H. S. Commager in *Scandinavian Studies presented to Henry Goddard Leach* (Seattle, 1965).

## (g) The Eighteenth Century

For the political history of Denmark in this period Holm's *Danmark-Norges Historie fra den store Nordiska Krigs Slutning til Rigernes Adskillelse 1720–1814* (7 vols., 1891–1912) remains fundamental; the author reached 1807 before his death. A good account in English of all aspects of Danish life is contained in B. Hovde's *The Scandinavian Countries 1720–1865: The Rise of the Middle Classes* (2 vols., Boston, 1943).* There is still no thoroughly satisfactory study of Struensee, but S. M. Toyne contributed a brief article on him to the first volume of *History Today** and aspects of his career are examined in W. F. Reddaway's 'Struensee and the Fall of Bernstorff' (*Eng. Hist. Rev.*, vol. 27) and 'King Christian VII' (*ibid.*, vol. 31). The same author wrote a chapter on 'Denmark under the Bernstorffs and Struensee' for the old *Cambridge Modern History*, vol. VI (Cambridge, 1909).* J. H. E. Bernstorff's political career in the reign of Frederik V is studied by Aage Friis in the second volume of his unfinished *Bernstorfferne og Danmark* (1919), and Christian Reventlow's life has been written by H. M. H. Jensen (1938). Britain's diplomatic relations with Denmark may continue to be studied in vol. III of *British Diplomatic Instructions* (see above, section f), to which may be added, M. Roberts, 'Great Britain, Denmark and Russia 1763–70' (in *Studies in Diplomatic History in Memory of D. B. Horn*, ed. R. M. Hatton and M. S. Anderson, London, 1970). The background to the British attack on Copenhagen in 1807 was examined in two articles by J. H. Rose: 'Canning and Denmark in 1807' (*Eng. Hist. Rev.*, vol. 11) and 'Canning—the Secret Intelligence from Tilsit' (*Trans. of the Royal Hist. Soc.*, New series, vol. 20). But the whole incident has been put in a wider context in A. N. Ryan's 'The Causes of the British Attack on Copenhagen in 1807' (*Eng. Hist. Rev.*, vol. 68). Denmark as an ally of Napoleon is well treated in R. Ruppenthal's 'Denmark and the Continental System' (*Journal of Modern History*, vol. 15). A full examination in a brief space of Danish economic policy in the seventeenth and early eighteenth century is provided by A. Olsen in 'Nogle synspunkter for dansk merkantilistik Erhvervspolitik' (*Scandia*, vol. 3). Danish trade with Asia is the subject of a recent full-length study in English by O. Feldbæk, *India Trade under the Danish Flag 1772–1808* (Copenhagen, 1969), summarized in 'The Danish trade in Bengal 1777–1806' (*Scandinavian Econ. Hist. Rev.*, vol. 12). In volume 8 of the same journal is K. Glamann's 'The Danish Asiatic Company 1732–1772'.

(h) *The Nineteenth Century*

Hovde's book (see above, section g) is a good introduction for the period up to 1865, but English readers are fortunate in now having W. Glyn Jones's *Denmark* (London, 1970),* which, after an introductory chapter on earlier Danish history, treats the nineteenth and twentieth centuries in considerable detail. P. Engelstoft and F. W. Wendt's *Håndbog i Danmarks politiske Historie fra Freden i Kiel til vore Dage* (1934, reprinted 1964) is a

## Suggestions for Further Reading

recognized textbook. The standard history of the *Rigsdag* is *Den danske Rigsdags Historie* (6 vols., 1949–53). The period 1848–66 is perhaps still best approached through Niels Neergaard's *Danmark under Junigrundloven* (3 vols., 1892–1916), while in *Venstre og Forsvarssagen 1870–1901* (Århus, 1960) Kristian Hvidt has examined one of the great political debates of the period before the 'change of system'. Its leading protagonists are surveyed in E. Henrichsen's *Mændene fra Forfatningskampen* (2 vols., 1913–14), and there are more recent lives of *Jacob Brønnum Scavenius Estrup* by T. Thaulow (1940) and *J. C. Christensen* by F. Aagaard (1941). The Schleswig–Holstein Question has been well catered for in English with L. D. Steefel's *The Schleswig–Holstein Question* (Cambridge, 1932), on the second and better known of the two wars, and W. Carr's *Schleswig–Holstein 1815–48* (Manchester, 1963), though both authors tend to look at it from a German viewpoint. Holger Hjelholt has devoted three volumes to *British Mediation in the Danish–German Conflict 1848–50* (1965–71), and there is a useful article on 'Danmarks Krise 1863' by E. Arup in *Scandia*, vol. 3. The effects of the loss of the Duchies on the Danish economy are discussed by O. Hornby in 'Industrialisation in Denmark and the Loss of the Duchies' (*Scandinavian Econ. Hist. Rev.*, vol. 17) and industrialization generally in K. Glamann, 'Industrialization as a Factor in Economic Growth in Denmark since 1700' (*First International Conference of Economic Historians: Contributions*; Paris, 1960). A more detailed examination is provided by L. Jörberg, *The Industrial Revolution in Scandinavia 1850–1914* (transl. P. B. Austin, London, 1970),* which also gives due weight to agriculture. In Danish there is E. Olsen, *Danmarks økonomiske Historie siden 1750* (1962). Thomsen and Thomas's work (see above, section f) should also be referred to in view of the great importance of Anglo-Danish trade from this time onward. 'Danish emigration prior to 1914' (*Scandinavian Econ. Hist. Rev.*, vol. 14) is a pioneer study by K. Hvidt which he has followed with a full-length work in Danish on the subject entitled *Flugten til Amerika* (Århus, 1971). For social history, there is *Dagligliv i Danmark i det nittende og tyvende Åruhundrede* (3 vols., 1963–9), edited by Axel Steensberg.

# Suggestions for Further Reading

## (i) *The Twentieth Century*

V. La Cour's *Danmarks Historie 1900–1945* (1950) is a good survey in two volumes. In English the best account of the whole period is given in Jones's *Denmark* (see above, section h). Denmark's part in the First World War forms part of E. F. Heckscher *et al.*, *Sweden, Norway, Denmark and Iceland in the World War* (New Haven, 1930), and C. C. Tansill has provided a detailed study of *The Purchase of the Danish West Indies* (Baltimore, 1932). The great political crisis at Eastertime 1920 has recently been examined by Tage Kaarsted in *Påskekrisen 1920* (1970). He has also come nearer the present time with *Dansk Politik i 1960'erne* (1969). Harald Westergaard Andersen's *Dansk politik i går og i dag* (1967) is a useful survey of developments since 1920. Several very detailed accounts of the German Occupation have appeared in Danish, including: J. Brøndsted and K. Gedde (eds.), *De fem lange Aar* (3 vols., 1945–7); A. Friis, *Danmark under Verdenskrig og Besættelse* (5 vols., Odense, 1946–8); and H. Frisch *et al.*, *Danmark besat og befriet* (3 vols.). Brief post-war accounts in English are D. Lampe, *The Savage Canary, the Story of the Resistance* (London, 1957), and B. Outze (ed.), *Denmark during the German Occupation* (Copenhagen, 1946).* For the diplomatic build-up, see V. Sjøquist, *Danmarks Udenrigspolitik 1933–1940* (1966). There is a study of Stauning consisting of a number of essays by different contributors edited by B. Schmidt (1964).

# Index

254

# Index

142; eighteenth-century, 143–5, 148; nineteenth-century, 185, 205; twentieth-century, 205, 218, 221, 240

Århus (Jutland), in Viking times, 38; medieval, 47, 49, 56, 87; seventeenth-century, 116; nineteenth-century, 195; twentieth-century, 221, 240, Plate 12

Aristocracy, *see Nobility*

Arkona, 56

Armed Neutrality, Leagues of, 138, 150, 157, 161

Army, medieval, 51, 63, 71, 76; sixteenth-century, 104; seventeenth-century, 112, 115–16, 122, 137; eighteenth-century, 145–6, 149; nineteenth-century, 174, 188; twentieth-century, 202, 206–7, 228

Arrebo, Anders Christensen (1587–1637), 128–9

Art, *see* Painting, Sculpture, etc.

Asiatic Company, 147–8

Asser, Archbishop of Lund (d. 1137), 47–8

Augustenborg, Dukes of, 171, 187

Austria and Denmark in the nineteenth century, 179, 186–9

Bager, Oluf (*c.* 1521–1602), 106

Ballads, 73, 75, 88, 108

Ballet, eighteenth-century, 156–7; nineteenth-century, 185; twentieth-century, 221, 240

Bang, Herman (1857–1912), 197

Bang, Jens (*c.* 1575–1644), 111

Bang, Nina (1866–1928), 215

Banking, nineteenth-century, 164, 167, 174, 183; twentieth-century, 207, 214

Barkær (Jutland), prehistoric village at, 20

Bartholin, Rasmus (1625–98), 129, 134

Bartholin, Thomas (1616–80), 129

Baunsgaard, Hilmer (1920– ), 238–9, 244

Bengerd (Berengaria) of Portugal, wife of King Valdemar II (d. 1221), 60, 73

Bentzon, Niels Viggo (1919– ), 241

Berg, Christen (1829–91), 197, 200

Berg, Claus (*c.* 1470–*c.* 1532), 87

Bernadotte, *see* Charles XIV

Bernstorff, Count Andreas Peter (1735–97), 157, 160

Bernstorff, Count Christian Günther (1769–1835), 160

Bernstorff, Count Johan Hartvig Ernst (1712–72), 149–51, 153–4, 156

Berntsen, Klaus (1844–1927), 203–4, 207, 213, 243

Best, Werner (1903– ), 227–8

Bible in Danish, 101–2

Bing & Grøndahl, 204

Bismarck, Count Otto von (1815–98), 187–9

Bjerg, Johannes (1886–1955), 241

Black Death, 76

Blekinge, 42, 77, 95, 111, 135

Blicher, Steen Steensen (1782–1848), 173

Blixen (-Finecke), Karen (1885–1962), 222

Bo, Jørgen (1919– ), 240

Boats, *see* Ships

Boat-axe culture, 22

Bøggild, Mogens (1901– ), 241

Bogs, finds in Danish, 23–6

Bojsen, Frede (1841–1926), 199–200

Bornholm, prehistoric, 27; medieval, 47, 66, 70; seventeenth-century, 123–4; eighteenth-century, 146; twentieth-century, 218, 232, 241

Bornhøved, Battle of (1227), 59

Borremose (Jutland), prehistoric earthworks at, 25

*Børsen* (Copenhagen), 112

Bournonville, Antoine (1760–1843), 185

Bournonville, August (1805–79), 185

Boyesen, Kay (1886–1958), 220, 240

Brahe, Tyge (Tycho) (1564–1601), 107, 116

Brandenburg and Denmark in Middle Ages, 70, 73–4, 76, 89

Brandenburg-Prussia and Denmark in the seventeenth century, 116, 122–3 (*see also* Prussia)

Brandes, Edvard (1874–1931), 198

Brandes, Georg (1842–1927), 196–8, 205

Branner, Hans Christian (1903–66), 222, 242

Brávellir, Battle of, 28

Bremen, 112–13, 117, 122

Bridges, 220

Britain and Denmark, in Viking times, 30; in eighteenth century, 147, 152,

# Index

256

# Index

# Index

# Index

# Index

# Index

# Index

# Index

19, 121, 123-4, 131, 133; in eighteenth century, 141-3, 147-8, 150, 156; in nineteenth century, 164-5, 177; in twentieth century, 222-3, 232, 235

Notke, Bernt (c. 1440-c. 1509), 87

Nyborg Castle (Fyn), 56, 71

Nydam (Slesvig), prehistoric boat from, 26

Nyrop, Martin (1849-1921), 205

Odense (Fyn), 26; Viking, 35; medieval, 45, 47, 49, 52, 77, 87; sixteenth-century, 106; seventeenth-century, 115; nineteenth-century, 195; twentieth-century, 205

OEEC, 233

Oehlenschläger, Adam Gottlob (1779-1850), 167-8, 184

Olav Haraldsson (St. Olav), King of Norway (1016-30), 36

Olav Tryggvason, King of Norway (995-1000), 35

Oldenburg, 141, 150

Olof, see Oluf

Oluf (I) Hunger, King of Denmark (1086-95), 45-6

Oluf II, King of Denmark (c. 1140-3), 46

Oluf III, King of Denmark (1375-87), 60, 78, 80-1

*Ombudsmand*, 233

Ongendus, Danish prince (c. 730), 33

Ørsted, Anders Sandøe (1778-1860), 180, 243

Ørsted, Hans Christian (1777-1851), 175

Oscar I, King of Sweden (1844-59), 186

Øsel, 103, 118

Oxe, Peder (1520-75), 104-5, 107

Oxe, Torben (d. 1517), 91

Painting, medieval, 67, 77; sixteenth-century, 105; seventeenth-century, 117; eighteenth-century, 148, 156; nineteenth-century, 168-9, 205; twentieth-century, 205, 217-18, 240-1

Palladius, Peder, Bishop of Roskilde (1503-60), 101

Palmerston, Henry John Temple, Viscount (1784-1865), 186

Paludan, Jacob (1896– ), 217

Papacy and Denmark, 55, 71-2, 88, 97

Paris, Viking attacks on, 30-1; University of, 58, 65

Parker, Admiral Sir Hyde (1739-1807), 161

Passage-graves, 22

Paul I, Tsar (1796-1801), 149-50

Peasantry, medieval, 61, 67, 69, 73, 75-7, 79-84, 86, 92; sixteenth-century, 94-5, 99, 105-6; seventeenth-century, 116, 126, 137-8; eighteenth-century, 142, 145-6, 150-1, 154, 158-9; nineteenth-century, 159, 164, 166

Pedersen, Christiern (1480-1554), 101-2

Pensions, Old Age, 214, 216, 235, 238

*Permanente, Den* (Copenhagen), 221

Peter III, Tsar (1762), 149

Petersen, Carl (1874-1923), 218

Petersen, Nis (1897-1943), 222

Philipsen, Theodor (1840-1920), 197

Pietism, 143-5, 148

Pilo, Carl Gustav (1711-93), 148

Pio, Louis (1841-94), 196

Place-names, 27, 31, 34, 37, 61

Plague, 76, 124, 129

Plessen, Christian Siegfried von (1646-1723), 137

Ploug, Carl (1813-94), 170, 177, 186

Pomerania, 58-9, 83, 114, 117

Pontoppidan, Erik, Bishop of Bergen (1698-1764), 151

Pontoppidan, Henrik (1857-1943), 197, 217

Poor relief, 159, 199, 202, 219

Poppo, Bishop of Slesvig (c. 960), 33

Population, prehistoric and Viking, 18, 24, 27, 36-7; medieval, 61, 67, 76; seventeenth-century, 111, 124, 135; eighteenth-century, 141; nineteenth-century, 159, 166, 195

Porcelain, 157, 204

Postage stamps, 184

Pottery, prehistoric, 19-20 (*see also* Porcelain)

Premonstratensians, 52

Printing, 88

Prussia and Denmark in eighteenth century, 149, 161; in nineteenth century, 177-9, 186-9

265

# Index

# Index

# Index

Stone Age, Old, 17–20
Stralsund, Treaty of (1370), 78
Strikes, 196, 204, 207, 213, 219, 227–8, 231, 235–7
Struensee, Johan Friedrich (1737–72), 153–5, Plate 8
Sture, Sten (the Elder) (*c.* 1440–1503), 86, 89
Sture, Sten (the Younger) (*c.* 1492–1520), 92
Sunesen, Anders, Archbishop of Lund (d. 1228), 58
Svane, Archbishop Hans (1606–68), 124–6
Svend (I) 'Forkbeard' (*Tveskæg*), King of Denmark (986–1014), 33, 35–6
Svend (II) Estridsen, King of Denmark (1047–74 or –76), 42–4, 46–7
Svend (III), Grathe, King of Denmark (1146–57), 46
Svolder, Battle of (*c.* 1000), 35
Sweden and Denmark, in prehistoric and Viking times, 28, 32; in Middle Ages, 42, 45, 52, 73, 75, 77–87, 89, 91–2; in sixteenth century, 93–6, 99, 102, 104; in seventeenth century, 109, 112, 114, 117–18, 121–4, 132, 135, 138–9; in eighteenth century, 147, 149, 161; in nineteenth century, 163, 177, 186–8; in twentieth century, 222, 228, 232, 235
Sweyn, *see* Svend
Syberg, Fritz (1862–1939), 205

Tacitus, Cornelius (*c.* 55–120), 25
Tallin, 59
Tariffs, in seventeenth century, 110; in eighteenth century, 150, 159; in nineteenth century, 183; in twentieth century, 215–16
Tausen (or Tavsen), Hans (1494–1561), 96, 97, 101
Taxation, medieval, 75–6, 82, 84–5, 94; sixteenth-century, 99, 104–6; seventeenth-century, 115, 122, 125, 127, 133, 136–7; eighteenth-century, 142, 144, 154; nineteenth-century, 164, 174, 182, 191, 198; twentieth-century, 200, 216, 231, 234, 237–8 (*see also* Finances)
Telegraph, 184
Teutonic Knights, 76, 87, 103
Teutons, 25

Theatre in Copenhagen, 143–4, 148, 157
*Things*, 39–40, 48, 51–2, 64, 81
Thirty Years War (1618–48), 112–14, 117
Thommesen, Erik (1916–  ), 241
Thomsen, Christian Jürgensen (1788–1865), 17
Thralls, 38–9, 67
Thorvaldsen, Bertel (1770–1844), 169, Plate 9
Thurah, Laurids de (1706–59), 144–5
Tietgen, Carl Frederik (1829–1901), 183, 196
*Tøjhuset* (Copenhagen), 112
Tollund (Jutland), 'bog man' from, 25
Tønning (Slesvig), 139
Torstensson, Count Lennart (1603–51), 117–18
Towns, Viking, 37; medieval, 62, 77, 82, 86, 91–2; sixteenth-century, 97, 106; seventeenth-century, 111, 127, 135; eighteenth-century, 142; nineteenth-century, 166, 182, 195
Toys, 240
Trade, prehistoric and Viking, 19, 22–7, 29, 36–8; medieval, 49, 55, 59, 62–3, 67, 77, 82, 86–7, 89, 91; sixteenth-century, 95, 103–4, 106, 108; seventeenth-century, 110, 112, 117, 120, 123–4, 138; eighteenth-century, 141–2, 147–8, 150, 154, 159–61, 163; nineteenth-century, 164, 166, 182–3, 193–4, 196; twentieth-century, 204, 206–7, 209, 212, 214–16, 218–20, 225, 231, 233–6, 238–9
Trade unions, 204, 209–10, 213, 216, 235
Trankebar (India), 110, 141, 208
Travendal, Treaty of (1700), 139
Treasurer, office of, 107, 127
Treasury, 127, 154
Trelleborg (Zealand), Viking camp of, 35
Troldebjerg (Langeland), prehistoric site at, 22
Trolle, Gustav, Archbishop of Uppsala (1488–1535), 92
Trundholm (Zealand), prehistoric find at, 23
Tyra, Queen (d. *c.* 935), 32

268

# Index